imagine otherwise

imagine otherwise

on Asian Americanist critique

Kandice Chuh

Duke University Press   Durham & London

2003

© 2003 Duke University Press

All rights reserved

Designed by C. H. Westmoreland

Typeset in Monotype Joanna by

Keystone Typesetting, Inc.

Library of Congress Cataloging-

in-Publication Data appear on

the last printed page of

this book.

to my parents, with love and gratitude

contents

preface: imagine otherwise   ix

introduction: on Asian Americanist critique   1

1
against uniform subjectivity: remembering
"Filipino America"   31

2
nikkei internment: determined identities / undecidable
meanings   58

3
"one hundred percent Korean": on space and
subjectivity   85

4
(dis)owning America   112

conclusion: when difference meets itself   147

notes   153

works cited   187

index   211

preface:

imagine otherwise

> That life is complicated is a theoretical statement that guides efforts to treat race, class, and gender dynamics and consciousness as more dense and delicate than those categorical terms often imply. It is a theoretical statement that might guide a critique of privately purchased rights, of various forms of blindness and sanctioned denial; that might guide an attempt to drive a wedge into lives and visions of freedom ruled by the nexus of market exchange. It is a theoretical statement that invites us to see with portentous clarity into the heart and soul of American life and culture, and to track events, stories, anonymous and history-making actions to their density, to the point where we might catch a glimpse of what Patricia Williams calls the "vast networking of our society" and imagine otherwise. You could say this is a folk theoretical statement. We need to know where we live in order to imagine living elsewhere. We need to imagine living elsewhere before we can live there.
> —Avery Gordon, *Ghostly Matters: Haunting and the Sociological Imagination* (1997)

This book takes its title from Avery Gordon's call to evoke the potential transformative power of envisioning life and culture in ways deeply cognizant of the diverse and intricate forms they assume. The idea of imagining otherwise captures my sense of Asian American literatures—of how they articulate the complexities of power and personhood involved in imagining and narrating relations to the nation, America, which is at the same time the same as and more than the U.S. nation-state. It evokes how they at once critique the ways of knowing forwarded in the name of "America," but also work prophetically, presaging the elsewhere of Gordon's "folk theory." I mean this title, this idea, to inscribe Asian American literatures as epistemological projects engaged in a politics of knowledge. *Imagine Otherwise* advances a critical approach to the study of Asian American literatures that conceives of that work as theoretical devices that help us apprehend and unravel the narrative dimensions of naturalized racial, sexual, gender, and national identities. I argue for a definition of "Asian American" that relies not on the empirical presence of Asian-raced bodies in the United States for its intelligibility, but for one that instead emphasizes the fantasy links between body and subjectivity discursively forged within the literary and legal texts considered here. *Imagine Otherwise* attempts to demonstrate how this understanding can provide grounds for continuing to mobilize and deploy the term "Asian American" in light and in spite of contemporary critiques of its limitations. Informed by poststructural insights into the nature of language and knowledge, my interest here is in investigating the structures of power and meaning that give rise to identity and difference as national and racial epistemes. To imagine otherwise is not simply a matter of seeing a common object from different perspectives. Rather, it is about undoing the very notion of common objectivity itself and about recognizing the ethicopolitical implications of multiple epistemologies—theories about knowledge formation and the status and objects of knowledge—that underwrite alternative perspectives.

Although the title of this book draws from Avery Gordon, its arguments and, indeed, the very fact of its completion owe much to the critical generosity of many others. Most immediately, I acknowledge with deep thanks Lisa Lowe, whose rigorous readings of multiple drafts of the manuscript—always offered in a spirit of constructive, collaborative effort—were in so many ways crucial to this endeavor. I am grateful to Ken Wissoker, at Duke University Press, who had an astonishing faith in this project when, at times, there was perhaps little reason to do so. I have also had the inestimable benefit of the sustaining friendship and intellectual camaraderie of Karen Shimakawa, who continues to shape my thinking in all of the important ways. Likewise, Nicole King and William Cohen were the most necessary of touchstones as I worked to complete this book. Both reached across distances and differences of various kinds to offer critical input and boundless support.

What I am describing in relation to all of those acknowledged here is precisely the practice of critical generosity. The phrase comes from David Román and is particularly appropriately used here because he was instrumental to the development of the initial germs of this project during my years as a graduate student. Carolyn Allen, Tani Barlow, Evan Watkins, Shawn Wong, Traise Yamamoto, and, especially, Susan Jeffords have my great thanks as well in this regard. And I have been enormously fortunate to find colleagues at the University of Maryland who are equally critical and generous. In that context, I thank Jonathan Auerbach, Susan Leonardi, and particularly Robert Levine and Sangeeta Ray for offering truly helpful commentary on various chapters. Let me acknowledge also students at the University of Maryland with whom I have the privilege of working. The ways in which they challenge my thinking and energize my efforts are embedded in this book.

I am glad also to have the opportunity to thank Leti Volpp, who shares her work and engages with mine in the most productive of ways; and K. Scott Wong, whose critique was enormously important to the final shape of chapter 4 in particular. The insights I have mined from illuminating exchanges over the many years it has taken to complete this work with, variously, Cathy Davidson, Rosemary George, Gayatri Gopinath, Neil Gotanda, Judith Halberstam, Laura Hyun Yi Kang, Daniel Kim, George Lipsitz, Nayan Shah, Mary Helen Washington, and Lisa Yoneyama in many ways animate the arguments here. And Christine Dahlin, Rebecca Johns-Danes, and Fred Kameny at Duke University Press have my thanks for their work in shepherding this project through the publication process.

My parents, to whom this book is dedicated, patiently awaited and encouraged the completion of this work with characteristic sustaining love. Patricia Chuh, my extraordinary sister, made sure that I had what I needed both materially and emotionally to write this book. And Joshua Green, my partner in every way, suffered through the difficult parts of writing and celebrated with me the big and small accomplishments associated with this project. For buttressing my work efforts with unbounded support and teaching me daily the joys of living in difference, I am grateful. Various iterations of Browns, Greens, Gucks, and Gulnicks constitute the remainder of the amazing family network that I have relied upon in writing this book.

An earlier version of chapter 3 was previously published as "Transnationalism and Its Pasts" in *Public Culture* 9, no. 1 (1996): 93–112.

introduction:

on Asian Americanist critique

> Asian American culture is the site of more than critical negation of the U.S. nation; it is a site that shifts and marks alternatives to the national terrain by occupying other spaces, imagining different narratives and critical historiographies, and enacting practices that give rise to new forms of subjectivity and new ways of questioning the government of human life by the national state.—Lisa Lowe, *Immigrant Acts: On Asian American Cultural Politics* (1996)

> Justice remains, is yet, to come. Perhaps, one must always say for justice.—Jacques Derrida, "Force of Law" (1992)

> We need to remember as intellectuals that the battles we fight are battles of words. . . . What academic intellectuals must confront is thus not their "victimization" by society at large (or their victimization-in-solidarity-with-the-oppressed), but the power, wealth, and privilege that ironically accumulate from their "oppositional" viewpoint, and the widening gap between the professed contents of their words and the upward mobility they gain from such words.
> —Rey Chow, *Writing Diaspora* (1993)

The Hawaiʻi of Lois Ann Yamanaka's novel, *Blu's Hanging* (1997), is anything but paradisical. Filled with poverty and meanness, with violence and uncertain futures for the Ogata children who anchor the novel, *Blu's Hanging* directly challenges edenic images of the islands. It is indeed a challenging book on many fronts, depicting as it does vivid accounts of child abuse entwined with cruelty to animals, and culminating in the rape of the novel's eponymous character. And it does so in a lyrical prose that underscores the intolerability of the situation presented by juxtaposing poetics with violation.

In some perhaps perverse sense, it seems fitting that this thematically provocative novel should have animated the intense discussions that reached a climax at the Association for Asian American Studies' 1998 Annual Conference, held in Honolulu, Hawaiʻi. Practitioners of Asian American studies will no doubt be familiar with the controversy surrounding the novel. Briefly, criticized for its putatively racist representations of Filipino Americans, the novel's naming as Best Fiction by the association incited impassioned debate that led ultimately to the rescinding of the award and concomitant en masse resignation of the association's executive board.[1] For many, the awarding of this prize to *Blu's Hanging* signified the validation of racist representations by the Association itself, charges especially troubling for an organization in a field that emerged in large part precisely to counter racism. Perhaps for all, it provoked debate regarding freedom of artistic expression and critical evaluation—a thematization of the relationships between politics and aesthetics forwarded by this kind of association and award. In one sense, this controversy functioned as a crucible for testing the politics and practices of the association and its membership, dramatically highlighting marginalization and exclusionary knowledge politics within Asian American studies. And certainly, though these events are contemporary, these issues are not. They have circulated in the field since its inception in the 1960s and 1970s, as the grounding assumptions of to whom and to what "Asian American" refers, of the nature and constitution of the object of knowledge of Asian American studies, have faced repeated interrogation. Criticized for its homogenization of peoples, artifacts, and histories, and for its sometime deployment with masculinist and heteronormative biases and tacit East Asian orientation, "Asian American" as a term of criticism has never functioned as a label free of dispute. Through this controversy, perhaps because it seemed that the future of the association—one of the relatively few institutional sites for Asian American studies—was in jeopardy, attending critically to marginalization has gained a sense of field-wide immediacy.

In the aftermath of these events, as the association has rebuilt itself and many have attempted to apprehend their precipitating conditions, that multiple issues of concern for Asian American studies collided around the award has become evident. In retrospect, allegations of marginalization seem to have referred not only to biases in terminology and critical practice, but obliquely to the very orientation of the field as well: Activist or academic? Practical or theoretical? Had the association, the field, become too institutionalized, cut off from not only its membership, but also and maybe more importantly, "the community"? Had it lost, through that disconnection, a clear sense of how to conduct antiracist work?

Such questions arise at a time when discourses like transnationalism and postcolonialism solicit examination of the implicit framing principles of nation-based fields like Asian American studies. Propounding, or at least auguring, the end of the dominance of the nation-state as the preeminent unit of global organization, transnationalism recognizes contemporary flows of capital and information that seemingly find national borders irrelevant and "patriotic" loyalties displaced from nation-states to differently configured collectivities. It suggests that it is no longer clear—if it ever was—that the subject ("American") is a discretely bounded, discretely knowable entity merely modified by a specific adjective ("Asian"). Postcolonial studies, too, has mounted its own interrogations of the nation-state form, especially regarding its viability as a site of post-colonial liberation. Although with an emphasis on European colonialisms and their consequences in Asia and Africa, postcolonialism in the U.S. academy has of late become increasingly important to illuminating U.S. practices of empire. The critiques of modernity emergent under the rubric of postcolonial studies both inform and compel investigation of the U.S. nation-state, the putative and self-proclaimed representative of the achievement of modernity's principles of the Rule of Law, Democracy, and Equality. The already complex matter of understanding the position of U.S. racialized minorities is further complicated by recognizing the United States as an imperial metropole. I wonder, in hindsight, if the award controversy did not perhaps find especially fertile ground in light of these broad-based incitements to rearticulate the field.

Imagine Otherwise undertakes a critical consideration of Asian American studies, motivated in part by questions that arose through the award controversy, questions that give added impetus to revisit its framing assumptions in light of critiques of the (U.S.) nation-state emergent through postcolonial and transnational studies. I mean to ask after the coherency and object(ive)s of Asian American studies and to understand its work as both an academic field and an explicitly political project. I take the award controversy as my point of departure because it brings into sharp relief the significant differences too easily elided by the rubric "Asian American," differences both enumerated and complicated in part through the critiques mounted by postcolonial and transnational theorizing. Asian Americanists continue to search for ways to negotiate such differences so that the field can remain a politicized tool for social justice; this book attempts to contribute to such a project. My focus, in working through Asian American literatures toward that end, results from working in both Asian American studies and U.S. American literary studies as my two primary field locations. What motivates "Asian American" in the face of infinite heterogeneity among its referents? What does it mean to be a practitioner of Asian American studies when the anchoring terms—"Asian" and "American"— seem so fatally unstable? Does field coherency depend on political consensus, and, if so, what are the terms of those politics? What are the connections between the political and the literary? Is "Asian American" literature to be read/evaluated somehow differently from "American literature," and if so, how?

These questions animate Imagine Otherwise. In their interrogations of referentiality and calls for reflexivity in discourse and politics, they register this book's engagement with poststructural theorizing and its influence on the contemporary U.S. academic scene. Investigation of the currency and intelligibility of "Asian American" occasions scrutiny of that influence as an exigent condition of contemporary knowledge production. Arguably inaugurated by Ferdinand de Saussure's theorization of the arbitrary nature of the linguistic sign in the opening decades of the twentieth century, poststructuralism's radical destabilization of fixity and transparency in language has been manifested in what is often understood as the postmodern phenomenon of the assertion and recognition of the constructedness of "the real." That is, under the name of postmodernism, and underwritten by the social and political movements of the 1960s and 1970s that similarly demanded a radical interrogation of authority, poststructuralism's insights articulate to a critique of European master narratives of progressive subjective enlightenment characterizing modernity. And in the U.S. context, that articulation has conditioned the emergence of multiculturalism, which can thus be seen as a consequence of challenges to and the unraveling of structuring meta-narratives.[2] A paradigm that acknowledges the limitations of meta-narratives of Identity and History, multiculturalism is often evoked as justification for fields like Asian American studies. In other words, Asian American studies may be seen as a formation of the critical landscape configured by a (poststructural) problematization of referentiality, which facilitates the (postmodern) jettisoning of the authority of the meta-narrative.

Despite these genealogical links to poststructural theory, Asian American studies has yet, I believe, to contend thoroughly with their implications. And at least two reasons for this are immediately apparent. First, the dominant narrative of Asian American studies consistently foregrounds political activism, especially in the language of community work and social transformation, an emphasis that derives from its rootedness in the socio-political movements of the 1960s and 1970s. Student strikes in that era on the campuses of San Francisco State University and the University of California at Berkeley compelled the academic institutionalization of Asian American studies, a process that continues today at various sites around the nation. The vitality of this narrative, which has in many ways been instrumental to establishing Asian American studies in institutional locations over the past three decades, has tended to overshadow other possible narratives of the field's emergence.

And second, it is arguably politically suspect to claim or adopt a relation to poststructuralism, a deeply Eurocentric philosophical tradition that makes difficult immediate political intervention by means of its destabilization of subjectivity itself.[3] In undermining the knowability of "knowledge," poststructural thinking corrodes the authority of the "knowing" subject, whose grounds for action are consequently called into question. Here, subjectivity is conceived as an unstable construct of repressive/constructive orders of knowledge.[4] Neither "subject" nor "knowledge" has within this framework immanent authority/validity/stability.

Despite, on the one hand, the value of the political activist narrative of Asian American studies and, on the other, the questionability of tracing Asian American studies through poststructuralism, I believe that investigating the object(ive)s of Asian American studies in relation to poststructural theorizing illuminates ways that the field may productively imagine itself within the contexts and currents of the present historical moment. This is done in part to enable us fully to contend with the impact of liberal multiculturalism, arguably the dominating paradigm of U.S. academic culture today. Multiculturalism, contradictorily, attempts to retain a liberal conception of subjectivity while simultaneously claiming to take seriously radical critiques of precisely the liberal subject. In so doing, it occludes and effaces the historicity of racism and the deep-rootedness of racialization as a technology through which the United States, also contradictorily, has perpetuated a self-stylization as the achievement of the universalist Enlightenment values of equality and liberty. This kind of multiculturalism manages at once to sediment Asian Americanness in a narrative of otherness that achieves cohesiveness through an emphasis on (previous) exclusion and powerlessness, and to erase the continuities of the materialities underwriting such positions by insisting on the irrelevance of the past.[5] In light of these effects, what does recognizing Asian American studies as a formation of multiculturalism mean in efforts to conceive Asian Americanist discourse under contemporary historical conditions?

The current moment includes globalized practices of capital that have instituted demographic and immigration patterns in such ways as to prompt deliberate attention to how the "national" articulates to the "global." It is by now commonplace to recognize that globalization has made it an increasingly difficult task to determine with any certainty what peoples and cultural practices belong to or originate from where.[6] Globalization refers to the transformations of economic, political, and social organization set in motion by the emergence of transnational capitalist practices, especially since the 1970s. Unlike the multinational corporations of the previous iteration of capitalism, transnational corporations are unanchored in a given nation but rather are highly flexible and mobile in their pursuit of the locales that will best maximize their accumulation of capital.[7] Transnational corporations in fact prompt the development of new nation-specific laws that serve their interests, a phenomenon that signals the erosion of the sovereign power of nation-states. Transnational capitalism is a global mode of production that is globalizing in its attempts to integrate all sectors of the world economy into its logic of commodification. Class exploitation in contemporaneous forms, articulated in racialized and gendered differentiation and layered unevenly across the north/south, first/third world divides, aggressively inscribes this globalized terrain.[8] Multilateral cultural and information flows, enabled by contemporary technologies and driven by jagged relations of power, circulate across this landscape.

The shifts referred to by globalization include the changing economic significance of the Asia–Pacific region, which has affected the demographics and subjectivities of Asian-raced peoples in the United States. The U.S. 1965 Immigration and Nationality Act coincided with the post–World War II burgeoning strength of Asian economies, a difference in circumstance from earlier conditions that has resulted in a resurgence of immigration from Asia to the United States. But now, at least in part, no longer are Asian nations perceived, Eurocentrically, primarily as sources of labor and raw materials for "Western" capitalism. Rather, some are recognized exporters of capital and are influential nodes in the multilateral trajectories of transnational capitalism. Accordingly, while an underclass of immigrant laborers characterizes present as it did past flows of migration to the United States, today there is also a large professional, managerial class whose migrations may be multilateral and whose members are not necessarily interested in formally attaching themselves to the United States by way of citizenship.

Because the 1965 legislation favored the latter cohort of migrants, the roughly fivefold increase between 1970 and 1990 in the population of persons of Asian descent living in the United States has meant dramatic alterations to "Asian America" along multiple identificatory axes, including nativity and citizenship. Theorization of subjectivity follows suit, as earlier models of subject formation face revision to better correlate with this globalized scene. "Oppression," "marginalization," and "resistance," keywords in dominant narratives of Asian American studies, are terms that each require redefinition within this globalized context, as "by whom" and "against what" are questions that are increasingly difficult to answer with certitude. The uneven power relations and disparate distribution of resources to which these terms refer have not dissolved; rather, they have been articulated into new forms, necessitating investigation of the "scattered hegemonies" that characterize the present (Grewal and Kaplan 1994).

This moment too is characterized by discourses like feminism that also prompt concerted efforts to conceptualize subjectivity in ways that privilege difference over identity through interrogations of the racialized, gendered, classed, and sexualized ideologies underwriting U.S. national subjectivity. The convergence of these socio-discursive movements that critically recognize diversity and those that illuminate the operations and effects of globalization compels the generation of epistemologies that bear a renewed sense of the difficulties of defining (much less achieving) justice given shifting material terrains and the irreducible complexities of life, culture, and politics.[9] Poststructuralism or, more specifically, a "deconstructive attitude" contributes to this process by emphasizing the need to interrogate "identity-as-such," as R. Radhakrishnan has put it (1996, xxiii). The maintenance of a deconstructive attitude keeps contingency, irresolution, and nonequivalence in the foreground of this discourse. Such a stance helps the interrogation of field coherency in the face of multiple kinds of differences, precisely by its emphasis on difference as anterior to and irresolvable in identity.

Recall that deconstruction is neither method nor technique; rather, it is the state of internal contradiction itself, of the constitutive difference within any seemingly stable term (*différance*). "Asian American," because it is a term *in difference from itself*—at once making a claim of achieved subjectivity and referring to the impossibility of that achievement—deconstructs itself, is itself deconstruction. "Deconstruction takes place," Jacques Derrida theorizes. "It is an *event* that does not await the deliberation, consciousness, or organization of a subject" (1988a, 4). In other words, deconstruction is a state of becoming and undoing in the same moment. "Asian American" is/names racism and resistance, citizenship and its denial, subjectivity and subjection—at once the becoming and undoing—and, as such, is a designation of the (im)possibility of justice, where "justice" refers to a state as yet unexperienced and unrepresentable, one that can only connotatively be implied. Arguably, the overarching purpose of Asian American studies has been and continues to be pursuit of this (im)possibility, the pursuit of an as yet unrealized state of justice by tracing, arguing, and critiquing, and by alternatively imagining the conditions that inscribe its (im)possibility. Justice is understood here not as the achievement of a determinate end, but rather as an endless project of searching out the knowledge and material apparatuses that extinguish some (Other) life ways and that hoard economic and social opportunities only for some.

As the discussion that follows will show, a deconstructive understanding of "Asian American" emphasizes a necessary reflectiveness of Asian Americanist discourse upon itself. In part, this serves as an effort to intervene in multiculturalist ways of subjectifying and conceiving Asian American and other ethnic studies fields, to work through and against, in other words, the liberal legacy of negotiating identity and difference in such a way as to flatten power relations. But also, this deconstructive attitude attempts to shift the grounds of intrafield debates about Asian American subjectivity that seem to resort to some version of identity for intelligibility. To imagine otherwise is not about imagining as the other, but rather, is about imagining the other differently. It is, to borrow from Gayatri Spivak, "to *recognize* agency in others, not simply to comprehend otherness" (1997, 473; emphasis original). By emphasizing the internal instability of "Asian American," identity of and as the other—the marginal, the marginalized—is encouraged to collapse so that the power relations to which it referred may be articulated anew, as the basis and effect of an Asian Americanist discourse grounded in difference.

I recognize that in interpreting Asian American studies in these particular ways, I am prioritizing the role of literary studies despite its constitution by multiple disciplines. Clearly, my own disciplinary biases are in play. At the same time and not unrelatedly, I will suggest that approaching Asian American studies literarily traces the internal work (the deconstruction) of individual disciplines necessary for Asian American studies to work interdisciplinarily in more than name alone. And that remains a project of some significance for Asian American studies, lest its transformative energies be deflated by cooptation of its practitioners into traditional disciplinary divisions, a point to which I shall later return.

Imagine Otherwise argues that current conditions call for conceiving Asian American studies as a *subjectless discourse*. I mean subjectlessness to create the conceptual space to prioritize difference by foregrounding the discursive constructedness of subjectivity. In other words, it points attention to the constraints on the liberatory potential of the achievement of subjectivity, by reminding us that a "subject" only becomes recognizable and can act as such by conforming to certain regulatory matrices. In that sense, a subject is always also an epistemological object. If Asian Americanists have mounted sophisticated interrogations of representational objectifications of Asian-raced peoples in the United States, of dehumanizing images that affiliate certain object-ive meanings to certain bodies, we have not, I think, always paid such critical attention to "Asian Americans" and to "Asian

American studies" as "subjects" that emerge through epistemological objectification. Part of the difficulty in doing so results from the powerful demands of the U.S. nation-state's celebration of citizenship, or national subjectivity, held out as "natural" and tantamount to achieved equality and so long denied to Asian-raced peoples. In spite of claims about the death of the Subject heralded by postmodernism, the idea and importance of a consummate subjectivity remains unabashedly vital in the state apparatuses of the law. As the uniquely authorized discourse of the nation, and in contrast to the postulation of the modern era that subjects (to monarchal power) have transformed into consensual citizens (of a nation-state), law requires subjection/subjectification.[10] The centrality of citizenship and subjectivity to the politics of modernity both motivates and explains Asian American studies' central concerns with representation and representational politics in similar terms. The importance of political/legal subject status telescopes into the importance of discursive subject status; the metaphor of marginalization manifests the distance between these—between, that is, the "American" and the "Asian American." And clearly, as long as the state demands subjectivity and wields its particular kinds of power, Asian Americanists cannot simply dismiss those terms altogether.

At the same time, and despite how enormously enabling citizenship continues to be in the garnering of access to certain material resources, subjectivity itself, alone, cannot remedy injustice. Recognition of the subject as epistemological object cautions against failing endlessly to put into question both "Asian American" as the subject/object of Asian Americanist discourse and of U.S. nationalist ideology, and Asian American studies as the subject/object of dominant paradigms of the U.S. university. Otherwise, Asian American studies can too easily fall into working within a framework, with attendant problematic assumptions of essential identities, homologous to that through which U.S. nationalism has created and excluded "others." Subjectlessness, as a conceptual tool, points to the need to manufacture "Asian American" situationally. It serves as the ethical grounds for the political practice of what I would describe as a strategic anti-essentialism—as, in other words, the common ethos underwriting the coherency of the field. If we accept a priori that Asian American studies is subjectless, then rather than looking to complete the category "Asian American," to actualize it by such methods as enumerating various components of differences (gender, class, sexuality, religion, and so on), we are positioned to critique the effects of the various configurations of power and knowledge through which the term comes to have meaning. Thinking in terms of subjectlessness does not occlude the possibility of political action. Rather, it augurs a redefinition of the political, an investigation into what "justice" might mean and what (whose) "justice" is being pursued.

In the context of a globalized world in which corporate economies are often larger than nations' and racialized and gendered class exploitation has corollary renewed vitality, it may seem that a project such as this, that emphasizes discursive constructedness and problematizes the possibility of achieving justice through legal means, moves in the wrong direction. My vantage point as a U.S. academic and citizen undoubtedly underwrites the orientation of this argument. At the same time, I think that precisely these contemporary conditions, including the institutionalized setting of Asian American studies and its practitioners, warrant reflection on what and how Asian Americanist discourse can contribute to ways of thinking and producing knowledge about identificatory categories and subject formations that might interrupt the concepts that justify the sustenance of grossly unjust political and economic practices. Subjectlessness as a discursive ground for Asian American studies can, I think, help to identify and trace the shifting positionalities and complicated terrains of U.S. American culture and politics articulated to a globalized frame, by opening up the field to account for practices of subjectivity that might not be immediately visible within, for example, a nation-based representational grid, or one that emphasizes racialization to the occlusion of other processes of subjectification. It is an approach to conceiving of field coherency that consistently puts the field's own boundaries into question in an effort to resist turning into a properly disciplined academic discourse.[11]

Though I draw from and speculate that there may be implications of this argument for other minoritized discourses, I believe this move toward a subjectless ground is especially important for Asian American studies, given the uniqueness of the "Asian/American" dynamic. As David Palumbo-Liu has argued, "Asian American social subjectivity now vacillates between whiteness and color," and always, "its function is . . . to trace a racial minority's possibilities for assimilation" (1999, 5). Palumbo-Liu uses the construct "Asian/American" to suggest this function, where, "[a]s in the construction 'and/or,' . . . the solidus at once instantiates a choice between two terms, their simultaneous and equal status, and an element of indecidability" (1999, 1). He explains that "as it once implies both exclusion and inclusion, 'Asian/American' marks *both* the distinction between 'Asian' and 'American' *and* a dynamic, unsettled, and inclusive movement" between them (1999, 1). "Asia" in the U.S. frame neither can be or has been completely segregated out of the national imagination nor absorbed into "America" such that distinctions do not remain. Modern America has come into being through mediations of the figure of Asia as a signifier of foreign nations and interests and as that figure is recognized already to be within America. The United States has negotiated both the conditions of its interiority (i.e., "Asians" already in residence) and global relations, a double mode of introjection and projection at work within a field of interplay between U.S. racial ideology and its economic interests. The irresolution of the United States' preoccupation with the "foreign within" manifests in such figures as the "model minority." That stereotypical image precisely bespeaks simultaneous inclusion and exclusion, thus bearing the particular function of being at once a signifier of assimilative potential and of the limitations proscribing that possibility. The distinctness of the Asian/American dynamic suggests ways that "Asian American," through such figures as the model minority, may be co-opted in the perpetuation of injustice. The model minority image stages the competitive divisiveness that deflects attention from systemic conditions that give rise to differential advantage along various identificatory axes (race, gender, class, sexuality, and so on). Precisely because of the co-optability of the Asian/American dynamic toward such ends, Asian American studies must mount redoubled efforts to undermine the essentialism and identitarian assumptions through which such divisiveness proceeds.

The modality of competitive divisiveness registers in the kind of intrafield dissent that the Yamanaka book award controversy represents. Candace Fujikane's (2000) analysis of the controversy and the novel suggests that Asian American studies has clearly paid insufficient attention to intra–Asian American racisms. The counter-charge of censorship mounted in defense of Yamanaka's novel, Fujikane argues, covered over anti-Filipino Japanese racism palpable in the Hawaiian context. The uneven intra–Asian American positions of dominance and power underscored by her critique and by the award controversy itself testify to the ways that Asian Americanist discourse must identify those ideologies and structures that undermine projects of justice by compelling disunity through competition. I return to this discussion in the following chapters, and most explicitly in chapter 4. For now, my point is that a turn toward subjectlessness is driven both by recognition of how "Asian American" can be deployed in the service of conservative ends, and by the need to appreciate fully intra–Asian American difference.

Reconstituting Asian American studies in difference helps us to recognize that Asian Americanist critique must be consistently and insistently critical of both U.S. nationalism and its apparatuses of power, and of analytic frameworks that, however unintentionally, homologously reproduce U.S. nationalism's promotion of identity over difference. Part of the exigency underwriting this argument lays in the institutionalized settings of Asian American studies. The remainder of this introduction maps the term "Asian American" and examines its functions as a marker of "otherness" and as a sign of an academic discourse. That consideration underscores the importance of recognizing Asian American studies as unfolding within the spaces of the U.S. university, an institution, in David Lloyd's words, that "continues to organize crucial social functions" (1998, 15). Within this particular setting, I suggest, emphasizing the literary, discursive nature of the term "Asian American" helps make clear the necessity of revising what counts as "political" in Asian Americanist practices by revising understanding of the status of the subject(s) / object(s) of Asian American studies.

The awareness of contemporary historical and discursive conditions and the institutionalized location of Asian American studies rehearsed in this introduction grounds the encounters with the particular "Asian American" formations that focus each respective chapter. We begin in chapter one with consideration of the ways that the construct "Filipino America" challenges certain paradigmatic assumptions that have been important to cohering Asian American studies. As the Yamanaka award controversy dramatized, the unresolved tension between "Asian American" and "Filipino American" articulates perhaps most immediately the need to reinvent Asian American studies in difference. Carlos Bulosan's *America Is in the Heart* (1988 [1943]) and Bienvenido Santos's "Immigration Blues" (1992 [1977]) anchor that chapter's discussion. Building on the growing body of scholarship that speaks to the specificities of "Filipino America," I argue in that chapter that one of the implications of critically recognizing such particularity is conceiving "Asian America" as a sexualized sign formed through the interplay of multiple systems of subjectification, including the nonequivalent technologies of race, nation, empire, and sexuality. By inviting us to prioritize sexuality as a way of understanding "Asian America," Bulosan and Santos help us to understand the limitations of uniform subjectivity as a construct regulating the boundaries both of the U.S. nation and of Asian American studies.

The arguments offered in chapter 1 are complemented directly by the discussion constituting chapter 4. There, I reestablish the limitations of a discourse and politics framed by the paradigms of space and subjectivity made available through the form of the nation-state. In that chapter, I extend the consideration of Yamanaka's *Blu's Hanging* begun here and locate inquiry specifically within the context of Hawaiian history and politics. In so doing, I demonstrate how the "postcolonial" as an analytic critiques the borders of Asian American studies in such a way as to identify how Asian Americanist discourse might resist transformation into a depoliticized instrument of hegemonic nationalist pedagogy. Employing the insights garnered through the preceding analyses and echoing in particular the arguments of chapter 1, I ask after what is lost when a text like Yamanaka's is evaluated primarily in terms of race and racism, and what broadening the terms of criticism might do to our understanding of the novel and the issues raised by it.

Bracketed by these linked discussions, chapters 2 and 3 do the work of exploring the potential of transnationalism as a discourse that offers alternatives to the frame of nation. Anchored by analysis of John Okada's *No-No Boy* (1992 [1957]), a novel "about" Japanese American internment during World War II, and by examination of Hisaye Yamamoto's story, "High-Heeled Shoes" (1998 [1948]), written in the same era, chapter 2 argues that the transnational as a critical frame in Asian Americanist discourse reaffirms the importance of maintaining a deconstructive attitude toward identity in generating and employing paradigms alternative to nation. The historic deployment of the "transnation" as a means for justifying internment points to ways that transnationalism may be used to reify specifically *national* boundaries through a reaffirmation of the identity of the "true" national subject. In that chapter, I argue that employing the transnational as an analytic helps us to recognize the *undecidability* of identity and contributes to the construction of an Asian American studies geared specifically toward undermining racial essentialism. Moreover and equally importantly, the transnational emerges from that discussion as a critical frame attuned to bringing to surface the practices of life and culture that unfold beneath the radar of state power. Okada and, especially, Yamamoto compel us to understand that even or perhaps especially when, as in the historic instance of internment, the U.S. nation's power is seemingly near-absolute, life continues in all of its complexities. Pointing not only to the nation-state's power but to its powerlessness as well, the transnational along these lines functions as a tool for identifying the variegated *spaces* of the U.S. nation.

Chapter 2's introduction of space as an axis of analysis translates in chapter 3 to a concerted focus on the spatial logic of U.S. nationalism and of Asian American studies. Chapter 3 extends consideration of transnationalism and Asian American studies and demonstrates the need to trace deeply the global contexts within which both national and transnational subjectivities are formed. Driven by the insights of Ronyoung Kim's *Clay Walls* (1987) and Chang-rae Lee's *A Gesture Life* (1999), I underscore in chapter 3 the ways that practices of Japanese imperialism participate in producing "Korean America" as a formation that is both national and transnational, as subjectivities that are demonstrably effects of apparatuses of subjectification, which are themselves effects of negotiations of unstable and changing global power relations. These writers help to illuminate the limitations of a territorial imagination that cannot account for the transnational dimensions of nationalized subjectivities. In so doing, they prompt us to understand the ways that Asian American studies' historic definition of itself as distinctly "about" here can effectively support a colonial epistemology contrary to the project of social justice.

This book unfolds largely by means of examining various legal narratives—cases and legislation—in conjunction with literary texts. As I have already begun to suggest (and as I discuss more fully below), because debates about the meanings and methods of Asian American studies center around questions of representation, literary and legal discourse, with their respective foundational concerns with representation and subjectivity, prove apposite sites from which to mount this study. I draw from especially critical race theory legal scholarship and feminist jurisprudential scholarship to understand how U.S. law works upon the assumption of the consensual subject—a subject anterior to politics—an understanding that drives identity-based models of political activism.[12] Consistently, as the discussions in the following chapters demonstrate, the modern subject of U.S. law does not and ontologically cannot represent, can neither fully stand nor act for, the racialized "other." The literary texts considered here schematize an understanding of subjectivity that takes issue with the assumption of modern subjectivity that the subject precedes politics. Along these lines, *Imagine Otherwise* conceives of Asian American literatures and U.S. legal discourse as functionally theoretical texts. They forward contrasting—though not necessarily directly oppositional—understandings of the nature of normative truth claims about race, gender, and sexuality as categories of nationalized/naturalized subjectivity, and about the nature and value of normativity itself. It is within these theoretical, philosophical, "disciplinary" contrasts that this book considers questions of justice; indeed, it is in part from the spaces of these differences that the imperative to work interdisciplinarily emerges, as I discuss below.

multiculturalism, or, why read literature as theory

If the questions driving *Imagine Otherwise* arise through reflecting on Asian American studies, they also engage in ongoing conversations in U.S. American literary studies. Among these, especially persistent and pertinent to this present project are those that take up the position of "minority" literatures (the "multicultural problem") and the place of "theory" (the "theory problem," which is also the problem of the "literary"). The multicultural problem has particular visibility in relation to canonicity and curriculum, and multiculturalism often serves as putative solution. The racialized, sexualized, gendered character of debates over what gets taught, by whom, and how is easily recognized.[13] It will no doubt be familiar to those who work with such texts that within that frame, minoritized literatures tend to be coded as "(multi)cultural." Meanwhile, the "literary" is reserved for canonical writers and texts. This solution to the multicultural problem retrenches a divide between "high" (literary) and "low" (minority) culture, effectively racializing the idea of culture itself. It thus exemplifies what Rey Chow has described as "an institutionalization of racialization of intellectual labor . . . resulting in an aristocracy and a subordinate class in terms of the production and dissemination of 'knowledge'" (1998a, xvi). Dismissively referred to as a symptom of identity politics or political correctness, this kind of logic minoritizes (re-racializes and re-hierarchizes) even as it "celebrates diversity." It reduces the rationale for offering courses like Asian American Literature to a matter of demographics (as in, "X percentage of students on this campus are of Asian descent and, therefore, Asian American Literature").

This version of multiculturalism is recognizably, as Minoo Moallem and Iain Boal have argued, a "multicultural nationalism," an iteration of liberal ideology that "operates on the fault line between a universalism based on the notion of an abstract citizenship that at the same time systematically produces sexualized, gendered, and racialized bodies, and particularistic claims for recognition and justice by minoritized groups" (1999, 245). Inasmuch as the modern (U.S.) university is tasked with producing citizens vis-à-vis multicultural nationalism, efforts within the academy to prioritize and protect difference must negotiate structural elements designed to herald the possibilities and promises of abstracted citizenship. As David Lloyd cogently explains:

> The [U.S.] university is modeled . . . on a European system that promoted not so much a mono-ethnic culture as . . . a universalist culture which, though mediated through national differentiations, is assumed to supercede local or ethnic values or knowledges. The disciplinary structure of the university further reinforces this model by dividing the sciences from the humanities and from the social sciences, a division that corresponds to a postenlightenment (that is, Western and modern) division of a universal human reason into "faculties," and in turn into the larger differentiation of spheres of practice within Western society: the technological/economic, the political, and the cultural. The disciplinary as well as the curricular structure of the university is profoundly "Western" and conforms in all respects to the West's notions of modernity, academic objectivity, relevance, and hierarchy of bodies of knowledge. (1998, 20)

Debates about canonicity and curriculum in relation to multicultural literary studies in this sense are symptomatic of the structural barriers to attending to difference in light of the university's liberal mission to abstract and universalize. "Ethnic and minority positions as such always emerge in differential relation to the unifying tendencies of the state and its apparatuses, and this differential formation of positions produces the contradictions in which the pluralist model founders: the *plures* out of which the *unum* should emerge are in fact constitutively, not merely accidentally, antagonistic to it" (Lloyd 1998, 21). Lloyd argues the need to work proactively to change the structure of the university as part of a far-reaching project of investigating modern political subjectivity. Such an insight, though perhaps implicitly, drives the interdisciplinary focus of fields like Asian American studies, a point to which I shall later return. Articulated specifically to the parameters of American literary study, it also, I think, requires resistance to the return of referentiality that characterizes the sedimentation of "multicultural literatures" as expressions of "other" cultures. For the multiculturalism enabled by the poststructural/postmodern undoing of Authority articulates to the structural economies of the U.S. university in such a way as to promote a version of otherness, as the identity of the other, against which Asian Americanists must work.

The constitutive antagonism to which Lloyd refers in other words plays out in the failure of U.S. multiculturalism to allow for the complexity of "ethnic literatures," which are effectively coded as transparent, self-evident expressions.[14] Such a positioning obviously makes difficult an engagement with minoritized literatures as anything other than ("authentic") artifacts of an ethnography of the Other. Otherness, here, appears principally as an *idea*, one devoid of the contradictions and complexities that inscribe and describe people's lives.[15] In other words, an already determined idea, a predetermined *ideal*, of minoritized cultures, of otherness, predicates acceptable versions of alterity. Importantly, the idea/ideal of otherness animating U.S. multiculturalism enables what Rey Chow has termed "self-subalternization" (1993): since this multiculturalism is a model of sameness-in-difference, then anyone and everyone is an other. This includes not only the assertion of the sameness of "white" and "non-white" (or "multicultural"), but also of researcher/scholar and subject. Within this scheme, the other is no longer oppositional, but simply another, and the researcher/scholar's privileged and empowered position is quickly effaced. The conservative effect of this resolution of the multicultural problem precisely registers in the racialized distinction between the literary and the multicultural.

One way of challenging this flattening of otherness into otherness-as-the-same may be to appropriate and redirect the logic of multiculturalism by introducing a third term, "theory." That is, if the literary (through multiculturalism's logic) excludes the multicultural, and if theory putatively excludes the literary, then we might write Asian American literatures into the space of theory itself. Theory, to borrow from Jonathan Culler, names works that "exceed the disciplinary framework within which they would normally be evaluated and which would help to identify their solid contributions to knowledge" (1982, 9). Asian American literatures' excessiveness, its uncontainment by the literary, dramatizes this definition. Moreover, conceiving of Asian American literatures as theory recognizes that, as Barbara Christian has explained, "people of color have always theorized—but in forms quite different from the Western form of abstract logic. And I am inclined to say that our theorizing . . . is often in narrative forms, in the stories we create, in riddles and proverbs, in the play with language" (1990, 38). Theorization by "people of color" in literary forms displaces the question of the relevance of theory to literary studies: Insofar as "people of color" and "Asian American" are designations of racial formations, this theorization, following Michael Omi and Howard Winant (1994), is interested and invested in the socio-historical apparatuses and processes through which racial categories are manufactured and signified. The material embeddedness of cultural expressions ("theory") emergent from positions of subjugated alterity re-injects power into the equation, creating a disequilibrium that unsettles sameness-in-difference. This move of defining Asian American literature as theory potentially effects both the disruption of the multiculturalist sedimentation of Asian American and other minoritized literatures as seemingly transparent vehicles of authentic otherness, and the unbounding of "theory." As Donald Goellnicht explains, it is "to appropriate to Asian American texts the power usually reserved . . . [for] what metropolitan Europeans and Americans at the center of academic power write" (1997, 341). Christian and Goellnicht remind us that the politics of knowledge that gives rise to such categorical divisions is a *racialized* politics, a locus of struggle over racialized power.[16]

This (re)definition of Asian American literatures prompts a reconceptualization of culture, from something one has either by nature (for "the multicultural" or "ethnic") or refinement (for "the literary"), to that which is a site in which the affiliation of meaning to individuals, ideologies, and social structures occurs in negotiation with the material conditions of existence shaped by politics and economics.[17] That is, in contrast to understanding "culture" as a referent of multicultural difference, and "culture" as a signifier of achievement ("high culture"), here culture is understood as the locus in which signification has a material life. Asian American literatures stand as the material traces of such practices of signification. From that vantage point, they offer a theory of the materiality and partiality of knowledge itself. "Theory oppresses," Trinh Minh-ha reminds, "when it wills or perpetuates existing power relations, when it presents itself as a means to exert authority—the Voice of Knowledge" (1989, 42). As the following chapters will show, the particular Asian American literatures considered here argue a different stance on knowledge by calling for scrutinization of the materialities underwriting in particular the authority of national subjectification as a process of signification—of "knowing."

To be clear, I do not mean to rebound Asian American literatures tightly as "theory." Rather, I mean to emphasize the ways that they offer "theoretical" knowledges, where "theoretical" refers in a common parlance sense to the "unreal." Weighted by the burden of authenticity, Asian American literatures seem to have some immanent, "real" meaning to them. Invoking the term "theory" in this sense is a tactic employed to problematize that kind of understanding of them. I offer Asian American literatures-as-theory as a provisional identification designed to undermine its definition as transparently "multicultural," not in order to reconcretize it.

deconstructing "Asian American"/ reconstructing Asian American studies

I have been arguing that unraveling distinctions between literature and theory may contribute to the project of challenging the hierarchical racialization that effects the subordinate status of Asian American literary studies in the realm of U.S. American literary studies. That doing so, in other words, intervenes in the conservative effects of U.S. multiculturalism. The deconstruction of other distinctions, like those between "activist" and "academic," can help, I will suggest in this section, the broader project of transforming the work and idea of the university.

"Asian American" emerged in the 1960s as a representational sign alternative to the predominating image of the forever-foreign, unassimilable "Oriental" through which Asianness in the United States had historically been coded. With its grammatical assertion of an American identity, activists of the era put forward the term as part of a cultural nationalist strategy of "claiming America."[18] Gary Okihiro offers an enlightening summary: "Asians in America, historically and within our time, have been and are rendered perpetual aliens, strangers in the land of their birth and adoption. Simultaneously, Orientalism has conflated the diverse ethnicities that constitute Asian America and therewith has exacted similar treatment of and tribute from those dissimilar groups. Those commonalities—the ties that bind—arose within the context of the United States. Little wonder that activists and intellectuals seized upon the United States as the site for contestation, to claim as a politicized, pan-Asian people its spaces and its ideals" (1999, 441). Rooted in this cultural nationalism that proclaims a pan-ethnic unity based on experiential similarity as a strategy of antiracist activism, "Asian American" has since faced criticism as part of the critique of such paradigms for their heteronormative and masculinist biases, as well as their erasure of diversity.[19] As the demographic, historical, and experiential diversity among Asians in the United States has proliferated, the difficulties of using "Asian American" descriptively have become increasingly apparent.[20] Those who might identify as "Asian American" may be newly arrived immigrants or have generations-old roots in the United States; they inhabit the widest range of social and economic and political positions; and they may refuse the pan-ethnic designation in favor of more or less particularized terms of identification. Organized around identity, the term homogenizes diversity such that recognizing "differences among" fractures its intelligibility. Attempts to resolve fragmentation by pluralizing its designated referents (as in Asian American literatures and histories), while successful in indicating multiplicity, appear able only to recognize (as in the multicultural models discussed above) rather than account for difference.[21]

Such adjustments, through pluralizing or through expansion, as in "Asian Pacific Islander American," are clearly corrections designed to enhance the term's accuracy, its reflectiveness as a representational sign. Remaining in a descriptive mode, "Asian American" and its various permutations in this sense serves as a positivist identity category: correcting the term's inaccuracies indicates an understanding of the nature of language as referential, and of identity as more than less stable. This "Asian American" in effect implies a normative subject. Definitional debates along these lines cannot but end in a dead end, where one either is or is not found to be a "real" Asian American, whether a particular representation is or is not found to be "authentic."[22] Here we might recall that the grounds for deploying "Asian American" are inseparably connected to a history of (racist/refused) representation both in the literal sense of "acting for" and in the figurative sense of "standing for." The parameters of what constitutes politics itself has productively shifted as a result of these kinds of definitional debates such that connections between representation and politics can be more explicitly identified and more readily analyzed. But perhaps precisely because of this connection between "acting" and "standing," "Asian American" in this regard serves as a unit of a normalizing discourse not wholly dissimilar from the ways that U.S. legal discourse works to establish and sustain norms of behavior and identity.

And this is an important connection. For this descriptive "Asian American" works in accord with the civil rights discourses dominating the U.S. social and political landscape in the 1960s, its moment of generation. Rights are fundamental units of U.S. jurisprudence and bespeak its rationalist, Enlightenment underpinnings. They function upon the assumption of autonomous individuals who possess rights as a matter of both nature and social contract, and such possession defines the importance and parameters of individual autonomy. Justice, within this economy, is derived by proclaiming a denial of rights that "ought" to be in one's possession, by claiming standing as the implied, proper subject of the law.[23] Only by claiming position as, or identity with, the legal norm can one achieve this version of justice. This is a situation that has meant for Asian-raced peoples in the United States the need to claim standing as national subjects, as deserving of everything from rights to immigration and citizenship to property ownership and miscegenation—all historically refused to "orientals."[24] A persistent domestic focus in Asian Americanist work registers this legal/political/representational history. As Sau-ling Wong summarizes, "Asian American studies began with an activist commitment to 'local' (as opposed to 'homeland,' i.e., 'Asians in Asia') politics; an emphasis on the experiences of American-born, Anglophone Asians; and a strong anti-Orientalist agenda that, in extreme cases, led to a studied avoidance of Asian connections by cultural critics" (2001, 135). At the same time that working in terms of the nation (i.e., working for rights, for example) has garnered certain forms of "justice," doing so also plays into myths of Americanness that cover over the material contradictions of U.S. culture and politics.

There is a certain contradictoriness, a certain inadequacy, in working within this hegemonic national paradigm with its attendant celebration of a rights-endowed subject status (citizenship) as a means to promised freedom and justice. In *Immigrant Acts: On Asian American Cultural Politics* (1996), Lisa Lowe demonstrates how the racialization of immigrants from Asia has been a state technology employed to suture together the conflicting demands of capital and of the U.S. nation-state. In so doing, she argues the limitations of the liberatory potential of the liberal nation-state form and its corollary citizen-subject. Lowe limns the ways that capital requires differentiation while the nation-state must unify its members largely through advancing Enlightenment liberalism's universal citizen-subject. In this sense, racialization and universalization are concomitant processes in the U.S. context, and thus citizenship itself is found to be complicit in the inequitable distribution of power and resources that results from capitalist practices. The racialization of Asian immigrant labor has consistently served, though in varying forms, to cover over this contradiction. Lowe reminds us that "the U.S. nation was founded exactly by establishing citizenship as a legal and political category for white male persons that historically excluded nonwhites and women and that guaranteed the rights of those male white citizens over nonwhites and women" (1996, 27). The advancement of the concept of citizenship as abstract and universal and thus accessible to any and all, which is central to American mythology, precisely disavows this exclusionary history. When recognized, it becomes impossible to rely on national subjectivity as a means of liberation. At the same time, it becomes possible to see "Asian American culture as an alternative formation [at a distance from national culture] that produces cultural expressions materially and aesthetically at odds with the resolution of the citizen in the nation" (1996, 6). "Asian American," in short, cannot stand as the national subject, nor can it be understood outside the context of the material conditions of its formation.

And yet, despite such insights, the normalizing valence of a subject-based definition of "Asian American" continues to circulate, registered in continuing debates over the academic ("theory") versus activist ("practice") orientations of the field and its practitioners. The imperative to articulate whatever scholarship, whatever critical practices, in the language of social transformation and political efficacy, plays out explicitly in these terms where the standard of value is contribution to community or, more specifically, to the community. In its inaugural moments, activists and intellectuals were seen as one and the same. Struggles to establish Asian American studies in universities were part of the efforts of ethnic studies movements generally to democratize the university, and being connected— "giving back"—to the community served as controlling ideology. The inclusion of Asian American studies was to remedy previous exclusion, to serve as an avenue of access for Asian Americans née orientals. "Activist" is the privileged term within this context. And while this debate has usefully focused attention on making and recognizing connections between what happens within universities and without, it is worth revisiting the underlying assumptions about the stability of such terms as *community, activism/practice*, and *academic/theory*. It is perhaps most readily apparent that the idea of "the community" presents some difficulty in light of the multiple communities in which one might participate or claim belonging and, indeed, in light of the fact that an "Asian American community" may not be a readily available formation at all. And as the problems of defining the community become clear, so too do the difficulties of adjudicating academic work as activist, of applying the standard of community contribution in a consistently intelligible way.

In another register, privileging "practice" over "theory" seems especially troublesome for the ways in which it deploys the selfsame logic that maintains the minoritized status of the field. As I discussed above, that distinction plays into a racialization of intellectual labor. While at first glance a rejection of "theory" may appear to be a way of undermining such hierarchization, *within the institutionalized setting of Asian American studies*, it effectively enables a return of referentiality, a reification of the idea of Asian American culture as transcending historical circumstance. Moreover, these terms of debate occlude recognition of the university as a national-statal institution. Far from being isolated bastions of abstract knowledge production, universities are sites of investment for corporate capital and military interest; they are shaped and sustained by government investments; and in these and myriad other ways, are precisely Ideological State Apparatuses. And indeed, this understanding undergirds the motivations of the movements of the 1960s and 1970s that sought to intervene in this particular site. In brief and crude terms, democratizing the university is in itself a "real world" project, and refusing the opposition of academic and activist is necessary to keep this in mind.

This is not unrelated to the ways in which interdisciplinarity might also help transform the university toward these ends. In recent years, disciplinary differences have been more explicitly considered as critics have responded to the imperative to be reflective about analytic methods and modes, and about the assumption of authority and the meaning of the political that accrue to those methods. Michael Omi and Dana Takagi have summarized that the influence of "postmodern" theorizing in Asian American studies "has created a curious intellectual divide within the field. On the one hand are historians and social scientists who vigorously defend concepts of 'social structure,' and on the other are literary and cultural studies intellectuals who, heavily influenced by postmodern thought, privilege 'discursive practices' " (1995, xi). And while they are quick to point out that "this is a gross characterization of the intellectual differences in Asian American Studies," they explain as well that "while we acknowledge the artificial, constructed, and continually shifting nature of this divide, we also feel that the split is real. Moreover, we would argue that it is one that profoundly affects the work produced and the claims made about it" (1995, xi). I agree with their conclusion that "While claiming to be interdisciplinary, the reality is that most of the scholarly work in Asian American Studies today follows strict disciplinary lines with respect to theory and method" (1995, xiii). This is, as they suggest, arguably a consequence of the professionalization of the field, including the institutional demands by tenure and promotion on faculty members, as well as the growth in numbers of Asian Americanist practitioners, among whom I count myself, trained disciplinarily and without the kind of participatory relationship to the social movements of the inaugural moments of Asian American studies. Indeed, I would add that many of us are now institutionally located "east of California," a commonly used phrase in Asian American studies meant to indicate the particularities of working outside of California, the historically dominant site of both practice and research for Asian Americanists. And, moreover, many are working in settings in which Asian American studies programs are nonexistent and the very idea of the field is still quite novel if not dismissed altogether. Many of us, too, are ourselves "new immigrants," a designation of the cohort of migrants to the United States whose entry was precipitated by the 1965 Immigration and Nationality Act that did away with the national-origins quota systems that had been in place since the 1920s and installed new regulatory mechanisms in their place. As Gayatri Spivak has suggested, this is a pattern of migration motivated by a desire for "justice under capitalism," by a desire, that is, to escape the wages of imperialism, recoded as global capitalism, by, perhaps ironically, removal to the global capitalist "metropole," the United States. This shared desire, Spivak argues, "is what unites the 'illegal alien' and the aspiring academic" and what should motivate us to "reinvent this basis as a springboard for a teaching that counterpoints these times" (1997, 470). There are no pure positions within "these times" (or ever, one may presume), and only by "teaching ourselves and our students to acknowledge our part and hope in capitalism" can we "bring that hope to a persistent and principled crisis" (1997, 474).

From Spivak's suggestion that "since we are imprisoned in and habituated to capitalism, we might try to look at the *allegory* of capitalism not in terms of capitalism as the source of authoritative reference but in terms of the constant small failures and interruptions to its logic, which help to recode it and produce our unity" (1997, 483; emphases original), I take a model for understanding the contradictory position of Asian Americanist work within the institutionalized site of the U.S. university.[25] Within this site, the concept of interdisciplinarity may serve the project of transforming the university both by working at the level of struggling for structural changes, and by working to insist upon the partiality of the knowledges produced by and logics of any given discipline—by insisting upon the *allegorical* nature of the idea of disciplined knowledge. That is, the concept of interdisciplinarity may be a way of tracing the deconstruction of individual disciplinary formations themselves. This task seems especially important given the contemporary conditions of dissimilarities in relationships to the history of Asian American studies and the disparate constraints and ofttimes isolated locations in which Asian Americanists work. Part of this work must be to undermine persistently the multicultural, positivist narratives of otherness that suggest a concrete knowability. That, for me, demands a deconstructive account of "Asian American," a move toward embracing the a priori subjectlessness of discourse.

Such an account works to unify Asian American studies by holding the category "Asian American" under erasure so that its provisional nature and its constructedness cannot be forgotten. Work like Oscar Campomanes's emphasis on the "categorical act" (1992, 1995) and Dana Takagi's (1996) articulation of the differing apparatuses through which racialized and sexualized identities become legible, I understand to function along these lines. For, both of these are examples of efforts to renovate "Asian American" in ways that resist the normativizing impulses of the term as a descriptor. Participating in the broad-ranging de-essentializing projects that have constituted so much of the academic work undertaken over the past several decades, arguments like Campomanes's and Takagi's emerge from an understanding of the (non)referentiality of language that might arguably be described as deconstructive. This kind of work invokes the inaugurating impetus of the term as a representational *sign*. As such, it is arbitrary but inscribed; it comes to have meaning through and within and as an effect of specific structures of social/power relations that are themselves ideologically valenced constructs. "Asian American" in this regard connotes the violence, exclusion, dislocation, and disenfranchisement that has attended the codification of certain bodies as, variously, Oriental, yellow, sometimes brown, inscrutable, devious, always alien. It speaks to the active denial of personhood to the individuals inhabiting those bodies. At the same time, it insists on acknowledging the enormous capacity for life that has triumphed repeatedly over racism's attempts to dehumanize, over the United States' juridical attempts to regulate life and culture. "Asian American" provides entry into these histories of resistance and racism. It transfers the properties of the racialized and gendered nation onto bodies—of people, of literatures, of fields of study. Far from being a transparent, objective description of a knowable identity, the term may be conceived as a mediating presence that links bodies to the knowledge regimes of the U.S. nation. "Asian American" is in this sense a *metaphor* for resistance and racism.

There is, in other words, a *literariness* to the term. "Asian American," as a deliberate and self-reflective term of representation, calls attention to the workings of language, to its structures and functions. It is connotative and evocative and, in that way, perhaps even poetry in itself.[26] There is, indeed, an aesthetic dimension to it—an inquiry into such matters as beauty and truth. In this regard, "Asian American" is *literary*. For this reason, approaching Asian American studies via literary studies may be particularly illuminating. My interest here is not in attempting to fix a definition of the "literary." Rather, it is to direct attention to critical methods and attitudes that attend to the literariness of "Asian American." As Jonathan Culler has suggested, attempts to "theorize the distinctiveness of literary language or the distinctiveness of literature" have "always functioned primarily to direct attention to certain aspects of literature. By saying what literature is, theorists promote the critical methods deemed most pertinent and dismiss those that neglect what are claimed to be the most basic and distinctive aspects of literature. . . . To ask 'what is literature?' is in effect a way of arguing about how literature should be studied" (2000, 276). Likewise, to underscore the literariness of "Asian American" is to argue for studying the ways that it aestheticizes and theorizes the social relations and material conditions underwriting the resistance and racism to which it refers.

As a ground for Asian American studies, what this literary, deconstructive understanding of "Asian American" does is work against the authoritativeness of any seemingly definitive knowledge. Always, it stands as a "partial fixation," to borrow from Ernesto Laclau and Chantal Mouffe (1985, 112)—a momentary configuration of meaning that is impermanent and overdetermined. Laclau and Mouffe have argued "the final impossibility of any stable difference and thus, of any objectivity" (1985, 122) in their theorization of the possibilities for pursuing a radical democratic practice. The " 'experience' of the limit of all objectivity" (1985, 122) they name "antagonism," which "constitutes the limits of every objectivity, which is revealed as partial and precarious *objectification*" (1985, 125; emphasis original). The process of objectification, the rules and methods of adjudication through which objects become "knowable," emerges as a principle focus of inquiry, and antagonism might be regarded as a point of entry for that investigation. This model is helpful to conceiving of Asian American studies as a field of *collaborative antagonisms*, collaborative in the doubled sense of working together and working subversively against, and antagonistic in the ways in which diverse approaches to knowledge critique and identify each other's limits. In this manner, difference and dissensus are more than simply acknowledged; they are valued as defining characteristics. The point is not to work toward resolving differences, to promote some version of assimilation, but is instead to insist on the productiveness of dissensus in demonstrating the impossibility of any objectivity, the irreducible inadequacy of any totalizing approach to or disciplining of knowledge. This conceptualization might displace the centrist metaphor of marginalization as organizing Asian Americanist knowledge politics, a metaphor organized by the idea of subject status problematized above. As a field of collaborative antagonisms, Asian American studies is interested in the irruptions of disciplinary formations. It is invested in facilitating those irruptions by emphasizing the ways that multiple processes of thematization characterizing both individual disciplinary practices and the idea of the university as a whole result in dissimilar subject-effects, the unevenness of which challenges the universal claims of the modern era/university. I do not mean this as a utopian celebration of dissensus. As, once again, Spivak has noted, "difference and conflict are hard imperatives. Difference becomes competition, for we live and participate—even as dissidents—within institutions anchored in a transnational capitalist economy" (1997, 471). For precisely this reason, they are *imperatives*, the imagined *ethical* grounds upon which we must find ways of uniting.

The chapters that follow elaborate the ideas and argument introduced here. By this book's end, I hope it will be clear that Asian American literatures may be seen to advance understandings of what it means to "know" America that cannot be captured by a subject-driven discourse where subjectivity bears the legacy of Enlightenment liberalism's celebration of the nation-state. These are understandings of the material embeddedness of such knowledges that limn the possibilities of an Asian American studies that accounts for difference through a model of what Avery Gordon (1997) has described as "complex personhood" rather than multicultural otherness—that, in short, help us to imagine otherwise in multiple senses.

1

against uniform subjectivity:

remembering "Filipino America"

> The interior of the category "Asian American" ought not be viewed as a hierarchy of identities led by ethnic-based narratives, but rather, the complicated interplay and collision of different identities.—Dana Takagi, "Maiden Voyage" (1996)

> Within the apparatus of colonial power, the discourses of sexuality and race relate in a process of *functional overdetermination*, 'because each effect . . . enters into resonance or contradiction with the others and thereby calls for a readjustment or a reworking of the heterogeneous elements that surface at various points.'
> —Homi Bhabha, quoting Michel Foucault,
> *The Location of Culture* (1994)

Despite the powerful critiques of cultural and state-driven racisms afforded by such paradigms as cultural nationalism, ongoing debates both motivated by and thematizing the tension between "Filipino America" and "Asian America" illuminate how such frameworks have seriously hindered the critical negotiation of difference through their emphasis on uniform subjectivity—on identity. I take in this chapter the difference between "Filipino America" and "Asian America" as exemplary point of entry for thinking through the limitations of critical models like cultural nationalism that are animated by the achievement of subjectivity as political objective. Guided by Carlos Bulosan's and Bienvenido Santos's respective works, together with the insights emergent from debates regarding the nonequivalence of "Filipino America" and "Asian America," I show here that a critical encounter with "Filipino America" compels us to hold as suspect the promise of justice through the achievement of subjectivity.[1] More specifically, I argue that this encounter calls for understanding that Asian American studies must consistently mount a twofold critique: of both U.S. nationalism and its promise of subjective equality, and of Asian Americanist reliance on paradigms that require uniform subjectivity for coherence—that, like U.S. nationalism, homologously equate subjectivity with achieved justice.

The paradigmatic exteriority of "Filipino America" from the dominant practices of Asian American studies to which this chapter speaks has long been argued. Symptomatic of the absence of empire as a formative analytic in Asian American studies, according to critics like Oscar Campomanes, even the discourse surrounding such exteriority has contributed to its sustenance. By a practice of rhetorically constructing what he calls "the Filipino case" through a series of "forgettings," both the construction and exclusion of "Filipino America" effectively support the aura of American exceptionalism central to U.S. nationalism (1995).[2] Indeed, the U.S. governmental and juridical narratives of the Philippines and Filipinos considered here register how such forgettings facilitate the naturalization of U.S. national identity. Concerned with contributing to ongoing efforts to challenge the effects of these forgettings, this chapter also asks, what function do these amnesiac acts have in Asian American studies? Or in other words, how might Asian Americanist discourse ensure that it does not participate in and perpetuate the kinds of disavowals that forgetting Filipinos represents?

In a literal way, "forgetting" is an especially apt term for describing the course that Asian American studies has taken to precipitate tensions between "Filipino American" and "Asian American." After all, the very first "Asian American" communities may be said to have been "Filipino American": in the mid-sixteenth century, small numbers of Filipinos established roots in Louisiana, far earlier than any other migrants from Asia. Working aboard Spanish galleons sailing to trade with Spain's holdings in North America, they jumped ship upon closing in on the continent and made their way to the Louisiana territory. Thus, if "Asian American" history "begins" upon arrival (putting aside for the moment the compelling reasons why this should not be the case),[3] it begins with Filipinos. And it is not the case that Filipinos have been consistently absent from "Asian American" histories—both Ronald Takaki's *Strangers from a Different Shore* (1989) and Sucheng Chan's *Asian Americans: An Interpretive History* (1991), standard histories in Asian American studies, offer treatments of the formation of Filipino American communities in the United States. And in the literary realm, the foundational *Aiiieeeee! An Anthology of Asian American Writers*, edited by Jeffrey Paul Chan, Frank Chin, Lawson Fusao Inada, and Shawn Wong, and first published in 1974, includes writings by and "about' Filipino Americans. I cite these examples to suggest that it is not that Asian Americanists have never known or have not been interested in "the Filipino case." So what begets the paradigmatic forgetting of Filipino Americans? The editors of *Aiiieeeee!* recognized that "Filipino America differs greatly from Chinese and Japanese America in its history, the continuity of culture between the Philippines and America, and the influence of western European and American culture on the Philippines. The difference is definable only in its own terms, and therefore must be discussed separately" (1991 [1974] xi). How is it that "its own terms" have not translated centrally to Asian American studies?

A critical encounter with "Filipino America" helps us to see that part of the explanation lies in the deployment of identity as a mechanism for furthering political representation. Recall that identity is a teleological narrative as used in a politics of identity, one that posits a common origin and looks toward a common destiny. It is in that sense assimilative, as difference must be elided to foreground resemblance. Another way to understand that elision is to recognize it as constituting the amnesia necessary to sustain a sense of stable identity.[4] We can perhaps see this most clearly in the ways that national identity attempts to assimilate difference by requiring those who claim it to forget the past (difference) in order to preserve and celebrate the present (identity).[5] As David Lloyd has pointed out, civil rights work precisely in this manner, as they are by definition and design those elements that designate and prioritize sameness (1991).[6] Thus it is that full endowment of rights signifies the achievement of abstract status as the citizen, defined as equal to/in identity with all other citizens and with the nation. This temporal logic of the difference/identity algorithm plays out even when the constructedness of identity for political purposes is recognized. In fact, that recognition might be seen as a conscious acceptance of that logic as it bespeaks a willingness to forego difference—*temporarily*, that is.

As arguably necessary as that politically driven assimilation of difference has been, because those strategic identities have been organized largely through paradigms of inclusion and exclusion most often articulated through the trope of immigration in Asian Americanist discourse, Filipino Americans have been repeatedly cast into the space of the difference that must be forgotten rather than the identity to be sustained. Histories of multiple colonizations make it impossible to fix definitive origins, as does the diversity of the social and cultural formations among people residing in the Philippine islands; the juridical regulation of immigration and citizenship for Filipinos cannot be narrativized by the trope of exclusion that highlights race-based management of the nation's borders; and the colonial era practice of benevolent assimilation has ensured that the racialization of cultural differences is problematized by enforced hybridization.

Moreover, as I argue here, to the extent that the axis of race has been privileged over that of sexuality in the conceptualization of "Asian American" identity, Asian Americanist paradigms have had difficulty in recognizing how "Filipino America" as a racialized category of socio-political identity was made operational through a particular process of sexualization. While recognition of the stereotype of the hypersexual "Filipino American" has increasingly come to influence the ways that the interactions of race, gender, and sexuality are studied in Asian Americanist discourse, such work arguably has taken as primary the important objective of the demonstration of anti-Filipino racism. By both adding to and thinking through the implications of such insights, as I intend to do here, we are able to see how "Filipino America" illuminates the cooperative workings of whiteness and heteronormativity. In this way, "Filipino America" advances understanding of the importance of *not* privileging race and ethnicity at the expense of other analytics in our study of social subjectivities. To put it otherwise, by functioning as a site of intersection among the variegated differences that discourses of sexuality, empire, race, and nation bring into critical visibility, "Filipino America" advances the reinvention of Asian American studies as a subjectless field. That is, it supports understanding that embracing the a priori subjectlessness of Asian Americanist discourse is a way of creating the critical space for remembering both complexity and difference.

Carlos Bulosan and Bienvenido Santos, whose writings are read in conversation with the legal adjudication of U.S. citizenship for "Filipinos" during the period in which the Philippines and the United States were joined together in a formally colonial union, represent "Filipino America" in ways that distinctly invite the use of the analytic of sexuality. By what I read as their respective critiques of the heteronormative and racialized masculinity of U.S. nationalism, Bulosan's novel *America Is in the Heart* and Santos's short story "Immigration Blues" bring to surface the sexualized demands and wages of the normative subjectivity required and promised by the U.S. nation-state. And in so doing, they call attention to the implicit heteronormativity of Asian American studies' historic promotion of uniform identity. In accord with the growing body of scholarship that undertakes to consider seriously how to attend to sexuality in Asian American studies in a way more adequate than, as Dana Takagi has put it, merely "toss[ing] the lesbian onto the diversity pile," Bulosan's and Santos's works challenge us to think specifically through sexuality in "reconsider[ing] . . . the theoretical status of the concept 'Asian American' identity" (1996, 26, 33).[7] Among other effects, examination of the construction of "Filipino America" through the representations afforded us by these writers contributes an important corrective to the common assertion of the representational emasculation of "Asian America" in popular discourse.[8] Namely, it argues the need for that assertion to be denied standing as exemplary of the "Asian American" experience. If the racism of U.S. nationalism manifested in various dissimilar ways throughout the nation's history has been the driving force behind Asian Americanist critique, these works guide us to affirming the signal importance of conceiving Asian American studies as a discourse of sexuality. The history of the formation of "Filipino" and "Filipino American" identity formations, from a U.S. perspective, is also a history of sexuality. It is a history that registers how sexuality coordinates the relationship of the U.S. nation to race, gender, and class as it shapes the relationships of individuals to the nation-state. Read in this way, "Filipino America" may be recognized as posing a radical challenge to paradigms incapable of addressing the intersectionality of the operations of nonequivalent but inseparably linked identificatory categories.

Relatedly and equally importantly, the attentiveness in Bulosan's novel and Santos's short story to the colonial relationship between the United States and the Philippines furthers the already unfolding integration of a "postcolonial" approach in Asian American studies. By prompting us to question not only the accessibility of an "American" subjectivity to "Filipinos" but also the very desirability of that subjectivity given the United States' imperialist practices, these works suggest the importance of sustained interrogation of precisely that desire. Postcolonial studies in the U.S. academy has traced the histories and legacies of especially European and U.S. colonizing endeavors, and that work has made significant strides in interrupting the exceptionalism that is so much a part of the self-aggrandizing practices of U.S. nationalism.[9] Increasingly making inroads into American studies, postcolonial studies in Asian American studies has of late garnered an energetic currency that in one sense may be seen as a revitalization of foundational precepts in U.S. ethnic studies generally.[10] But it is arguable that at least in Asian American studies, critique of the United States-as-empire has often given way to the exigencies of claiming the United States as "home." Such pressures have subsumed the early presence of empire as a critical frame in the field. Recent scholarship, driven in part by the ways that inattentiveness to empire makes difficult thorough engagement with certain "Asian American" formations like those with histories that trace to South Asian and Southeast Asian countries, has importantly testified to the necessity and productiveness of a postcolonial approach.[11] Bulosan's and Santos's works offer ways of understanding an "American" national subjectivity that are aligned with this scholarship. Especially by illuminating possibilities for and practices of life and culture that are indifferent to (in difference from) those promised and promoted by U.S. nationalism, they help us to understand that the achievement of identity with the nation is a limited and but one of myriad tools available for the sustenance of the lives and cultures of historically disenfranchised individuals and groups.

disruptive masculinities

By recognizing that in *America Is in the Heart*, Bulosan articulates his protagonist's journey to and into America as a search for masculine identity, we can begin to understand how this novel underscores the limitations of privileging race as the primary analytical category organizing Asian American studies. Bulosan defines Allos in terms of an "alternative" sexuality, not in the common parlance use of the term to designate nonheterosexual identities, but rather, in terms of an alternative to the demands of heteronormativity. Allos explains his initial departure from his family's village home as the beginning of his transition from childhood to "manhood" (A 30) and by the novel's close comes to embody a masculinity that is specifically in difference from heteronormativity. Masculinity here signals the process of affiliation of gender to bodies, and, through Allos, we see the inexhaustiveness of heteronormativity as the technology that works to encode normative genders. Beyond critiquing the imposition of a heteronormative heterosexuality, America, together with Santos's "Immigration Blues," helps us to imagine otherwise, to envision alternatives to acceding to demands for uniformity. In this way, they foster the development of critical practices geared toward mining and emphasizing such otherwise imagined identities as a strategy for remembering that even those who are systematically disempowered are never only or wholly powerless.

The novel from the start emphasizes Allos's awareness of his body and the constructedness of the relation between his body and his social identity by highlighting the several accidents that he has as a child and the chronic illnesses that plague him throughout his life. One of the most striking opening episodes of the novel recounts the physical torture of his brother and sister-in-law by members of the nearby community who, for reasons left largely unexplained, see her as the embodiment of immorality. Maintaining from this point forward a heightened awareness of the body as a site upon which power manifests, Allos's story is one that consistently examines the affiliation of social identities to bodies. His particular discomfort with his own body often figures colonialism, and sometimes explicitly, as when to earn money as a child of 11 or 12, Allos performs "nativeness" for U.S. tourists.[12] Making himself "conspicuously ugly," Allos recognizes that "what interested the tourists most were the naked Igorot women and their children. Sometimes they took pictures of the old men with G-strings. They were not interested in Christian Filipinos like me," he explains (A 67). "They seemed to take a particular delight in photographing young Igorot girls with large breasts and robust mountain men whose genitals were nearly exposed, their G-strings bulging large and alive" (A 67). Undressing for the tourists' camera, Allos "exposes" a purposefully falsified body, an identity that deliberately mimics and attempts to exploit the colonial imagination. His description suggests that he recognized though did not synthesize that those bodies are grotesque in the eyes of the tourists. Moreover, his notation in this early scene of the sexualized character of the tourists' interests echoes throughout the novel, a representation through which Bulosan articulates U.S. colonization as a sexualized project. Despite his distinguishing himself from the spectacularized Igorots, never does Allos seem fully comfortable with his bodily identity, which may be read as an inability wholly to disarticulate himself from "them" as seen through the colonial imagination.

Significantly, it is a white American woman, Miss Mary Strandon, an artist-librarian relocated from Iowa to the Philippines, who removes Allos from his life as a "native" and catalyzes his desire for America. She evokes in him shame for his performance of the native and literally domesticates him until Allos "became adept at general housework" (A 69).[13] Introducing him to the figure of Abraham Lincoln, who appears here aggrandized into mythic proportions as representative of the promises of America, Miss Strandon personifies U.S. nationalist pedagogy. The constellation of the tourist and Miss Strandon in this episode mark the novel's driving interest in exploring the contradictions constitutive of America. Allos objectifies himself as a "native" to accommodate the colonial gaze, and yet it is that same gaze that teaches him to be ashamed for performing that expected, imposed identity.[14]

As Elaine Kim has noted, "It is often a white woman who symbolizes the America to which Bulosan's Filipinos want to belong" (1982, 51). Like Miss Strandon, the white women in the novel for the most part represent a generosity of spirit that Allos affiliates to America. Along his journey, we meet Judith, a kindly grocery store clerk "with brown hair and blue eyes" who "fascinates" Allos and furthers his American literary education (A 172–173), and Marian, the syphilitic prostitute who takes him in and earns the money he needs to pursue a formal education before she dies (A 209–218). There are Lily and Rosaline, who offer him hospitality and companionship as he travels from California to Seattle (A 220–221). We meet each of these figures immediately following an experience of usually violent anti-Filipino racism. Through these juxtapositions, Bulosan underscores the symbolic function of the white woman as evidence that counters America's violent unkindness. We meet as well Harriet Monroe, an editor of a literary magazine who not only supports his efforts to become a writer but also perceptively recognizes his physical hunger and feeds him unbidden (A 227–228), and Alice Odell, another writer, "sensitive and lonely," who teaches him that "her life and [his] were the same, terrified by the same forces" of poverty and disappointment (*A* 230) Both of these writers, we are told, become expatriates in order to pursue the ideals of America in light of the realities of the United States that make it seem impossible for those ideals to be realized at "home." Alice Odell's sister, Eileen, becomes Allos's longtime companion, bringing him food and books as he tries to recuperate from the tuberculosis that has debilitated him physically. Nurturing, educative, and maternal, none of these characters is fully developed. They are but shadows of women, consequential primarily because they figure Allos's idealism.[15] In contrast to the mostly violent white men whom Allos meets, these women are im-material: the idealized feminine is dislodged from the body. In this way, *America Is in the Heart* articulates the necessity of overcoming a particular and violent version of masculinity to allow for the realization of the feminine ideal.

The novel punctuates this point with a detailed scene that associates brutality with heteronormative masculinity. While working in the United States with fellow Filipinos to unionize laborers, Allos and his comrades, Millar and José, are kidnapped and beaten.

> Painfully, I crawled to my feet, knelt on the grass, and got up slowly. I saw them kicking Millar in the grass. When they were through with him, they tore off José's clothes and tied him to a tree. One of them went to the car and came back with a can of tar and a sack of feathers. The man with the dark glasses ripped the sack open and white feathers fell out and sailed in the thin light that filtered between the trees.
> Then I saw them pouring the tar on José's body. One of them lit a match and burned the delicate hair between his legs.
> "Jesus, he's a well-hung son-of-a-bitch!"
> "Yeah!"
> "No wonder whores stick to them!" (*A* 207–208)

Evoking the white racist fantasy of the hypersexual Filipino, Bulosan indicates in this scene an awareness of how, and with what sharply material consequences, the imagined can become the literal. While some of the other Filipinos with whom Allos associates through the course of the novel, including some of his brothers, and Allos himself go through a period of embracing violence, finally, his response to the threat of castration, metaphoric and literal, is not to reiterate but to reject this version of heteronormative masculinity. Bulosan's representations in this way appear to be geared toward illustrating the possibilities for living in spite of, and in difference to, this version of America.

Allos's idolatry of white women does not translate into a desire for miscegenation per se, but for the conditions that would make it unremarkable for Allos to be seen in the company of a white woman.[16] Bulosan thematizes the historical anxieties over miscegenation, yet his narration, more than critiquing the racism of antimiscegenationist logic, also interrogates the presumptive desire for heterosexuality that underwrites that logic. Allos's first experience of heterosexual intercourse expresses an alienation from that presumption. Literally forced by fellow laborers at one camp in which he worked into that experience, Allos articulates a disjuncture between the experience of the body and that of the mind.

> I was backing to the door when Benigno and two other men grabbed me. I struggled desperately. I knew what they would do to me. They carried me toward the wall of sheets, and the men who were holding them made way for me. I trembled violently, because what I saw was a naked Mexican woman waiting to receive me. The men pinned me down on the cot, face upward, while Benigno hurriedly fumbled for my belt. The woman bent over me, running her hands over my warming face. The men released me, withdrawing sheepishly from the wall of sheets. Then, as though from far away, I felt the tempestuous flow of blood in my veins.
>
> It was like spring in an unknown land. There were roses everywhere, opening to a kind sun. I heard the sudden beating of waves upon rocks, the gentle fall of rain among palm leaves. Was this eternity? Was this the source of creation? Then I heard a thunderclap—and suddenly the sound and stench of humanity permeated the air, crushing the dream. And I heard the woman saying:
>
> "There now. It's all over."
>
> I leaped to my feet, hiding myself from her.
>
> "Did you like it?" she asked.
>
> I plunged through the wall of sheets and started running between the cots to the door. Benigno and the other men laughed, shouting my name. I could still hear their voices when I entered my tent, trembling with a nameless shame. . . . (A 159–60; ellipsis original)

The nameless shame at having found pleasure in a situation in which his body was removed from his control fades into an ellipsis, marking a disappearance of sexualized desire. Heterosexuality appears here as a markedly homosocial ritual that disrupts its standing as a natural, inherently romantic phenomenon.[17] Because this eroticized violence occurs at the hands of fellow Filipinos, it may be recognized that the novel is critiquing heteronormative masculinity and not just its white iteration. Through these representations, we witness Bulosan literally formulating an identity resistant to heteronormativity.

While the novel has been read and criticized largely in terms of evaluating the extent to which it supports an assimilationist trajectory for "Filipino Americans," interpreting it with attentiveness to how sexuality operates in it begins to sketch the complexity of the picture Bulosan draws. By disrupting the assumption of a natural desire for heteronormative masculinity, that putative bastion of power and authority, Bulosan prompts us to interrogate rather than strive for ownership of that kind of power. In other words, this novel demands careful consideration of the means of empowerment used to challenge discriminatory systems. Self-critique, in the recognition that various systems create subjects of selves, emerges from *America* as crucial to the project of negotiating the United States.

Bienvenido Santos's "Immigration Blues" offers an understanding of "Filipino America" that is in many ways aligned with Bulosan's work, but that emphasizes even further how critique of the racialized demands of U.S. nationalism may be incisively mounted by working along the trajectory of sexuality. Like Bulosan's, Santos's work suggests that the ability to see certain racialized formations may well depend upon the use of sexuality as an interpretive lens. "Immigration Blues" demonstrates how heteronormativity may be coopted and deployed as a tool for resistance to racialized exclusionary immigration legislation and simultaneously as an instrument for community building. Santos stages in this story the circumstantiality of identity for Filipinos and Filipinas for whom the Philippines has been rendered an impossible site of return by virtue of (de)colonization. He highlights immigration as a technology of sexualized identity formation, which in the world of his story is one and the same as Filipino American identity. The protagonist Alipio's recognition of resemblance between one of the two women he sees out of his window as the story opens and his late wife Seniang's sister establishes the direction of the narrative and presages its thematization of marriage and the construction of family. The women, Antonieta Zafra and her sister Monica, have come uninvited to Alipio in the hopes that he will marry Monica and thus enable her to stay in the United States. With this fairly simple plot, the story invokes the complex historical conditions that motivate this particular use of marriage.

This is not, however, a mercenary vision of marriage as a business transaction devoid of emotion. Santos indicates otherwise by making clear that Alipio's marriage to Seniang under similar deportation pressures "was not . . . in name only." Effectively, this story reverses the heteronormative narrative trajectory that begins with love and ends with marriage, in a sense invoking the history of U.S. colonization that began with a formal union and was to result in a "loving" relationship between the United States and the Philippines. By showing how that reversal works to create community and de-isolate individuals, Santos illustrates how the lessons of the U.S. colonial venture in the Philippines have been learned so well as to be reiterable, only for different objectives. This story bespeaks, in other words, the ways that U.S. colonization and tutelage have conditioned the impossibility of effective or exhaustive regulation of the U.S. nation's borders against Filipinos.

Through Antonieta's history as a nun previous to marrying Carlito Zafra, an old friend of Alipio's, Santos parallels marriage to god and marriage to Carlito as mechanisms for evading deportation. Santos challenges the sacred and revises the romance of both narratives of immigration and settlement and of the missionary project of empire. But this story does not celebrate the absence of the sacred altogether, for we understand that Antonieta's decision to marry Carlito was a difficult one, requiring her to revise the values with which she had been raised. Changing material circumstances, according to this story, require a reinvention of sacrosanct values. Antonieta's marriage to Carlito is one presented as perhaps more instrumental than emotional, though she strongly affirms her husband's good-heartedness. Thus, this story does not valorize but rather concerns itself with commenting upon the driving historical forces that circumscribe and produce certain choices and the significance that accrues to them.

For Alipio, romance is found not in a person, but in fate and in words. The utterance of "extension" and "visa" "[break] into his consciousness like a touch from Seniang's fingers. It was quite intimate," we are told. They recall for him his community of "old timers," which bespeaks a time of fellowship rather than loneliness. Learning of his visitors' purpose animates

Alipio—"Boy, oh, boy!" he thinks, while "His gleaming dentures showed a crooked smile" (IB 18). Isolated after Seniang's death when "everything had gone to pieces" (IB 4), Alipio reads these women's appearance as a divine sign—"God dictates," is his favored refrain—and the story closes with his implied acceptance of Monica as his new wife. In this regard, this story might be understood as redefining the symbolic and practical function of marriage. Here, marriage is not the narrative closure to a story of individuals uniting in love, but signals instead the affirmation of community. Marriage for Alipio is a way of continuing a communal past.

Along these lines, this story articulates the experience of exile that, as Oscar Campomanes has suggested, pervades so much of Filipino American literature (1992). "[F]or Filipinos as 'colonial exiles,'" Campomanes explains, "the 'search for identity and the construction of a vision of home amount to the same thing.' In turn, this 'identity . . . condenses itself in the institution of creative genealogies . . . [and] mythic reinterpretations of colonial history'" (1992, 58; quoting Andrew Gurr).[18] Where Bulosan's novel undertakes such a reinterpretation on a grander scale, Santos's story speaks of the microlevel inventions of identity that proliferate to sustain life and create community. Both texts prompt us to displace the privileged centrality of race as the category by which we understand and investigate the formation of "Asian America." They help us to recognize that conceiving of Asian American studies *as* studies of sexuality, and of antiheteronormativity *as* antiracism, is necessary to the project of developing a politics of heterogeneity. Taking us into the space between subjectification and subjection, the inseparably coupled operations of technologies of subject formation, Bulosan and Santos identify that space as the locus for the emergence and survival of alternatives to normative subjectivities. Rather than striving for an American identity, in their respective ways, their works promote the reinvention of America by offering characters who, though residing in the United States, live otherwise.

If these insights are literarily offered, their productiveness in shaping the study of the historico-political formation of "Filipino America" becomes clear in pursuing the threads of history woven into and underwriting these narratives. That is, recovering the colonial past and tracing the ways that "Filipino" came to function as a socio-legal category in the United States illuminate the shortcomings of identity-based critical paradigms. As the following discussions illustrate, doing so challenges the exceptionalism of

U.S. nationalism and underscores the limitations of an emphasis on the achievement of subjectivity to account for the irremedial complexity of "Filipino America."

civilizing love and love of civilization

> The truth is, I didn't want the Philippines, and when they came to us as a gift from the gods, I did not know what to do with them. I walked the floor of the White House night after night until midnight; and I am not ashamed to tell you gentlemen, that I went down on my knees and prayed Almighty God for light and guidance more than one night. And one night late it came to me this way— I don't know how it was, but it came: 1) That we could not give [the Philippines] back to Spain—that would be cowardly and dishonorable. 2) That we could not turn them over to France or Germany, our commercial rivals in the Orient—that would be bad business and discreditable. 3) That we could not leave them to themselves—they were unfit for self-government—and they would soon have anarchy and misrule. . . . ; and 4) That there was nothing left for us to do but to take them . . . and to educate the Filipinos, and uplift and civilize and Christianize them, and by God's grace do the very best we could by them, as our fellow men for whom Christ also died. And then I went to bed and went to sleep and slept soundly.

This oft-cited speech by President William McKinley, David Traxel reports, concluded with his explanation that " 'the next morning, I sent for the chief engineer of the War Department . . . and . . . told him to put the Philippines on the map of the United States'—at this moment McKinley pointed to the large map on the wall of his office—'and there they are, and there they will stay while I am President!'" (1998, 284).[19] The year was 1898, and McKinley was hoping for ratification of the Treaty of Paris, formally ending the Spanish-American War and ceding the Philippines, Puerto Rico, and Guam to U.S. control. Textualized by this cartographic representation as well as by the treaty, which would be ratified by the U.S. Congress despite significant anti-imperialist protest and in part because of renewed patriotism inspired by the onset of the Philippine-American War, the Philippines became enmeshed in the history of American modernity as a figural presence.[20] The Philippines would "stay on the map" as part of the U.S. empire long after McKinley's tenure as president had ended.[21] After many promises and many delays, formal independence arrived finally in 1946.

The year 1898 was a crucial moment in the history of U.S. nation/empire building, as it marked the formal extension of its practices of colonization beyond the North American continent and inaugurated the pattern of willingness to conduct war in the Asian Pacific that would characterize the twentieth century. The strength of the U.S. Navy owes much to this moment, as the need for greater naval power to protect U.S. territories abroad became clear during this period of war first against Spain and then with the Philippines. The U.S. government's treatments of the North American continent's indigenous peoples and the institution of slavery were experiential precursors to its occupation of the Philippines and its racialized justification thereof (San Buenaventura 1998).

As in McKinley's speech, the justificatory rhetoric employed to support U.S. occupation repeatedly infantilized the Philippines and its residents, installing by force a distinctly paternalistic relationship between colony and metropole. Referred to as "little brown brothers" living "in a hopeless condition of ignorance" by William Howard Taft, the first Governor-General of the Philippines under U.S. rule, the islands' inhabitants experienced a transition from centuries-long occupation by Spain to U.S. colonization characterized by war, euphemistically couched as "benevolence." The Philippine-American War followed on the heels of the Spanish-American War and was driven by Philippine nationalists attempting to claim independence. One group, led by General Emilio Aguinaldo, who had been driven into exile as Spanish forces attempted to quell the anticolonial movements in the islands, returned to assist the United States in defeating Spain with the understanding that the Philippines would emerge as a sovereign nation. When that autonomy was not realized, nationalist forces mobilized against the United States.[22] In the United States, the war was perceived more as an insurgency than a battle between nations (Miller 1982), as the United States refused to recognize Aguinaldo or any other nationalist leader as a leader of a nation, instead identifying them as leaders of an insurgent guerrilla movement (Rafael 2000). Influential policymakers in the United States simply assumed that the Philippines would not want autonomy, and when that assumption proved incorrect, expressed surprise and narrativized the "unfitness" of Filipinos for self-government (Traxel 1998; Musicant 1998).

To sustain the United States' veneer of morality even while it conducted war against Philippine nationalists, conceiving of Filipinos as childlike was instrumental. Moreover, the rhetorical strategies employed in arguments for occupation register an arguably gendered image of the islands vulnerable to forcible penetration, accompanied by a not particularly surprising racialization. These images were authorized, as in McKinley's speech, by a simultaneous appeal to divine providence and an unapologetic capitalist logic. As one influential pro-imperialist senator, Albert Beveridge, proclaimed:

> The Philippines are ours forever. And just beyond the Philippines are China's illimitable markets. We will not retreat from either. . . . We will not renounce our part in the mission of our race, trustee, under God, of the civilization of the world. . . . It has been charged that our conduct of the [Philippine-American] war has been cruel. Senators, it has been the reverse. . . . Senators must remember that we are not dealing with Americans or Europeans. We are dealing with Orientals. (quoted in Zinn 1984, 17)

In Beveridge's fantasy, the Philippines was an evacuated territory awaiting domination: "A hundred wildernesses are to be subdued. Unpenetrated regions must be explored. Unviolated valleys must be tilled. Unmastered forests must be felled. Unriven mountains must be torn asunder and their riches of gold and iron and ores of price must be delivered to the world" (quoted in San Buenaventura 1998, 5). Beveridge's statement rather starkly indicates a derivation of pleasure from the potential for forcible power, evoking as it does an unmistakable eroticization of violence. Congress is charged with penetration, violation, and mastery as their duties, a vocabulary that articulates patriarchal, heteronormative masculinity as a technology of empire. For Beveridge, divinely sanctioned capitalism and civilization define the United States and Europe, whereas the Philippines are all but emptied of people, who are in any case dismissed as mere Orientals, subpar humans. If Beveridge's is a particularly virulent account, his sentiment is not exceptional to the imperialist rhetoric of the day.[23] Nor of course is this feminization of Asia and dehumanization of "Orientals" unusual in the discursive practices of "Western" imperialisms (Said 1978).

As Howard Zinn wryly observes, "Filipinos did not get the same messages from God" (1995, 306). The substantial military power of the United States violently quashed Philippine resistance by 1902, although guerrilla warfare would continue for the next decade. Despite the hundreds of thousands of lives lost, Taft nonetheless claimed that "there never was a war conducted, whether against inferior races or not, in which there was more compassion and more restraint and more generosity" (quoted in Rafael 2000, 20). Deftly effacing the wounded and the dead, as in Beveridge's description, Taft's narrative simultaneously justifies U.S. presence and subordinates Filipinos, positioning them as children who require discipline and training to appreciate the United States' attention.[24] Feminized and infantilized burdens of the white man, simultaneously to be "uplifted" and "mastered," the Philippines and Filipinos were to be made ready for self-government through *benevolent assimilation*.

"Tutelage," the practical arm of benevolent assimilation, offered a logic of exchange in attempting to pacify resistance. As Epifanio San Juan has explained, "Taft's policy of 'Philippines for Filipinos,' a slogan more revealing for its disingenuous opportunism than for its diplomatic substance . . . was really a strategy of cooptation articulated in terms of equal exchange. . . . What this hegemonic strategy performed with finesse is its formal conversion of a relation of domination into a relation of exchange, an exchange of services, a contractual relation. . . . In short, subjugation is transcoded into freedom" (1992, 6). In exchange for U.S. tutelage—for the "great brutality" with which the United States "ensur[ed] the political unification of the archipelago by smashing . . . all opposition," as Benedict Anderson has put it (1995, 10)—the Philippines would be given a better version of itself, one bettered (uplifted, civilized) through "Americanization."[25] Tutelage effectively linked metropole and colony and became self-sustaining through the state apparatuses installed by the United States in the Philippines. A bicameral legislature approximating the U.S. Congress was put into place, with a corollary educational system that would help to fill government positions with "appropriately" trained (i.e., Americanized) Filipinos. From the inception of U.S. rule independence was promised—only later. As San Juan summarizes, "U.S. policy required military force to destroy the revolutionary government and suppress the subsequent guerrilla insurgents who sustained the anti-colonial resistance until the end of the first decade of the century, while in the same breath promises of future independence after a period of tutelage were regularly offered" (1992, 26).[26]

Thus forcibly instilling a "love of civilization," to borrow from Vicente Rafael (2000, 21), the United States compelled cultural and political hybridization. Emptying the Philippines of its illimitable cultural, social, and linguistic diversities, the United States' rhetorical justification of its occupation created the "Filipino" as a desexualized child, an unenlightened being yet to be brought to maturity. That construction enabled the reaffirmation of the patriarchal supremacy of the United States, the consolidation of an American identity as a strong-handed masculine presence capable of meting out necessary discipline. As, among others, Gail Bederman (1995) and Amy Kaplan (1990) have demonstrated, U.S. empire-building has historically effected the stabilization of an American heteronormative masculinity, defined in terms of physical prowess and virility, at "home."[27] And as Rafael explains with specific reference to the Philippines, "The tropics opened up a terrain for the testing and validation of white masculinity at a moment of fantasized crisis stemming from the proximity of 'contaminating' nonwhite and nonmale others. The romance of empire was thus a means for shoring up an endangered white masculinity at home by spectacularizing the aura of its sovereign virility abroad" (2000, 55).[28] Narrativized in this way, this colonial history echoes Bulosan's and Santos's sexualized representations of "Filipino America." Neither "race" nor "nation" is sufficient to bring out this dimension of the project of U.S. empire, which is also in this instance the project of giving meaning to "Filipino" as a socio-political category.

threatening men

At "home," the "Philippine Problem" as it was often designated in congressional and popular debates of the era, coincided with ongoing anxieties about the "Negro Problem" and continuing anti-Asian exclusionist movements. As U.S. anti-imperialist voices argued, taking ownership of the Philippines clearly violated the ideals of freedom and equality claimed as exceptionally American and, more narrowly, contradicted the principles of liberty upon which the United States had at least in part entered into war with Spain—to "free" Cuba in particular. One of the issues at stake was the unconstitutionality of "taxation without representation." As Campomanes explains, "if the U.S. Constitution did not allow for 'taxation without representation—which the colonial incorporation of about six million Filipinos logically entailed—then a whole debate and series of resolutions . . . [would need to] be staged to adapt that sacred document" (1995). In 1901, a series of U.S. Supreme Court decisions known as the Insular Cases described the

Philippines as an "unincorporated territory" of the U.S. nation (subject to its jurisdiction yet ineligible for statehood) and concurrently made "American nationals" of the Philippines' residents (also subject to jurisdiction but ineligible for citizenship).[29] This served as a palatable compromise between pro- and anti-imperialist positions taken on the "Philippine Problem"—the latter encompassing "rabidly anti-annexationist Southern senators and constituencies who were fearful about adding another 'race problem' to the 'Negro problem' of the body politic" (Campomanes 1995).

Recall that citizenship, from the first moments that the U.S. Congress specifically addressed it, was explicitly articulated through race, as it was reserved through 1790 legislation to "white persons." From 1790 until the 1952 Immigration and Nationality Act, this racial prerequisite remained in place through multiple changes to requirements for naturalization enacted during that period.[30] One such change occurred in 1875, when Congress provided that "The provisions of this title [naturalization] shall apply to aliens being free white persons, and to aliens of African nativity and to persons of African descent" (section 2169, Revised Statutes). The judiciary confirmed and contributed to this legislated racialization of citizenship by adjudicating a series of challenges to the definition of "white" in ways that effectively created "yellow," "brown," and "red" to accompany "black" as legally recognized categories.[31]

In 1906, Congress passed legislation that intended to accommodate the peculiar situation of those from the Philippines and Puerto Rico seeking naturalization, but because it neglected to address the racial prerequisite, the law created confusion in the courts. Section 30 of the Naturalization Act of 1906 provided that

> All the applicable provisions of the naturalization laws of the United States shall apply to and be held to authorize the admission to citizenship of all persons not citizens who owe permanent allegiance to the United States, and who may become residents of any state or organized territory of the United States, with the following modifications: The applicant shall not be required to renounce allegiance to any foreign sovereignty; he shall make his declaration of intention to become a citizen of the United States at least two years prior to his admission; and residence within the jurisdiction of the United States, owing such permanent allegiance, shall be regarded as residence within the United States within the meaning of the five years' residence clause of the existing law. (34 Stat. 606)

Although the legislative record seemed clear enough in indicating that this provision intended to extend citizenship eligibility to Philippine and Puerto Rican "American nationals," federal courts around the country decided differently as to whether or not section 30 mooted the racial prerequisite.[32] In In re Alverto, for example, a 1912 case adjudicated in the Eastern District Court of Pennsylvania, the court denied petitioner Eugenio Alverto's application for naturalization based on "the opinion that Congress did not intend to extend the privilege of citizenship to those . . . of the Philippine Islands . . . unless they were free white persons or of African nativity or descent" (198 Fed. 688, 691). "Free white persons," according to this court, designated "members of the white, or Caucasian race, as distinct from the black, red, yellow, and brown races" (198 Fed. at 690).[33] Similarly, in In re Rallos, a 1917 case adjudicated in the Eastern District Court of New York, the court decided that petitioner Penaro Rallos, who otherwise had standing to petition for naturalization, "[was] not a white person" and therefore could not be naturalized, for the 1906 legislation had not explicitly repealed the racial prerequisites in place (241 Fed. 686, 687).[34]

Alverto and Rallos are particularly notable cases because the petitioners in both instances invoked their military service for the United States as part of their arguments for naturalization. Filing under an 1894 statute providing for accelerated naturalization upon service in and honorable discharge from the U.S. military, Alverto reminded the court of his record of seven years in and honorable discharge from the United States Navy.[35] The court, however, again found that the racial prerequisites trumped this other statute and denied the relevance of Alverto's military service to his petition (198 Fed. at 690). The New York court adjudicating In re Rallos followed suit (241 Fed. at 687). These decisions indicate that even a willingness to die for the U.S. nation is insufficient to warrant fully enfranchised representation.

At the same time, on the other side of the continent, the Northern District Court in California interpreted the 1906 act to allow for naturalization of Filipinos. In In re Bautista, a 1917 case, the court held that Engracio Bautista should be admitted to citizenship despite the racial prerequisites still in place. The justices explained:

> We think we have clearly shown by the proceedings in Congress that . . . [the 1906 act expressly amended the naturalization laws in place] so as to admit to citizenship all persons not citizens who, owing "permanent allegiance to the

United States," and possessing the other qualifications provided by the statute, became residents of any state or organized territory of the United States. This was done by the Congress with full knowledge that the Filipino belonged to the Malay or brown race. It must therefore have been the purpose of Congress to so modify [the 1875 provisions reserving naturalization to "free white persons and to aliens of African nativity and to persons of African descent"] as to admit to citizenship the Filipino otherwise qualified for citizenship, notwithstanding he is not an alien of the white race nor an alien of African nativity or descent. (245 Fed. 765, 769)

Bautista, who, like Alverto and Rallos, had also served in the U.S. Navy, "[came] to court with proof of good moral character from his superior officers," the court explained (245 Fed. at 767). In admitting Bautista to citizenship, the court summarized that "He has rendered the necessary naval service, has been honorably discharged from such service, and has twice been recommended for re-enlistment, and has the intelligence to understand and appreciate our form of government and the constitutional principles under which it is administered" (245 Fed. at 772–773). Bautista appears to exemplify for this court the success of benevolent assimilation in producing Filipinos capable of understanding and appreciating "our form of government."

These divergent interpretations of Filipino eligibility for U.S. citizenship can be understood as manifesting the contradictions embedded in the construct "American national." A compromise category, one created to resolve the rupture to American exceptionalism that U.S. occupation of the Philippines represented, it did not address so much as cover over underlying incongruities narrated as the "Philippine problem." The inconsistencies across these adjudications of U.S. citizenship eligibility manifest the irresolution of that "problem." U.S. ambivalence over its occupation of the Philippines, together with its attempts to regulate the racialized identity of America, conditions the uncertainty of the Filipino case in the eyes of the law. That is, that the courts could make such contrary decisions evidences how Filipino subjectivity has been constitutively constructed to resist sustainable visibility within the representational grids of the U.S. nation.

If it comes as no surprise that both legislation and adjudication relied on racial qualifications that ultimately excluded Alverto and Rallos from U.S. citizenship, we might nonetheless take note of the courts' dismissal of military service in these cases. Service in the armed forces, this particular expression of patriotism that manifests a willingness to die for the nation, is in one sense the penultimate expression of national loyalty, and one that genders such commitment as heteronormatively masculine. One way of reading these cases is to interpret them as denying access to and/or possession of that masculinity. In those cases, by defining the representative national body in racialized terms, the courts effectively disaffiliate heteronormative masculinity from Filipinos. The physical body, represented by Alverto's and Rallos's willingness to lay it down, literally, for the nation, acquires a political materiality only through negotiation with the U.S. body politic. Their bodies in essence cannot enact an American masculinity; in effect, they are juridically gender-less.[36] Moreover, while the federal court located in California in In re Bautista by this logic "gendered" the Filipino as American, California proved to be the state in which, throughout the 1920s and 1930s, growing antagonism against Filipinos, figured in the racist popular imagination specifically as hypermasculine, became most visible.

The coincidence of the 1907–1908 Gentleman's Agreement that halted most immigration from Japan, the continuing need of industry and agriculture for cheap labor, and the open travel status that Filipinos had as American nationals contributed to the growing numbers of Filipino immigrants, especially in Hawai'i and California through the early 1930s. As with migrants from China before them, laborers hailing from Japan had been actively recruited by sugar planters in Hawai'i and agribusiness in California; limitations to their immigration turned capitalist focus toward the Philippines. By 1930, about 110,000 Filipinos, of whom roughly 65,000 resided and worked in Hawai'i and 45,000 were laborers mostly residing in California, were counted as part of the census; the census two decades prior had numbered their population at just under 3,000. The rapid population increase and relative localization of Filipinos in California and in agribusiness made them an especially visible target for the largely economics-driven antagonisms these immigrants faced. Most (93 percent) of these migrants were men between the ages of 16 and 34; labor recruiters tended to prefer unattached men, the better to economize on living quarters and because they were seen as more likely to move willingly as crop cycles lived through their ebbs and flows and, in a heteronormative logic, as less likely to "settle down" and establish their own farms and businesses (Espiritu 1996a). Additionally contributing to this sex imbalance, in some

Catholic communities in the Philippines, emigration by women was actively discouraged as being against cultural mores (Takaki 1989).

To some extent already "tutored" into familiarity with "America" before having departed the Philippines, these early Filipino migrants faced antagonism for precisely this acculturation. With greater immediate facility in negotiating the social and political structures they confronted in the United States, Filipinos posed a particular kind of threat to the fantasy of the white ethnicity of America. Because of the colonial relationship between the United States and the Philippines, Filipinos could not simply be excluded as were Chinese, nor could they be treated out of the domestic space, for there was no sovereign nation with whom the United States could negotiate, as it did with respect to Japanese migrants. This marks one of the signal distinctions of Filipino from Chinese and Japanese immigration histories. Although they have in common the needs of U.S. capitalism for inexpensive labor, and likewise, "the same economic antagonism," as Leti Volpp has put it, "the primary source of antagonism [against Filipinos] appeared to be linked, even more dramatically, to sex" (2000a, 804).

In her study of the relationship between Filipinos and antimiscegenation laws in California, Volpp summarizes that "Anxiety about what was called the 'Third Asian invasion' was expressed primarily around three sites. First, the idea that Filipinos were destroying the wage scale for white workers; second, the idea that they were disease carriers—specifically, of meningitis, and; third, the idea that they were sexually exploiting 'American and Mexican' girls" (2000a, 805–806).[37] The last of these charges appeared to stem from anxieties about the social contact between Filipinos and white women, especially as taking place in the "taxi dance halls" where "a dime a dance" allowed for intermingling.[38] One particularly vocal nativist agitator, Judge D. H. Rohrback, described Filipinos as "little brown men attired like 'Solomon in all his glory' strutting like peacocks and endeavoring to attract the eyes of young American and Mexican girls" (quoted in Osumi 1982, 18). Characterized by other contemporaries as creating problems by virtue primarily of their putatively voracious sexual appetites, Filipinos became the target of popular violence and juridical attention. Rhetoric and sentiment like this led to such violence as the riots in Watsonville, California, in 1929. A Filipino man had been arrested after being seen socializing with a white woman. Though released after her parents explained their approval of the relationship, the incident sparked an anti-Filipino rampage. As

Ronald Takaki reports, "Within [the] context of hysteria whipped up by local white leaders, four hundred white men attacked a Filipino dance hall. During four terrible days of rioting, many Filipinos were beaten and one was shot to death" (1989, 328).[39]

The Watsonville riots were but the most visible incidents in a pattern of such violence directed at Filipinos. Their association with a Spanish heritage appears to have contributed to the hypermasculinization of Filipinos in the popular imagination, as racist stereotypes about the "Latin lover" were mapped onto Filipinos as well (Melendy 1977; Volpp 2000a). Often with darker skin color than their Japanese and Chinese counterparts, Filipinos were likely to be seen in terms of savagery and primitiveness in ways that analogized them with racist conceptions of black Americans, again confirming a threatening masculinity. Fear of miscegenation of course did not begin with Filipinos; U.S. antimiscegenation laws are an outgrowth of slavery and articulate to "Mongolians" in the nineteenth and twentieth centuries as immigration from various Asian countries increased the numbers of Asian-raced peoples in the United States. As Megumi Dick Osumi, quoting the above-referenced Rohrback, summarizes, "Most Californians of the early 1900s believed in the polygenetic concept of the superiority and purity of the white race. They were convinced that an 'eternal law of nature is decreed that the white cannot assimilate the blood of another without corrupting the very springs of civilization'" (1982, 13). Everything from weakness of mind to an inevitably debilitated body has been ascribed to "multiracial" individuals and groups (Spickard 2000).[40] In the late nineteenth century, California enacted antimiscegenation legislation between white and "Mongolian," extending its already standing prohibition against marriage between white and "negroes or mulattoes." In the 1920s and 1930s, the state faced pressure by anti-Filipino activists to bar marriages between white and "Malay" as well. Almost immediately following the 1933 *Roldan v. Los Angeles County* decision, California amended its legislation in that direction.

Roldan is the final case in a series of civil actions mounted around this issue, all of which required the adjudication of color, specifically the color of Filipinos.[41] Salvador Roldan had applied for license to marry "a woman of Caucasian descent." Roldan, "found to be a 'Filipino,' . . . born in the Philippine Islands of Filipino progenitors whose blood was co-mingled with a strain of Spanish," fought the decision of the county denying his application (18 P.2d 706, 707). Roldan was defined as Filipino and "not a Mongolian," a class of persons already restricted to marriage to "white persons," and hence both the lower and appeal courts of California issued a writ of mandate in his favor. The appellate court's concluding advice seemed to consolidate movements toward antimiscegenation legislation identifying Filipinos: "this is not a social question before us, as . . . [races restricted] . . . was decided by the legislature at the time the Code was amended [in 1905]; and if the common thought of today is different from what it was at such time, the matter is one that addresses itself to the legislature and not to the courts" (18 P.2d at 709).

I read the California legislature's amendment of relevant legislation as the suturing together of the crisis that Filipinos represented to the white body politic and, in particular, the threat it posed to white heteronormative masculinity. As the figure of the white woman is reconfirmed as the embodiment of U.S. national spirit, antimiscegenation legislation bespeaks recognition of the ways that "nonwhite" could successfully challenge the primacy of that masculinity. Given the logic behind benevolent assimilation, neither the crisis posed nor the fact that it has been articulated in sexualized terms is particularly surprising. Benevolent assimilation implied that "little brown brothers" could grow up to be (like) "big white men." Racial difference alibis the reaffirmation of patriarchal heteronormativity in these antimiscegenation laws and popular discourse surrounding Filipinos. Simultaneously, sexuality instruments the regulation of the racialized identity of the nation. That operation too has its own legal history, one that might arguably be dated from 1855, when Congress first enacted legislation that enabled the derivation of noncitizen women's naturalized citizenship by marriage. The year 1907 witnessed the extension of this sexualized gendering of citizenship as Congress put in place legislation that would strip U.S. citizen women regardless of race of their citizenship should they marry noncitizen men. In 1922, the Cable Act revised that legislation to apply only in marriages to men ineligible for U.S citizenship, namely, "Asians."[42]

By annexing the Philippines, the federal government had complicated its reliance on immigration regulation as a tool for managing national identity, and, thus, the project of doing so fell to local state authorities. While receptive to anti-Filipino exclusionist sentiment, especially as the United States entered into the Great Depression, until Philippine independence was formally achieved, the U.S. Congress could not exclude Filipinos on a wholesale basis. Exclusionists, anti-imperialists, and Filipino nationalists together, with grossly different motivations and yet with converging purpose, promoted the passage of the 1934 Tydings-McDuffie Act providing for Philippine independence by 1944.[43] World War II, particularly Japan's occupation of the Philippines in 1941, would delay independence until 1946.

These related histories of a colonial past and of domestic adjudications of the legal and cultural status of "Filipinos" suggest that "Filipinos" be conceived along the lines that Bulosan and Santos begin to trace. That is, brought into being at precisely the juncture of subjectification and subjection, as those men who must be threatened precisely because the histories they represent threaten U.S. exceptionalism, "Filipinos" may be understood as a category of critique rather than identity. It is an analytical category through which we can plainly see the a priori emptiness of identificatory terms, one that bespeaks the constructedness and constitutive instability of seemingly purely descriptive terms. The threat that "Filipino America" poses might be understood along these lines as even more radical for Asian American studies than its work of laying bare the United States' imperiousness implies. In addition to, perhaps even more than, arguing for the integration of sexuality as an analytic category and an awareness of historical particularity as central features of Asian Americanist practice, "Filipino America" distinctly prompts interrogation of the epistemological assumptions underwriting Asian American studies. In its resistance to definitional certitude within a single frame of reference, whether that be national or colonial subjectivity, "Filipino America" shifts the focus of critical inquiry from questioning the exclusion of "Asian America" from full participation in the U.S. nation to the first-order work of identifying and interrogating the systems and technologies that would have us believe that such membership is desirable.

Constitutively, by definition, a category that is always already eroding, "Filipino America" defies understanding by means of an identity-based narrative that operates within the frame of nation and that must assimilate difference for coherence. Indifferent to nation, which is to say that it is constitutively in nonidentity not just with U.S. national identity but also with the assumption of possibility of attaining such identity, "Filipino

America," precisely *because* of its categorical flux, is an ideal construct around which to organize Asian American studies. It is, in other words, an explicitly antagonistic force that refuses to allow Asian American studies to solidify the boundaries of what constitutes its proper objects of knowledge. Developed through this antagonism, Asian American studies emerges as a discourse critical of identity, of uniform subjectivity and its promises of equality, whether those constructs be found in hegemonic U.S. nationalism or in academic critical practices.

2

nikkei internment:

determined identities/undecidable

meanings

> Writing is dangerous from the moment that representation
> there claims to be presence and the sign of the thing itself.
> —Jacques Derrida, ". . . That Dangerous Supplement . . ."
> (1997 [1967])
>
> Deconstruction . . . is a persistent critique of what one cannot
> not want.—Gayatri Spivak, "Bonding in Difference" (1996)

As I suggested in the last chapter, a critical encounter with "Filipino America" argues for the displacement of identity-based paradigms in Asian American studies in part by raising awareness of the generativeness of sexuality as a critical frame of analysis. In so doing, it undermines the assumption of a uniform "Asian American" subjectivity as either object of analysis or political objective while also illuminating the ways that sexualization operates to sustain the inseparably coupled project of U.S. nation- and empire-building. We might recognize as well that such an encounter also points to the productiveness of conceptualizing racial identities beyond the frame of nation. While, to be sure, critical awareness of the proximate particularities marking the distinctiveness of racial identities remains of vital importance, that such identities may well be formed and operate across or in ways indifferent to national boundaries cannot be ignored. "Filipino America" makes this clear by compelling us to acknowledge its *transnational* dimensions. Resisting fixation either as naturally issuing from the Philippines or as emergent strictly within the U.S. context, "Filipino America" traverses the conceptual boundaries of nation. Spanish and U.S. colonization of the Philippines effectively created a transnational arena of identity formation rather inadequately encompassed by either "Filipino" or "Filipino American" as terms of reference. Along these lines, "Filipino America" prompts us to consider the possibilities of employing a transnational imaginary as a conceptual frame better suited for producing knowledge of "Asian American" identities and for mounting critique of U.S. nationalism's use of gendered and sexualized racialization as an instrument of power.

In this chapter, I take up the exploration of such possibilities. Drawing on the variegated discourses of transnationalism and anchored once again by both legal and literary narratives, I consider the potential of a transnational approach to understanding the processes by which "Asian American" social identities are constructed.[1] Internment of Japanese Americans during World War II focuses this discussion. Analyses of the historical and legal record leading to internment and to Supreme Court decisions in such cases as *Hirabayashi v. United States*, considered here, distinctly posit the need for such an examination of the potential of the transnational as a conceptual frame for Asian American studies. For what they show is the conversion of the threat of Japanese empire into Japanese (American) racial difference by governmental and legal apparatuses of U.S. nationalism through what I will suggest is a "transnationalization" of Japaneseness. That conversion into a "nikkei transnation" enabled the justification of internment as necessary to contain that threat. The subjugating use of the concept of transnationality in the historic instance of internment thus troubles an easy embrace of a transnational imaginary in Asian American studies. Indeed, what Neil Gotanda (1999) has described as the process of *Asiatic racialization*, that U.S. nationalism has repeatedly denied or "nullified" political citizenship by creating "Asians" as different from "Americans," gives pause in moving toward a transnational paradigm.[2] Asiatic racialization defines Asianness as ineffably foreign and inassimilable to America. Highlighting the transnational dimensions of "Asian American" identity formation seemingly bolsters that process of differentiation whereby both entry into and participation in the socio-political and cultural life of the U.S. nation have been regularly denied "Asians." Historically, it has been in response to such exclusionary practices that Asian Americanists have long advanced the belongingness of "Asians" to the United States.

And yet, under the current pressures of globalization, the significant inadequacies of conceiving of "Asian America" primarily within the frame of the U.S. nation and principally in relation to its difference from U.S. national identity cannot be ignored. We have already seen how such a circumscription of critical inquiry hinders understanding of the historic formation of "Filipino America," understood as exemplary of the limitations of the representational grids of nation and nationalism to contend with, perhaps especially, the formative effects of colonial pasts and presents. And the explanatory power of narratives of immigration and settlement into an "Asian American" identity knowable in the frame of nation have been sharply called into question by discourses that illuminate the transformations wrought by globalization. Demographic shifts and multilateral migrations characterizing the present and the near past trouble the ability of such narratives to account for the subjectivities and cultural practices of Asian-raced peoples living in the United States. In this light of globalization, the already unruly heterogeneity terminologically elided by "Asian American" succeeds in fracturing its standing as a declaration of identity.[3]

In this chapter, I use the occasion of internment to explore the problematics and potential of thinking transnationally given Asiatic racialization on the one hand and the historic and current pressures to conceive racial identities beyond the conceptual confines of the nation-state on the other. I argue that actively deflating the referential authority of "Asian American" allows us to articulate transnationalism as a critical tool in Asian American studies, one that recognizes the historic denial of the material advantages accruing to identity with the U.S. nation, but that also thinks beyond the nation in conceiving of "Asian America" as the figure of a particular kind of critique. I suggest that it is precisely because U.S. nationalism has constituted "Asian America" as a transnational identity that it has power as an analytic in exposing the failures of the U.S. nation-state's promises of universal equality. From that vantage point, that it is the reciprocal relation between racial essentialism and U.S. nationalism that must be challenged to dismantle racial differentiation as an apparatus of U.S. national identity formation becomes clear.

I proceed by means of pursuing the particular resonance I see between transnationalism and Asian American studies in terms of their interests in national borders. More specifically, because transnationalism speaks of such borders and their permeability, it models the attentiveness in Asian American studies to the simultaneous significance and irrelevance of official U.S. citizenship given Asiatic racialization. As the following analyses suggest, Asiatic racialization may be understood as the technology of the production of an imagined transnationality ascribed to Asian-identified individuals and groups. In this manner, transnationalism might be seen as a discourse that advances investigations of the technologies of race and U.S. national identity formation, or perhaps more pointedly, the technology of race *as* a technology of U.S. national identity.

Here, I show how understanding Asiatic racialization through the language of transnationalism helps us to recognize the radical and permanent *undecidability*, to borrow from Jacques Derrida, of identificatory terms like "Asian American." The analyses that follow illustrate how such terms garner meaning only as an effect of various and varying historically embedded relations of power that manifest as racism and nationalism, or more particularly in this context, as *patriotism*. I work in this chapter with narratives regarding and facilitating the internment of Japanese and Japanese Americans (collectively, *nikkei*) living in the United States during World War II. Internment testifies to the need to be critically aware of both the discursive and material registers within which knowledge is produced and circulates, and of the ways that imaginings can transform into visceral consequences. Nikkei internment holds the dubious honor of exemplifying the broad-scale institutionalized forms of anti-Asian racism that characterize U.S. history. Irreducible to a matter of individual pathology, the racism manifested in state narratives of internment testifies to the systemic embeddedness of anti-Asian racist epistemes. Internment exemplifies the suturing of the unity of the U.S. nation by means of differentiating between those who do and do not belong through the deployment of race, a category that in this context signifies national origins. In this way, internment speaks of knowledge produced by racism and patriotism, the promulgation of devotion to the father(land) that demands different demonstrations of loyalty from the nation's would-be sons and daughters. Because governmental narratives of internment produce race through the affiliation to certain bodies of foreignness, of being naturally and immutably of and belonging to another country, they exemplify the process of Asiatic racialization. In this regard, they may be seen to utilize *transnationality* to justify internment.

I use *transnationalism* to refer to the constellation of academic practices and interests noted above. *Transnation* designates cross-border collectivities and identity formations, and *transnationality* refers to the conception and condition of membership in those organizational forms. Transnations and transnationality are delocalized, not contingent upon territoriality for unity.[4] Meanwhile, *transnational* has two functions here. First, it names in a more literal sense border crossings, as in transnational alliances and transnational capitalism. This is the sense of meaning I understand to accrue to "transnational paradigm," a framework that underscores the importance of critical awareness of cross-border flows of people, capital, and cultures in the production and evaluation of knowledge. And second, I mean transnational as a cognitive analytic that traces the incapacity of the nation-state to contain and represent fully the subjectivities and ways of life that circulate within the nation-*space*. In this second sense, transnational refers to border crossings without literal movement, to a conceptual displacement of a national imaginary in order to allow for discursive and critical acknowledgment of those political and cultural practices illegible in the official discourse of the U.S. nation-state.

My concern in this chapter is with demonstrating how conceiving of the transnational as an analytic provides a way of attending to the particularities marking Asiatic racialization. John Okada's novel *No-No Boy* (1992 [1957]) and Hisaye Yamamoto's short story "High-Heeled Shoes" (1998 [1948]), the literary texts anchoring the latter half of this chapter, help us to understand that at stake in employing the transnational in this manner is a radical challenge to the credibility of official, state-produced knowledge. Okada's novel articulates a gendered experience of citizenship nullification that registers the production of identity as an effect of state power. Interrogating the justificatory rationale underwriting the state's production of Japaneseness, *No-No Boy* emphasizes the insubstantiality of such knowledge and, in doing so, points directly to the need to confront and contest racial essentialism. For the transnational to work as a critique rather than an instrument of state power, this novel implies, it must be distinctly disarticulated from that epistemic practice. Yamamoto's story further advances this understanding, while also crucially emphasizing the nation-*space* as site of critical inquiry. Through her story, Yamamoto invites us to articulate the transnational as a critical frame that deliberately recognizes the circumstantiality of knowledge. Pointedly, her story unfolds in a space circumscribed but not wholly defined by the nation-state. Thus, it affirms the importance of conceiving the transnational as a cognitive entryway that takes us into the variegated spaces of nation, which here serve as sites from which alternative lifeways may be imagined.

Collectively, these legal and literary narratives compel us to identify the *process* of the affiliation of meaning to certain bodies as the collectivizing problematic anchoring and necessitating Asian Americanist discourse. In this way, transnationalism may be seen at once to problematize "Asian American" by its highlighting of multivalent changes under globalization and its underscoring of ensuing heterogeneity, and to facilitate a reconstruction of Asian American studies geared to attend to intractable diversity. Once again, we shall see the necessity of contesting both U.S. nationalism and Asian Americanist employment of nation-based paradigms that functionally rely on a seemingly stable and knowable prediscursive identity for objective coherence. Once again, that is, we will be guided to emphasizing and acknowledging critically the productiveness of understanding the a priori subjectlessness of Asian Americanist discourse.

producing America/producing nikkei transnationality

In this section, I rehearse the ways that the interarticulation of racism and nationalism underwrote the fantastic construction of nikkei as enemies to the U.S. nation, an imagining that was a necessary precondition to internment. I argue that the governmental and juridical narratives that register and articulate such fantasies themselves argue for a persistent awareness of signification as giving rise to racialized social and political identities. Accordingly, they promote the adoption of deconstruction as an important critical orientation in Asian American studies in advancing its critique of U.S. nationalism.

In the context of World War II, not surprisingly, American identity functioned as a site in which anxieties about national security played out. Domestically, World War II served to isolate nikkei by particularizing a tradition of enmity against Asian-raced populations in the United States. The history of that animosity has been well documented: phases of public hysteria throughout the nineteenth and twentieth centuries about the "yellow peril" generally culminated in the enactment of some law—from various immigration exclusion acts to antimiscegenation laws—that juridically legitimated and thus perpetuated the national cultural fantasy of the "Asian" as villain, a fantasy that tended to realize itself around one Asian-raced group at a time.[5] Japan's alliances in World War II relegated this position to nikkei: "The lot of persons of Chinese, Korean, Filipino, and Asian Indian ancestry improved because their ancestral lands were allies of the United States" (Chan 1991, 121).[6] Concomitantly, nikkei were firmly established as the "enemy alien" despite intelligence reports that had concluded that there was no reason to fear sabotage or espionage by either *issei* (Japanese nationals) or *nisei* (Japanese Americans) living in the United States. As Ronald Takaki reports, Lieutenant General John L. DeWitt, head of the Western Defense command, disbelieved such reports: "We are at war [and] . . . I have little confidence that the enemy aliens are law-abiding or loyal in any sense of the word. Some of them yes; many no. Particularly the Japanese. I have no confidence in their loyalty whatsoever" (quoted in Takaki 1989, 387). In advising the U.S. government to go forward with plans for internment, DeWitt described Japanese as "an enemy race" whose "racial affinities [were] not severed by migration" and whose "racial strains" remained purportedly strong even among U.S. citizens (Chan 1991, 125; Takaki 1989, 391). Joined by the popular press and various patriotic organizations, the movement toward internment intensified quickly.

Even those most adamantly in support of internment recognized the constitutional issues that would be raised should American citizens, even if of Japanese ancestry, be interned. Secretary of War Henry L. Stimson wrote in his diary shortly before the signing of Executive Order 9066 providing for internment, "The second generation Japanese can only be evacuated either as part of a total evacuation . . . or by frankly trying to put them out on the ground that their racial characteristics are such that we cannot understand or trust even the citizen Japanese. This latter is the fact but I am afraid it will make a tremendous hole in our constitutional system to apply it" (quoted in Takaki 1989, 390). Attorney General Francis Biddle affirmed that given the absence of any evidence of "imminent attack" or "planned sabotage," such mass evacuation would indeed be beyond the scope of authority proscribed by the Constitution (quoted in Takaki 1989, 391). Subsequently, calling on the Constitution's War Powers clause, President Roosevelt grasped "military necessity" as the justification for what amounted to the citizenship nullification of Japanese Americans and, on February 19, 1942, signed Executive Order 9066.[7]

At issue during these negotiations was the formulation of a racialized U.S. national identity. The rhetoric used by DeWitt and Stimson iterates a belief in the immutable unassimilability of a specifically Japanese "race." In effect, DeWitt and Stimson imagined a nikkei transnation out of a belief in the essential and delocalized sameness of Japanese regardless of borders, nativity, or citizenship. Linking foreignness with race, they constructed a fantasy in which Japaneseness overflowed Japan's sovereign territory to constitute a simultaneously internal and external threat to the United States. The United States–Japan relationship, historically one of competition, facilitated this production of the nikkei transnation. Japan, conceived in the United States as a modern nation capable of challenging "us" on "our" own terms, constituted the United States' most intense Asian adversary (Lipsitz 1997; Igarashi 1998).[8] That challenge motivated the "feminization" of Japan in the U.S. popular imagination, figuring "her" as thus able to be mastered by the "manly" United States (Igarashi 1998; T. Yamamoto 1999). The possibility that Japanese expansionism across the Asia Pacific would result in prohibited access to the raw materials of Southeast Asia, upon which the United States had relied to support its economic empire, alarmed the United States into establishing a complete embargo on iron and oil in 1941, by some accounts precipitating Japan's attack on Pearl Harbor (Zinn 1995, 401). Unlike U.S. citizens and residents of Italian and German descent, nikkei were associated with a foreign power conceived to be in direct competition with the United States' economic interests.[9] Japan's attack on Pearl Harbor cast Japan as an enemy in close proximity, delocalizing Japanese nationality and further catalyzing the coherence of an imagined Japanese transnationality. Racism, patriotism, and the expansionist demands of capital together formed the basis for the U.S. governmental construction of the nikkei transnation.

Internment's success relied on the favorable adjudication of challenges to that construction, to the phantasmatic imagining that would lead to the alienation of putatively inalienable rights from U.S. citizens. By October 30, 1942, 112,000 nikkei, of whom roughly two-thirds were U.S. citizens, were imprisoned in internment camps in the interior regions of the United States. Perhaps not surprisingly, given the government's participation in these proceedings, few nikkei looked to the legal system for assistance in resisting the military orders of curfew and evacuation that constituted some of the apparatuses of internment. At issue was the abrogation of the rights of U.S. citizens to due process of law as codified in the Fifth Amendment.[10]

Gordon Hirabayashi, one of a dozen or so who sought legal remedy, refused to comply with and was subsequently convicted of violating the orders imposing curfew and commanding evacuation. He surrendered to authorities in May 1942 and explained his resistance in a written statement titled "Why I refused to register for evacuation." He explained:

> This order for mass evacuation of all persons of Japanese descent denies them the right to live. It forces thousands of energetic, law-abiding individuals to exist in a miserable psychological and a horrible physical atmosphere. . . . Hope for the future is exterminated. . . . Over sixty percent are American citizens. . . . If I were to register and cooperate under those circumstances, I would be giving helpless consent to the denial of practically all of the things which give me incentive to live. . . . I consider it my duty to maintain the democratic standards for which this nation lives. Therefore, I must refuse this order for evacuation. (quoted in Irons 1983, 88)[11]

Hirabayashi's equation of "life" with "citizenship" argues for recognition of a deeply held affective desire for and need of recognized identification with America. In this statement, he conflates his own life with that of the nation: his "duty" to the "democratic standards of the nation" becomes indistinguishable from his "incentive to live." Expressing here a profound loyalty to America, Hirabayashi attempted to (re)claim standing as a legitimate member of the National Symbolic, what Lauren Berlant has described as the "*political* space of the nation" (1991, 4; emphasis original).

Five months after his surrender and subsequent indictment, Hirabayashi was brought to court. His attorney argued that "The curfew and evacuation orders . . . violated both the due process clause of the Fifth Amendment and the rights of Japanese Americans as a racial minority to equal protection of the law [under the Fourteenth Amendment]" (*JAW* 154).[12] In his decision, Judge Lloyd D. Black, according to Peter Irons, "substituted patriotism and paranoia" for legal analysis. Black wrote, "It must not for an instant be forgotten that since Pearl Harbor last December we have been engaged in a total war with enemies unbelievably treacherous and wholly ruthless, who intend to totally destroy this nation, its Constitution, our way of life, and trample all liberty and freedom everywhere from this earth" (*JAW* 155).

With this fervently patriotic context established, Black then dismissed the constitutional challenges by arguing that a "technical interpretation" of the due process clause in this context would potentially "endanger all of the constitutional rights of the whole citizenry" (JAW 155). Black's decision shifted Hirabayashi from his self-positioning as a member of the citizenry to standing as the personification of the danger of Japan to America.

Finally, as Irons summarizes, "At his one day trial in Seattle, U.S. District Judge Lloyd Black [again] referred to the Japanese as 'unbelievably treacherous,' and ordered the jury to convict Hirabayashi" (1989, 49).[13] The Supreme Court unanimously upheld Hirabayashi's conviction in June 1943.[14] Delivering the majority opinion, Chief Justice Harlan Stone argued that because nikkei had faced racism, they were more likely than other groups to be a danger to the United States: "The restrictions, both practical and legal, affecting the privileges and opportunities afforded to persons of Japanese extraction residing in the United States, have been sources of irritation and may well have tended to increase their isolation, and in many instances their attachments to Japan and its institutions" (JD 61). In other words, according to Stone, racism itself rationalizes internment and justifies conceiving of Japanese transnationality.

The government's and judiciary's imagining of a Japanese transnational threat to the United States subsumed the issue of the abrogation of Fifth Amendment rights. Thus Stone wrote in his opinion, "We cannot say that the war-making branches of the Government did not have ground for believing that in a critical hour . . . [citizens of Japanese ancestry] . . . constituted a menace to the national defense and safety, which demanded that prompt and adequate measures be taken to guard against it" (JD 61). Stone concluded his opinion with the following: "We cannot close our eyes to the fact, demonstrated by experience, that in time of war residents having ethnic affiliations with an invading enemy may be a greater source of danger than those of a different ancestry. . . . In this case it is enough that circumstances within the knowledge of those charged with the responsibility for maintaining the national defense afforded a rational basis for the decision which they made" (JD 63). In short, this decision positioned the rights of Japanese-identified U.S. citizens in conflict with the security of the United States on the basis of presumed "ethnic affiliations."

The Court was not unaware of the discriminatory nature of its rationale. Justice Frank Murphy's concurring opinion, which initially was prepared as a dissent, is evidence of this recognition (JD 49). Irons explains that "Murphy was talked out of his dissent by Justice Felix Frankfurter, who asserted that any break in unanimous support for the Army in wartime amounted to 'playing into the hands of the enemy.' Faced with this challenge to his patriotism, Murphy capitulated" (JD 49). In spite of his acknowledgment that, in his own words, "no less [sic] than 70,000 American citizens [had] been placed under a special ban and deprived of their liberty because of their particular inheritance," and that such action was tantamount to "sanction[ing] discrimination between groups of United States citizens on the basis of ancestry," called upon to prove his own loyalty to America, Murphy ultimately conceded to majority opinion (JD 69).

A similar rationale underwrites Supreme Court decisions in other cases that raised constitutional challenges to internment.[15] Collectively, they codify into an official realm a fantasy of a "genuine" American "race." Since upholding the 1790 Naturalization Act that reserved naturalized citizenship to "whites" and the legality of various race-based immigration exclusion acts and antimiscegenation laws, the judiciary has long reaffirmed the whiteness of America.[16] As Etienne Balibar argues, "It is [a] broad structure of racism . . . which maintains a necessary relation with *nationalism* and contributes to constituting it by producing the fictive ethnicity around which it is organized" (1992, 49; emphasis original). These narratives illuminate this reciprocal relation between racism and nationalism. While racism works for nationalism in the production of the fictive ethnicity of the nation, racism also relies on nationalism for legitimacy. As Balibar explains:

> Racism sees itself as an "integral" nationalism, which only has meaning (and chances of success) if it is based on the integrity of the nation, integrity both towards the outside and on the inside. What theoretical racism calls "race" or "culture" (or both together) is therefore a continued origin of the nation, a concentrate of the qualities which belong to the nationals "as their own"; it is in the "race of its children" that the nation could contemplate its own identity in the pure state. Consequently, it is around race that it must unite, with race—an "inheritance" to be preserved from any kind of degradation. (1992, 59)

Given the state's power to materialize this affiliation of race with nation, Hirabayashi, juridically defined as representative of the Japanese transnational race, could make no claim of identity with *the* American race. Regardless of formal citizenship, nikkei were therefore ineligible for American national subjectivity. Nikkei, in this regard, could only be members of the Japanese transnation.

The transnation in this context describes a process of literal and metaphoric imprisonment—into internment camps, into a concretized identity as ineffably inassimilable, alien, enemy, Japanese. These narratives that construct nikkei transnationality underscore the phantasmatic character of Americanness, a national identity built upon a fictive ethnicity. A discursive catapulting of nikkei into a fantastic, aterritorial transnation recursively defines the boundaries of the United States. Possession of the nation was literally denied to nikkei, whose belongings and belongingness transformed from private property into public obsession as they emerged as dispossessed national subjects.[17] These narratives of nikkei transnationality exhibit an epistemology of racial essentialism; they register racism's status as a regime of power that produces materially consequential "truths"—as *identities*—that appear to be merely interpretations rather than constructions of variously marked bodies. The government and judiciary effectively ascribed to Japanese-identified peoples living in the United States a transcendent loyalty to Japan based upon an essentialist and purposive conception of a relationship between race and national origins. Racializing loyalty served as a mechanism of differentiation, and in recognizing that operation we witness the precedence of difference over identity—the *différance* of identity. Along these lines, deconstruction of racialized identity emerges as a crucial critical orientation for contesting the material effects of racism.

Transnation and nation appear here as coextensive, as unfolding simultaneously and in intimate relation. This juxtapositional relationship of nation and transnation argues for conceiving a transnational imaginary not as an autonomously generated conceptual terrain, but as one that emerges in conjunction with the production of U.S. nationness. We are reminded that the very idea of a national identity is contingent upon what it is not; it is an inherently *comparative* construct, and in the terms of this present discussion, may be seen as constitutively transnational.[18] Internment may thus be understood as a particularly visible and material instance within which the comparative, transnational dimensions of U.S. national identity played out. What I am suggesting is that the imperative for Asian Americanists to think in terms of transnationalism arises not only from globalization but also from recognizing *the transnational within the national*, from understanding that Asiatic racialization traces and materializes the transnational dimensions of U.S. national identity.

no-no boys and high-heeled shoes

The foregoing analyses have identified governmental and juridical power as determining forces in the fabrication of both U.S. national and racial identities. Race and nation become significant because these forces affiliate to them certain meanings out of an infinite range of possibilities. Those meanings then manifest in internment, the materiality of which tautologically suggests the immanent substantiality of those definitions. What gets lost from view is precisely that these meanings are *determined*, that they are consequences of specifically motivated interpretive acts that produce and not merely reflect meaning.[19] The challenge, then, is to bring to surface their insubstantiality or, more specifically, what Jacques Derrida has described as their *undecidability*. Derrida explains that "Undecidability is always a *determinate* oscillation between possibilities (for example, of meaning, but also of acts). The possibilities are themselves highly *determined* in strictly *defined* situations" (1988b, 148; emphasis original). In this case, for example, loyalty and disloyalty are possibilities in the determination of what race means. Relations of power circumscribe which of the possibilities will be selected and made to matter; in and of itself, race, no matter which "race," has no meaning—it is situationally determined but fundamentally undecidable.

Signification thus always carries the specter of alternative possibilities, and, hence, the stability of meanings can be recognized as fragile. In the following discussion, I show how John Okada and Hisaye Yamamoto through their respective works imply precisely this insight, this importance of bringing to surface the purposive constructedness of and power behind meanings. In their treatments of life in and around the time of internment, both identify and explore the determining forces that render intelligible such terms as *race*, *gender*, and *nation*. Though in different ways, Okada and Yamamoto interrogate and illuminate the undecidability of meaning and implicitly suggest that unveiling that characteristic can support efforts to understand and perhaps transform those determining forces.

Okada's novel, first published in 1957 and set in the late 1940s, takes particular interest in loyalty and patriotism. Its title, *No-No Boy*, refers to possible responses to a "loyalty questionnaire" that internees were required to complete in February 1943, as the government began to explore resettlement plans.[20] Question 27 asked draft-age males, "Are you willing to serve in the armed forces of the United States on combat duty, wherever ordered?" And question 28 asked of all internees, "Will you swear unqualified allegiance to the United States of America and faithfully defend the United States from any or all attack by foreign or domestic forces, and forswear any form of allegiance or obedience to the Japanese emperor, or any other foreign government, power or organization?"[21] Those who submitted negative answers were known as "no-no boys." The novel explores the implications of that identity by following Ichiro, its protagonist, through his process of reentry into American public life upon release from the internment camps and imprisonment for refusing to serve in the military. Okada confronts the difficulties of understanding that particular nisei identity, one especially complicated because it seemingly involves an element of choice. While avoiding internment altogether was not an option, becoming a no-no boy was, in Ichiro's eyes. However, and sometimes in spite of Ichiro's thoughts to the contrary, the novel indicates that the semblance of choice was a false one to the extent that the available options had already been strictly defined by forces outside of his control. It becomes evident as the story unfolds that Ichiro needs to change his frame of reference, to question rather than adopt the meaning of no-no boy as defined by those forces as unforgivably disloyal, as a confirmation of not belonging to and in the United States. In this way, *No-No Boy* brings to light the undecidability and (in)determinate nature of meaning.

No-No Boy is organized by the question of whether choosing not to fight for the United States in the war constituted a treasonous act. Ichiro asks of himself and perhaps of the reader, "Why is it . . . that I am unable to convince myself that I am no different from any other American? Why is it that, in my freedom, I feel more imprisoned in the wrongness of myself and the thing I did than when I was in prison? . . . There is, I am afraid, no answer. There is no retribution for one who is guilty of treason, and that is what I am guilty of. The fortunate get shot. I must live my punishment" (NNB 82). The novel catalogues a range of responses to the experience of being asked to serve in the military of a nation that had presumptively defined respondents as disloyal.[22] Narrated largely through internal monologue, No-No Boy dramatizes these responses in a way that indicates the impossibility of determining with certainty, despite Ichiro's own sentiments, what the "right" response should have been. Ichiro remembers one fellow internee's response to being asked to fight for the United States:

> You, Mr. Judge, who supposedly represents justice, was it a just thing to ruin a hundred thousand lives and homes and farms and businesses and dreams and hopes because the hundred thousand were a hundred thousand Japanese and you couldn't have loyal Japanese when Japan is the country you're fighting and, if so, how about the Germans and Italians that must be just as questionable as the Japanese or we wouldn't be fighting Germany and Italy? Round them up. Take away their homes and cars and beer and spaghetti and throw them in a camp and what do you think they'll say when you try to draft them into your army of the country that is for life, liberty, and the pursuit of happiness? If you think we're the same kind of rotten Japanese that dropped the bombs on Pearl Harbor, and it's plain that you do or I wouldn't be here having to explain to you why it is that I won't go and protect sons-of-bitches like you. (NNB 32)

But Ichiro remembers as well that "For each and every refusal based on sundry reasons, another thousand chose to fight for the right to continue to be American because homes and cars and money could be regained but only if they first regained their rights as citizens, and that was everything" (NNB 34). In both tenor and substance, these recollections convey the immediacy of the experience of nullified citizenship. The words pour out in disordered chaos; no regulated syntax paces the narration or temporizes the sentiment. Equalizing the quotidian elements of life with the grand principles upon which the United States proclaims its exceptional status, these responses at once challenge the relevance of those principles and indicate the ordinary invisibility of the nation-state's power.[23] They point out, that is, that the ordinary and the grand are situationally determined, conditions contingent upon particular configurations of power relations. Moreover, by linking materiality with "the right to . . . be American," Okada emphasizes the concrete dimensions of citizenship nullification. In this way, his novel points to an inseparability between the discursive and the material, thereby identifying discourse as a potent site of politics.

Ichiro's struggles with his own reasons for becoming a no-no boy manifest in part in the tension between the well-ordered syntactical structure that begins his explanation and the less controlled flow that follows:

> I did not go because I was weak and could not do what I should have done. It was not my mother [who had urged him not to fight against Japan], whom I have never really known. It was me, myself. It is done and there can be no excuse. . . . I remember a lot of people and a lot of things now as I walk confidently through the night over a small span of concrete which is part of the sidewalks which are part of the city which is part of the state and the country and the nation that is America. It is for this that I meant to fight, only the meaning got lost when I needed it most badly. (NNB 34)

"America" in this passage is literally amplified as the sentence it anchors crescendos to conclusion. His meditation on the relationship between "the small span of concrete" and "the nation that is America" metaphorizes the citizen-nation relationship. The "meaning" that got lost is his own sense of the ordinariness of citizenship, the fact-ness of his belonging, just as the unremarkable piece of the sidewalk simply exists, and likewise exists simply, as part of the nation. Ichiro's self-castigation rings false, as his declaration of sole accountability seems disingenuous in the face of the overwhelming state power that had conditioned the need to engage in war in the first place, power that is recognized in Ichiro's recollection of other internees' responses previous to his own. As the novel unfolds, the more Ichiro attempts to claim autonomous agency for his decision to become a no-no boy, the clearer it becomes that his choices are circumscribed by broadly determining forces.

Ichiro's parents represent the binary logic that the U.S. government employed in constructing nikkei transnationality. In the Yamadas' world, Japan and the United States, Japaneseness and Americanness, constitute mutually exclusive poles. The novel's critical depiction of the Yamadas thus serves to criticize that logic. Mr. Yamada's alcoholism mirrors Mrs. Yamada's "sickness," a condition that, as Elaine Kim has suggested, "is 'Japanese' to the extent that it revolves around loyalty to Japan" (1982, 150). It is moreover inseparable from her implied usurpation of her husband's "rightful" role as head of the family. Though in different ways, both are hapless figures, symbolic embodiments of the insanity of reducing identity to binary terms. Unable and unwilling to accept that Japan has not emerged victorious from the war, finally, when forced to concede her position, Mrs. Yamada psychologically deteriorates and finally commits suicide. Symbolically figuring Japan, Mrs. Yamada stands as a literary representation of the feminization of Japan in the U.S. popular imagination. As Traise

Yamamoto has argued, conceiving of Japan as "femininely infantile and sexually exotic" was necessary to repress the threat that Japan posed to the United States (1999, 61). That Okada registers this feminization of Japan in his construction of Mrs. Yamada indicates the novel's own interest in recuperating a heteronormative masculinity for nisei men, a point to which I return in a moment.

Mrs. Yamada's story also figures the consequences of acceding to the imposed narrative of Japanese transnationality: the vitiation of mind and the end of life are its narrative closures. As Ichiro voices uncertainty about how to understand his mother, it becomes clear that the novel broadly comments on the contradictory demands made by the United States on the nikkei: "Was it she who was wrong and crazy not to have found in herself the capacity to accept a country which repeatedly refused to accept her or her sons . . . or was it the others who were being deluded, the ones . . . who believed and fought and even gave their lives to protect this country where they could still not rate as first-class citizens because of unseen walls?" (NNB 104). Okada highlights through Ichiro's questioning the impossibility of negotiating to a stable resolution the nation's simultaneous presumption of disloyalty and demand for self-sacrifice.

Okada represents through Ichiro the particular intensity of this paradox for nisei, official U.S. citizens and officially interpellated into a nikkei transnation. *No-No Boy* affirms the viscerality of citizenship, the intimate connection between materiality and discursivity. According to this novel, citizenship cannot be understood as an abstraction but rather must be seen as a particular condition of embodiment driven by patriotism to identify that body with the nation (Berlant 1991). The nisei of Okada's novel are, like their nonfictional counterparts, citizens who are "merely subject to the law: within its symbolic order but outside of direct control over its legislation. These citizens' bodies are not protected by the law that administers to them; these citizens' minds are not fully engaged in support of the state's manifest legislation" (Berlant 1991, 101). *No-No Boy* offers a sense of the deep-rootedness of this affective experience of nullified citizenship.

It does so in large part through contrasting Ichiro and Kenji, a nisei war veteran. Injured in the war, Kenji has a gangrenous leg that signifies the lethal consequences of attempting to claim Americanness in spite of the nation's determined efforts at exclusion. The decaying wound symbolizes the irresolvability of nation and transnation and in the end, Kenji's embodiment of this simultaneity ultimately kills him. "They were two extremes, the Japanese who was more American than most Americans because he had crept to the brink of death for America, and the other who was neither Japanese nor American because he had failed to recognize the gift of his birthright when recognition meant everything" (NNB 73). As Kim summarizes, "In the topsy-turvy world where Japanese American men are required and require each other to risk their lives and their manhood, to sacrifice their families and their wives, to prove their loyalty to America, Ichiro would change places with his dying friend if he could" (1982, 151). Ichiro's movement toward a willingness to die for the nation clearly indicates his yearning for an unfractured identity with America, and in this novel, that desire manifests itself in part as a need, again, for confirmation of heteronormative masculinity.[24] Interpellated into a nikkei transnation within a symbolic economy that feminizes Japan, Ichiro's search for uncontested identification with America unfolds as a search for such masculinity. His is a desire for identity as patriot, as the embodiment of the masculinized identity of the nation. The power of national identity according to this novel transfers from fathers to sons, and Ichiro, plainly put, has the wrong father.[25]

No-No Boy emphasizes throughout the simultaneous emptiness and significance of Americanness, of Japaneseness, of masculinity, and of loyalty and patriotism. Categories posited as bearing immanent meaning in the governmental and judicial narratives of internment, this novel critiques as becoming substantial and significant only by force of their determination. Internment transformed the ordinary into the extraordinary, according to Okada's work, inverting public and private dimensions of life, illuminating their interarticulation, and creating the cognitive disjuncture that accompanies the ascription of disloyalty on imagined grounds. The no-no boy stands as an impossible subjectivity, infinitely undecidable, one that cannot have stable meaning because it is refracted by so many determining forces. Specifically gendered and far from idealized, Okada's no-no boy is an apt figuration of an "Asian American" identity, emblematizing as it does racism and resistance in the same breath. We might recognize that as the no-no boy is unrepresentative of nikkei as a whole, literally reflecting only a particular portion of nikkei and fictively at that, neither does "Asian American" work denotatively. Rather, both function as signs, to borrow from Gayatri Spivak, of that which we cannot not want, namely, here, a permanent stability of a singular identity as patriot, as American, but also, as wholly oppositional. Earlier, I suggested that governmental and judicial narratives of internment indicate that U.S. national identity may be conceived as constitutively transnational, as having borders that are always already eroding even as they are materially effective. Okada's novel offers an analogous insight into the constitutive corruption of seemingly objective identities: there is no purity to identity, it is neither wholly self-generated nor exhaustively imposed by material conditions; it is neither completely assimilative nor oppositional. *No-No Boy* suggests that we must maintain a critical stance on the *desire* for such a purity or singularity, implying the political importance of persistently interrogating identity.

If Okada's text takes up these questions of identity specifically in relation to the nation-state's power as manifested in internment, Yamamoto's work importantly reminds us that that power is not necessarily all-consuming. In "The High-Heeled Shoes: A Memoir," first published in 1948, Yamamoto articulates a concern with power in relation to identity and knowledge that unfolds in the register of the personal, and in such a way that the personal may be recognized as historical. In other words, where Okada's work takes us from the historical event of internment to the interior life of his characters, Yamamoto's moves us from interiority out. The importance of attending to this different direction lies in the necessity of understanding that politics and life are practiced and lived beneath the radar of such critical frames as nation. A transnational imaginary may be seen to refer to the conceptual space in which those cultural practices and politics circulating in difference from the official discourse of the U.S. nation may be brought to surface. Yamamoto's story, by articulating the impurity and undecidability of identity in this personal-to-historical manner, confirms how crucial it is for our critical practices to account for the multiple regimes of relations of power that intersect to produce the situational stabilities we refer to as knowledge.

The first piece in *Seventeen Syllables: A Collection of Stories*, "The High-Heeled Shoes" is not among those that explicitly refer to internment. In fact, it is that it does not do so that I find it to be such a powerful critique of the logic of internment. For, conceiving that logic to ascribe, among its various demands, to the nation-state a near omnipotence and omnipresence, part of the challenge before us—even as we attend to the crucial work of interrogating state power—is to deny it such all-powerful status. As part of a critical reading strategy, in other words, the transnational helps us to keep in mind the unavoidable situation of having to negotiate state power without giving it total authority.

"The High-Heeled Shoes" opens with an ambiguous phone call: "In the middle of the morning, the telephone rings. I am the only one at home. I answer it. A man's voice says softly, 'Hello, this is Tony'" (SS 1). The narrator continues:

> I don't know anyone named Tony. Nobody else in the house has spoken of knowing any Tony. But the greeting is very warm. It implies, "There is a certain thing which you and I alone know." Evidently he has dialed the wrong number. I tell him so, "You must have the wrong number," and prepare to hang up as soon as I know that he understands.
>
> But the man says this is just the number he wants. To prove it, he recites off the pseudonym by which this household, Garbo-like, goes in the directory, the address, and the phone number. It is a unique name and I know there is probably no such person in the world. I merely tell him a fragment of the truth, that there is no such person at the address, and I am ready to hang up again. (SS 1)

Immediately, the mysteriousness of the phone call ensnares readers into the world of the story. Like the narrator who is "suddenly in a bad humor, suspecting a trap in which I shall be imprisoned uncomfortably by words, words, words, earnestly begging me to try some product or another, the like of which is unknown anywhere else in the world" (SS 1), readers are willingly or not entangled in this memory. Clearly, Yamamoto indicates the unavoidability of unwanted intrusions into private spaces, like the phone call that invades this household that, "Garbo-like," seeks sanctuary from external forces. This reference to Garbo, mythically compelled to obsessive hermetic existence by overwhelming outside forces, foreshadows the insights this story has to offer about engendered subjectivity, where gender signals relations of power.

The narrator takes a detour through a quietly humorous meditation on the "unrapturous life a salesman must often lead" before finally revealing that the ominousness implied by the caller's inappropriate knowledge is warranted: "'And just what is it you want?' I ask impatiently. The man tells me, as man to woman. In the stark phrasing of his urgent need, I see that the certain thing alluded to by the warmth of his voice is a secret not of the past, but, with my acquiescence, of the near future" (SS 2). Details are unnecessary to understand the allusion, and, indeed, Yamamoto does not provide them. Instead, immediately, the narrator detours again as she steps outside and describes Margarita, the seven year old who lives next door who "has never known any mother or father, only tias and tios who share none of her blood" (SS 2). The narrator's introduction of Margarita, intertwined with the description of the vivid colors of the pansies she selects to share with her young neighbor, serve as an "innocent disguise"[26] that disarms the reader moments prior to being reminded of the phone call: "all the time the hands are occupied with these tokens of arrived spring and knowing Margarita, the mind recalls unlovely, furtive things" (SS 2). Yamamoto here alternates among definitional registers, between thoughts and actions, between inside and outside, between nature and humanity, questioning throughout the efficacy of the boundaries that separate them.

"The High-Heeled Shoes" continues on this wandering and yet focused path, offering through similarly muted tones the story of sexual assault on a former housemate, Mary. Offered a "choice between one kiss and rape," a choice that clearly is not a choice, the narrator explains that Mary "indicated what seemed to be the somewhat lesser requirement" (SS 3). The narrator shows through this episode the potential threat of patriarchal power not only in recounting the assault itself, but also by explaining that Mary "came back [from the police] with the impression that the police had been much amused, that they had actually snickered as she left with their officially regretful shrug over her having given them nothing to go on" (SS 3). Only after Mary's boss "called the police and evidently made his influence felt" did they even gesture at assistance. "Thereafter, she and the rest of the women of the household took to traveling in style, by taxi, when they were called on to go forth at odd hours. This not only dented our budgets, but made us considerably limit our unescorted evening gadding" (SS 3). Plainly, Yamamoto is interested here in narrating unbalanced gender relations. "Mary" widens the scope of the story from the particular women in the story to "woman" categorically, invoking as it does Christian mythology. Naming the virginal mother, the impossible femininity to which "woman" is nonetheless supposed to aspire, Yamamoto's seemingly simple narration of memories magnifies into a multilayered critique of gendered relations of power. She suggests that these relations have both direct and indirect material effect, as Mary's visceral response of fear is recounted along with the household's behavioral modification.

Finally, following Mary's story, the narrator shares the incident involving the eponymous high-heeled shoes.

> Walking one bright Saturday morning to work . . . I noticed a dusty blue, middle-aged sedan parked just ahead. A pair of bare, not especially remarkable legs was crossed in the open doorway, as though the body to them were lying on the front seat, relaxing. I presumed they were a woman's legs, belonging to the wife of some man who had business in the lumberyard just opposite, because they were wearing black high-heeled shoes. As I passed, I glanced at the waiting woman.
>
> My presumption had been rash. It wasn't a woman, but a man, unclothed (except for *the high-heeled shoes, the high-heeled shoes*), and I saw that I was, with frantic gestures, being enjoined to linger awhile. Nothing in my life before had quite prepared for this. . . . (SS 3–4; emphasis original)

Nor had the story really prepared its readers for this particular image. And as the text continues, as for the narrator so too the reader, as "the incongruity of a naked man in black high-heeled shoes was something the mind could not entirely dismiss, and there were times afterwards when he, never seen again, contributed to a larger perplexity that stirred the lees around and around, before more immediate matters, claiming attention, allowed them to settle again" (SS 4). Yamamoto conjoins through these recollections, epitomized by the naked man in the high-heeled shoes, meaning and meaninglessness. Determinate meaning accrues and empties rapidly as foreknowledge that shapes interpretation ("I presumed they were a woman's legs") is refigured by changing circumstantial evidence. The ordinarily unremarkable shoes transform into markers of unintelligibility, signifiers detached from normative signifieds and affiliated incongruously. That incongruity lingers and haunts outside the presence of the man himself. Again like the narrator, readers are left without explanation that would make sense of the naked man in the high-heeled shoes.

The story turns to considering possible responses to these situations that resist being rendered understandable. The narrator returns us to Tony, considering first what it might mean to have "momentarily borrowed Gandhi's attitude to life and death," interpreted as an attitude of dogmatic non-violence, in answering the unexpected phone call. The possible responses she considers range from the "piously sober" ("I'm afraid you *do* have the wrong number") to the "enlightened woman's yap" ("I think a psychiatrist would help you quite a bit") (SS 5). In categorizing these responses as such, the narrator implies the proscription of possibilities, their generation through and inscription in particular discursive fields. These thoughts lead to a series of unanswerable questions about what she should have done and what might have happened had she done something else, and culminate finally in a sense of hopelessness.

> Whatever, whatever—I knew I had discovered yet another circle to put away with my collection of circles. I was back to what I had started with, the helpless, absolutely useless knowledge that the days and nights must surely be bleak for a man who knew the compulsion to thumb through the telephone directory for a woman's name, any woman's name; that this bleakness, multiplied infinite times (see almost any daily paper), was a great, dark sickness on the earth that no amount of pansies, pinks, or amaryllis, thriving joyously in what garden, however well-ordered and pointed to with pride, could ever begin to assuage. (SS 6)

Inexplicability itself has a powerful significance for this narrator, who is drawn unwillingly but relentlessly into the spirit of despair that she envisions for the intrusive caller. Though we are given his name, Tony, it is a meaningless designation except as a reference to the intrusion. The flowers to which she had been attending throughout her meditations and memories lose their ability to signal the pleasures of community and home. And yet, those are the forces that ultimately bring the narrator out of this circle of unanswerable thoughts, as she answers the phone again to aunt Miné's "slightly querulous but altogether precious" voice inviting her to dinner (SS 6), bringing her back into ordinary life as the story ends.

Yamamoto offers in this story a critique of authority, of imbalances in relations among differently gendered individuals, and of the powers and limitations of thoughts and words against the actions of others against the self. This story stands as a powerful testimony to gendered relations of power and the crucial counterbalancing importance of community. The insights she offers into unintelligible uses of power suggest that the experience of nullified citizenship—of the effective irrelevance of legal boundaries, of the law—that accompanied internment are not exceptional to that historical event alone. Here, state power, represented as the ineffectual and dismissive police, offers neither protection nor authority. It punctuates but does not integrally shape the lives narrated in Yamamoto's story. Given the imperatives to silence about internment in nikkei communities following the end of the war, perhaps this story might be read as an explicit literary treatment of sexual harassment that is also an allegory of internment. The naked man in the high-heeled shoes is as unfathomable as the drive toward internment seen in the light of the unessential nature of racial and national identities. But my interest is not in arguing for reading Yamamoto's story as a narrative of internment. Rather, what I find so compelling about her articulation of the difficulties of making sense, of making meaning, is that it points to the microlevel ways that the broad issues of power and knowledge raised by internment play out. Both the grand sweeps of history that Okada sketches and the quotidian elements of life that concern Yamamoto register the ever-presentness of relations of power that circumscribe signification. Together, they suggest that critical inquiry likewise be conducted deliberately on multiple levels and through paradigms that work with both the nation-state *and* the nation-space. They remind us that we need to develop critical reading practices capable of attending to scope and scale even to begin to bring to surface the infinite complexities that shape "Asian American" lives. Neither Okada nor Yamamoto invests in narrating identities as truthful or authentic or not. Rather, both leave us with a sense that at issue, finally, are the determining forces that give weight, materiality, to discursively constructed, fundamentally undecidable terms of knowledge.

I have offered the foregoing analyses to show how the particularities marking Asiatic racialization condition the especial and particularized usefulness of transnationalism for Asian American studies. The affiliation of an ineffable foreignness distinctly characterizes the kinds of relationships that those so marked are able to have with the U.S. nation. For that reason, the transnational as an analytic draws critical attention to Asiatic racialization as a technology of national identity formation. In helping to bring to surface the purposive determination of meaning through racial essentialism, the transnational limns the importance of a deconstructive approach to identity, of an insistence on undecidability. In the context of internment, when racialized identity became so extensively materially significant, we can see how identity came to have the appearance of presence, of referentiality, by sheer force of juridical power. Because the governmental and judicial narratives that materialized Japaneseness did so by making certain truth claims about nikkei, the temptation to respond in kind, by arguing their inaccuracy, perhaps arises. But it is, I think, precisely that temptation against which Asian American studies must guard, and which Okada and Yamamoto implicitly displace. If we follow their lead, we are guided to thinking in terms of signification and interpretation, of conceiving every (meaning that comes to stand as) truth as a version of the naked man in the high-heeled shoes: as that which requires interpretation and which is a deployment of a practice of power.

The importance of this shift lies in part in recalling that in internment, we witness the U.S. government and judiciary deploying a politics of identity, a certain truth game, as Foucault might say, whose rules are based in racial essentialism. We cannot for this reason simply ignore identity politics, but neither can we rely upon it to effect radical social change. It is along these lines that we are returned to the potential of deconstruction toward those ends. As Gayatri Spivak has explained, "Deconstruction does not say there is no subject, there is no truth, there is no history. It simply questions the privileging of identity so that someone is believed to have the truth. It is not the exposure of error. It is constantly and persistently looking into how truths are produced" (1996, 27). We might explicitly politicize this deconstruction by understanding that persistent interrogation into the production of truth is inquiring after, and contesting as necessary, its consequences as well as its conditions. Which is to say that such an interrogation includes investigating how and why, and for whose benefit, certain meanings, interpretations, and knowledges garner the semblance and authority of truth.

It is by helping us to move in these critical directions that transnationalism might be seen to assist Asian American studies in reinventing its cohering rationale. Out of these analyses emerges an understanding that what coheres the field is not that there is an object, the "Asian American," out there to be investigated. Rather, these narratives of internment testify to the ways that certain peoples and cultural practices and products are made to mean Japanese, different, foreign, inassimilable, and so on, *without immanent reason for doing so*. It is because the term is fundamentally undecidable and yet has material effectivity that critical investigation is warranted. It is in other words the *absence* of identity, the a priori meaninglessness of "Asian American," that collectivizes Asian American studies. *Undecidability rather than identity* provides the grounds for unity, and identifying and contesting the forces that control intelligibility, that affiliate meanings, emerge as crucial tasks for Asian American studies. Perhaps, then, we might begin to think in terms of "Asian American" *unification* rather than identity to frame the cultural and political collectivity that we have asked the construct of identity to do for us. However we can further deflate "Asian American" from its seeming presence as a knowable identity, it is that such a shift is necessary that I have been attempting to argue here.

By way of closing this chapter, let me note that although my discussions have focused on a historic set of narratives, such issues as the materialization of racialized identities in negotiation with the borders of the nation clearly have contemporary currency. Regularly, ships transporting would-be immigrants from cross-Pacific locales, migrants who commonly make the journey with insufficient food and water and in lethally unsanitary conditions, are detained and generally turned away by INS officials. At the nation's southwestern borders, "Operation Wetback" aggressively works to close those borders to the "illegal aliens" who cross into the United States. California's invidious Proposition 187, denying education and social services to undocumented immigrants, and the Federal Welfare Reform Act of 1996, enabling individual states to deny welfare to legal residents who are not U.S. citizens, represent the continuing power of state border regulations deployed against those already within the United States' geographic boundaries (Chang and Aoki 1998). The recently enacted U.S.A. P.A.T.R.I.O.T. Act promises to pose a continuing threat for those constituted as foreigners, a category that is clearly a euphemism for certain racialized peoples. As George Lipsitz has put it, "Race is as important as ever; people are dying every day all around the world because of national narratives with racist preconditions" (1997, 348).[27]

Furthermore, as Keith Aoki and Robert Chang have suggested, the end of the Cold War, in depriving the United States of its "ideological Other," may effectively have conditioned an inwardly focused such for its "enemies." "For the United States," they explain, "which is not at much risk of literal invasion by another nation-state, its cultural identity and national sovereignty may be at greater risk of 'invasion' by immigrants and would-be immigrants" (Chang and Aoki 1998, 321).[28] Fear of the foreigner within shapes at least in part the contemporary terrain of U.S. culture and politics, as does the continuing concretization of the nation's juridical and geographic borders against certain bodies.[29] Such insights bear even greater resonance in the current moment, when "immigrant" and (potential) "terrorist" seem to be increasingly closer in meaning. In this light, while undoubtedly the United States' relationships with its residents and citizens as well as its negotiation of the globalized world are changing, such constructs as citizenship clearly continue to matter. Moreover, because of the distinctness of Asiatic racialization as proceeding through transnationalization, through the affiliation of an unbounded foreignness, that Asian American studies must remain attentive to the ways that "Asian American" comes to mean in relation to the relationship between an Asian-raced individual and the U.S. nation becomes clear. Even assuming that contemporary migrants have little interest in formally attaching to the United States by way of citizenship, the point is to examine modes of citizenship nullification and racialized national identity formation. To be clear, such examinations would not necessarily be for the point of arguing for citizenship, but would be geared toward illuminating how and with what consequences the U.S. nation differentiates between those who can and cannot identify as American. Functioning not as a positivist identity but as a term of criticism, "Asian American" makes no claim to verisimilitude and instead anchors investigation of the ways that the U.S. nation employs racialization as a technology of power.

3

"one hundred percent Korean":

on space and subjectivity

> We are in an era of the simultaneous, of juxtaposition, of the near and the far, of the side-by-side, of the scattered. We exist at a moment when the world is experiencing, I believe, something less like a great life that would develop through time than like a network that connects points and weaves its skein. Perhaps we may say that some of the ideological conflicts that drive today's polemics are enacted between the devoted descendants of time and the fierce inhabitants of space.—Michel Foucault, "Different Spaces" (1994 [1967])

> Just as space, time, and matter delineate and encompass the essential qualities of the physical world, spatiality, temporality, and social being can be seen as the abstract dimensions which together comprise all facets of human existence. More concretely specified, each of these abstract existential dimensions comes to life as a social construct which shapes empirical reality and is simultaneously shaped by it.—Edward Soja, *Postmodern Geographies: The Reassertion of Space in Critical Social Theory* (1989)

We have thus far seen how "Filipino America" and "Japanese America" in their respective ways function as critical devices that illuminate the limitations of disciplining constructions of uniformity in both U.S. nationalist and Asian Americanist paradigms. Animated by the possibilities and promises of uniformity, neither U.S. nationalism nor such an Asian Americanist paradigm is capable of making legible the complexities of history, culture, and socio-politics that underwrite the emergence of "Filipino American" and "Japanese American" formations. Their production both as and in difference along the nonequivalent axes of gender and race, empire and nation, and in political and cultural discourse, rises to the surface as they are examined through a critical approach that foundationally embraces the prediscursive meaninglessness of identificatory terms like "Asian American." I have been suggesting that these encounters with "Filipino America" and "Japanese America" accordingly argue for the development of critical practices that advance a politics of heterogeneity in lieu of those that work with the kind of equality-through-identity promised by U.S. nationalism. In a politics of heterogeneity, difference is neither celebrated nor subjugated, but is instead historicized and particularized.

"Filipino America," by taking us on a journey through sexuality and, as well as the sexuality of, nation and empire, and "Japanese America," by helping us to articulate the transnational within the national, together imply that the development of such critical practices depends upon our ability to rethink the spatial imagination organizing Asian Americanist discourse. For, analyses of their historic production lead to an interrogation of the imagined and practical relationship between nationness and territoriality that forms a cornerstone of the modern nation-state's operation. Territoriality literalizes nation, lending to it a palpability that contributes to its sense of inevitability. Hence, as Keith Aoki points out, U.S. legal discourse is littered with metaphors that work from and perpetuate the notion that there is an appropriate one-to-one connection between certain land and specific nation (1996). Embedded in such terms as "immigrant" and "exile" and in the difference between "native" or "birthright" and "naturalized" citizenship is this spatial logic. Theoretically, according to U.S. nationalism, departure from *there* and arrival *here* is a narrative whose closure may be found in being made like one was native-born through naturalization. Positing the naturalness of the relationship between the native-born and the nation, such an ideology depends upon territoriality for coherence and, more specifically, upon a spatialized logic that holds as discretely and naturally distinct "here" and "there." As Smadar Lavie and Ted Swedenburg summarize, "the notion that there is an immutable link between cultures, peoples, or identities and specific places . . . has served to ground our modern governing concepts of nations and cultures. In these still powerful conceptual frameworks, there is a homology between a culture, a people, or a nation and its particular terrain, and both the culture and its associated place are regarded as homogeneous in relation to other cultures/places" (1996, 1).[1] The preceding discussions have already suggested how this logic is troubled by critical consideration of "Filipino America" and "Japanese America" through an approach that does not posit assimilation into identity with the U.S. nation as objective or as standard of evaluation. In this chapter, I pursue that line of inquiry and examine the implications of contesting this spatialized logic for the conception of Asian Americanist discourse.

Working here with literary narratives that thematize the construction of "Korean American" identities in the middle of the twentieth century, I argue the importance of bringing to surface a potentially transgressive transnational cartographic imaginary articulated in these narratives, one that is suppressed in both U.S. nationalist and Asian Americanist nation-based paradigms. Despite significant differences between them, Ronyoung Kim's *Clay Walls* (1987) and Chang-rae Lee's *A Gesture Life* (1999), the novels anchoring this chapter, structurally and thematically both illustrate the critical power of defying a nation-based territorial imagination. Their combined insight contributes to the project of dislocating the dichotomous spatial logic that has long held together the boundaries of the field. In large part a response to Asiatic racialization's conflation of "Asian" with "Asian American" and the consequences that ensue, Asian American studies has conceived its distinctness as an academic field as arising partly from the difference between, as Sau-ling Wong has put it, "Asians in America" and "Asians in Asia" (1995). The exigencies of contesting the formal exclusion of "Asians" from the U.S. body politic that characterizes U.S. history promulgated a grammatically encoded emphasis on the *American* of "Asian American." Effectively, Asian Americanist practices that developed along these lines homologously reproduced the territorial logic of U.S. nationalism. Thus, little conceptual space was left in which to contend with the limitations of explanatory narratives that attempt to account for "Asian

American" subjectivities and cultural practices principally in the frame of nation.

Ongoing efforts in Asian American studies to generate alternative narratives as prompted especially by the kinds of demographic diversities of Asian-raced peoples currently residing in the United States make clear that those limitations cannot be ignored. Such efforts engage in the investigation of the methods and implications of epistemologies that translate the physical world into human and cultural differences that are then parceled out into seemingly naturally discrete objects of study. Drawing from them allows us to see that refusing the territorial logic of U.S. nationalism, in addition to inducing more adequate explanatory narratives into emergence, allows for a sharper critique of the knowledge politics that have organized Asian American studies. That is, as I discuss further in a moment, we shall see how the practice of holding "Asia" at a cognitive distance sustains a certain kind of imperialist epistemology responsible for conceiving Asian-raced peoples, among others, as Others. Thus the inadequacy of nation as conceptual parameter for understanding the complexities of subject formation is understood here as not simply a question of accuracy, but rather as one that is specifically ideological.[2]

Clay Walls and *A Gesture Life* advance the work of inviting Asian Americanist discourse to revisit its spatial groundings by narratologically emphasizing the synchronic character of the multiple systems of subjectification that converge to produce social identities. These novels point to Korean nationalism, Japanese colonialism, and U.S. racism as distinguishable but inseparably linked historical narratives that simultaneously underwrite the production of Korean and Korean American subjectivities. In so doing, they help us to recognize that "Asians in America" and "Asians in Asia" can only be held as separate and distinct within a symbolic economy that, more than refusing recognition of the "Asian" as "American," does not accord standing as equal person to those racialized as "Asian." In other words, if Asian Americanists have been invested in unraveling the metaphoric knot equating "Asian" with "foreign" by means of emphasizing literal presence, what we shall see are the ways that the different geography mapped by these novels implicitly undermines the colonial ontology underlying that signification.

To understand this point, we might take a brief detour through the conception of the distinction between Asian American studies and Asian studies, which on one level can be explained by the spatial logic organizing

Asian Americanist discourse. But precisely the ease with which this logic maps onto holding Asian studies as distant and distinct should give pause in light of the ways that it reproduces a deeply racialized process of signification. The genealogical underpinnings of Asian studies in the U.S. academy, and of area studies more generally, include an orientalist conception of humanity both perpetuated by and sustaining of holding separate in spatial terms the knowing subject from the areal object of study.[3] As Pheng Cheah explains,

> *Area* is shorthand for an expanse that is spatially distinct from the academic researcher or scholar—the knowing subject—and this distinctness implies the bounded nature of the area, the impossibility of the knowing subject's confusion of the area with the location from which he or she cognizes it. Moreover, since the knowing subject is almost always explicitly nationally marked as "American," the area that is studied is also qualitatively distinct in the sense of being "alien" or "foreign" in historical, social, or cultural terms. Thus, *non-Western* is inevitably a cognate, even a synonym of *area*. (2000, 38)

The "area" of area studies in other words serves as more than a disinterested description. Rather, it sediments the narrative of the genesis of the United States as rooted in Western Europe, erasing on one hand the significance of physical, territorial proximity while, on the other, actively distancing the "non-West."[4] In this regard, the installation and maintenance of distance as a metaphor for hierarchized difference between the United States and the areas of area studies may be seen both to register and to give rise to a series of cognitive binaries, all of which accord the United States greater power: the knowing Subject and passive Object, the universal and the particular, and the theoretical and the empirical. Such a map distinctly supports Eurocentrism by effectively creating two classes of humanity that, as Naoki Sakai explains, are conceptually organized into center and periphery.

> Until recently the global circulation of academic and intellectual information has customarily been imagined to follow cartographic visions which map two distinct flows. The first is a centripetal flow of "raw" and particularistic factual data from peripheral sites to various metropolitan centers "in the West." The second is a centrifugal flow of information about how to classify domains of knowledge, how to evaluate given empirical data, how to negotiate with the variety and incommensurability which is inherent in the body of empirical data from the peripheries, and how to render intelligible the details and trivia

coming from particular peripheral sites to "a Western audience." Academic information of this second kind is generally called "theory" and, in contrast to the particularistic nature of the first kind, it is believed to be universalistic and hostile to the presumption that only those who are involved in the locale can tell what it is that they are concerned with. (2000a, v)

Those from whom *information* flows are sedimented into objects of (area) study, whereas those from whom *knowledge* flows are coetaneously empowered with the subjective authority to evaluate that information.[5] The knowing subject sees him-herself as such against the passive object of study. Moreover, this "conceptual matrix governing [area studies'] institutionalization . . . predetermines the non-Western areas [as] . . . a priori distinct from a self-conscious subject of universal knowledge" (Cheah 2000, 47). Effectively, areas are prohibited from the possibilities of attaining self-knowledge, from attaining status as the knowing subject.[6] Relying as it does on physical space, on seemingly natural distance, this logic is in a way quite brilliant in its capacity to absorb challenges by resorting to a claim of natural environs as justification.

Distance-as-difference emerges from such analyses as these as terms of an epistemology that reinscribes its own dominance by perpetuating the understanding that knowledge flows unilaterally, emanating from a center to its peripheries. In this light, I would suggest that however unintentionally, maintaining as a distinguishing feature of Asian American studies the difference between "Asians in Asia" and "Asians in America" supports this Eurocentric, "othering" way of knowing.[7] An alternative, arguably transnational spatialization has potential to challenge such colonial modes of knowledge, and it is that different territorialization that the novels considered here help to articulate.

Though in different ways, both Kim's and Lee's works model a transnational conception of the lurching, sometimes irascible processes of subject formation that directly undermines the unilateral seamlessness of the immigration narratives forwarded by U.S. nationalism. Confined to the period of colonial Korea (officially 1910–1945), Kim's *Clay Walls* maps a field in which Korean/Korean American subject formation is largely wrought *against* Japanese colonialism and *in reaction to* the heightened racist nativism in the United States during that era. Lee's *A Gesture Life*, on the other hand, encompasses a broader time span, from roughly the 1920s to the present, and less distinctly identifies racism, nationalism, or colonialism as immediate to Korean/Korean American subjectivities. In the postindependence era, when the relations of power codified in Japanese occupation of Korea have mutated, and in the U.S. frame, when the de jure achievements of the civil rights era have transformed the particular shape of racism from its earlier iteration, the distinct exigencies of the earlier period that manifested in a desire to claim identity with anticolonial nationalism no longer operate with such urgency. As the difference between these novels instantiates, conceiving of a transnational arena of subject formation means understanding that that arena is itself inscribed by historical circumstances and therefore is constantly changing. Or to put it in other terms, in the irresolvable vacillation embedded in the construct "Korean/Korean American," which, as these novels do, raises the question of how one becomes or knows oneself by these identificatory terms, we witness the need to mark the historical conditions within which that signification occurs.[8] Thus, even as both Kim's and Lee's works reject the spatial metaphorics and related knowledge paradigms that underlie the critical practice of holding "Asia" at a distance from Asian American studies, they also argue that the generation of alternative territorial imaginaries must be mindful of the specific relations and formations of power shaping history at any given moment. The readings of *Clay Walls* and *A Gesture Life* that follow focus on their respective deployments and interrogations of "Korean" and "Korean American" identities as metaphors for different kinds of relations of power that we shorthand as colonialism, nationalism, racism, and sexism. I explore in this chapter how critique of these representations provides insight into the ways that Asian American studies constitutes itself as a body of knowledge.

borders, boundaries, bodies

When Faye at the end of *Clay Walls* declares, "Gosh, Momma, being one hundred percent Korean isn't easy" (301), she does so in recognition of the loss of any official or physical connections to the geopolitical territory called Korea. The comment has multiple meanings. It refers to the differing relationships that Haesu and Chun, Faye's parents, and Faye and her brothers each has to the real territory referenced by and to the imagined construct, "Korea." It also connotes the history of Japanese colonization that decisively transformed the meaning of Koreanness, ineradicably complicating what it means to be "one hundred percent Korean"—a condition already made impossible by the complex histories underwriting the emergence of Korea as a modern nation-state. And it is an expression of a desire to be able to quantify identity, to make it knowable in some tangible way. Faye's remark is incited by learning that the land in the northern part of the peninsula that her mother had clung to throughout their years living in the United States, with the division of Korea into north and south upon the end of World War II, had become completely inaccessible to her. Holding onto the land, which had been in her family's possession for generations, had represented for Haesu the possibilities of returning to claim a place in a Korea liberated from Japanese rule, and of returning to claim her former identity as a member of the privileged *yangban* class. The irony that the achievement of Korean independence means the loss rather than confirmation of that tangible connection and the deflation of those possibilities resonates in these closing pages of the novel.

It is unsurprising that *Clay Walls* should end on such a note, as from its beginning throughout, irony serves to organize its thematics.[9] Unfolding in three parts, titled "Haesu," "Chun," and "Faye," respectively, *Clay Walls* illustrates the shared temporality but vastly different lives of these characters.[10] Thus Kim structurally emphasizes the heterogeneity that circulates under the broader narratives of exile and immigration that frame this family's life. Moreover, it becomes increasingly clear that this shared temporality refers to the coeval unfolding of Japanese modernization and related colonialism, Korean anticolonial nationalism, and U.S. racism, simultaneously occurring narratives that collectively produce the unsettled subjectivities of this novel's characters. History, in this fictive world, is constitutively ironic, playing out through incongruities and contradictions. This broader sense of history telescopes into this family's history of migration to and life in the United States.

Rather schematically, the multiple historical narratives, the technologies of subjectification that coincide in *Clay Walls*, might be sketched as follows:

(1) Japanese modernization, most often dated to the 1868 Meiji Restoration, conditions its subsequent standing as a modern imperial power. With heightened awareness of the potential for domination by the European and U.S. powers that had aggressively expressed interest in the Asia Pacific region throughout the mid-nineteenth century, Japan's linguistic and cul-

tural unities were transformed by its rulers into the seemingly ever-present nation-ness of the land and its residents (Sakai 1991).[11] With a newly industrialized economy and constitutional mechanisms for governance in place by the end of the century, Japan emerged as the first modern nation-state in Asia.[12] Thus, in form prepared to compete with European and U.S. expansionism on its terms, Japan "modernized" itself into an imperial power. Exercising its version of "gunboat diplomacy," the favored foreign relations practice that the United States had been wont to employ to compel the establishment of trade relations with various polities in Asia, Japan "opened" Korea with the Kangwha Treaty of 1876, setting the stage for the formal occupation to follow.

(2) The first modern treaty into which Korea entered, the Kangwha Treaty, nearly marks the genesis of Korean modernization. Dissatisfaction with the then dominant feudalism of the peninsula grew through the mid- to late nineteenth century, coinciding with the growing threat of occupation by foreign powers, the combined force of which led to the Tonghak Rebellion of 1894, recognized as the first mass people's movement in Korea (M. Kim 1997). Japan and China, in their respective efforts to undermine each other's control over the peninsula, compelled the entry of Korea into the global arena as an independent nation-state. When the Tonghak Rebellion broke out, Korean rulers appealed to China for assistance in quashing the unrest; both Chinese and (uninvited) Japanese forces appeared presumably to give aid but ultimately ended up in beginning the Sino-Japanese War—fought on the Korean peninsula. The Japanese forces succeeded in overpowering the Tonghak movement and in defeating China by mid-1895. Following a decade of complicated maneuverings among various powers that led to the Russo-Japanese War (1904–1905), Korea unwillingly emerged as a Japanese protectorate in 1905. While "Koreans protested through riots and uprisings throughout 1905 and 1906 . . . [a]ll the . . . protests . . . simply accelerated the establishment of the Japanese military and civilian police networks" (Kim-Gibson 1999, 35). The year 1910 saw the formal annexation of Korea to Japan. As Min-Jung Kim explains, "Previously concerned primarily with reforming or transforming the nation, nationalism [thereafter] focused exclusively on national independence from Japan" (1997, 359). Korean nationalism of that era was in short born of both endogamous transformative energies and invasive colonizing pressures.

(3) On the U.S. front, the early decades of the twentieth century witnessed the nation celebrating its successful expansion beyond the continent to establish its presence in the Asia Pacific sphere. From the mid-nineteenth to the mid-twentieth centuries, by entering into a series of international treaties and by means of various immigration laws, the United States negotiated its contradictory need for differentiated labor and for the unity of its peoples. Through such official means, the U.S. nation relied on immigrant labor while effectively denying political and cultural citizenship to those differentiated as "non-white" (Lowe 1996). Emigration from Korea was severely limited by Japan after 1905, a factor contributing to the relatively few numbers of migrants from the peninsula to the United States during that period. White nativist resentment of Asian-raced laborers turned toward those from Japan as their numbers increased subsequent to the changes in migratory patterns effected by the 1882 Chinese Exclusion Act. Japan's standing as a modern and powerful nation-state indicated that the United States could not simply enact exclusionary legislation in this case. Instead, the Gentleman's Agreement of 1907–1908 was negotiated between the two governments. Under the terms of this agreement, "the Japanese government refrained from issuing travel documents to laborers destined for the United States. In exchange for this severe but voluntary limitation, Japanese wives and children could be reunited with their husbands and fathers in the United States" (Hing 1993, 29). Not until the 1924 Immigration Act did the United States enact legislation that prohibited immigration from Japan. Koreans, under Japanese jurisdiction, fell under the regulatory schemes of the treaties negotiated between Japan and the United States and were further prohibited from migration by the Japanese government, which saw potential for anticolonial nationalist mobilization among emigrating Koreans (Takaki 1989).

These three historical fronts, to varying degrees of explicitness, find expression in Kim's novel. And given their interarticulation, there is little wonder that they should coincide in this literary register. By emphasizing their simultaneity, *Clay Walls* argues for an approach to understanding Korean and Korean American subject formation that is at once vertically and horizontally oriented. Verticality describes the temporal axis of historical narratives, that is, the contiguities and disjunctures characterizing Koreanness understood *over time*. Horizontality refers to the spatial axis of narrative, that is, the *geographic* terrain bounding Koreanness. *Clay Walls* limns the inseparability of these axes as it literarily schematizes this transnational paradigm, narratively crossing borders but all the while remaining cognizant of the historical embeddedness of particular configurations of subjectivity.¹³

Readers learn that Chun had been mistakenly identified as an anti-Japanese student protestor in Korea, a mistake that compels his hurried marriage to Haesu and their subsequent migration to the United States. The mistaken identity transforms into irony as readers recognize Chun's utter disinterest in participating in anticolonial liberation movements. In exile by misrecognition, Chun never finds an anchor for identity, drawn increasingly to gambling, incapable of making and sustaining connections with anyone, including his family, until finally, he dies in isolation. As Chung-hei Yun has summarized, "Drifting from one place to another in search of work and exhausted from his futile wandering, [Chun] dies . . . an exile and homeless even in death" (1992, 88). Chun stands as representative of a consequence of failing to develop a sense of Korean nationalism; his demise symbolically figures the possible success of Japanese colonialism in the extermination of Korea in the absence of concerted resistance.

Kim's invocation of fate through Chun's addiction to gambling marks this novel's interest in exploring the possibilities of negotiating forces beyond individual control, an interest that includes colonization as well as patriarchal power. In contrast to Chun, Haesu perceives herself increasingly to be distinctly Korean during their years in the United States. A mobilizing force in the small community of immigrants from Korea inhabiting the novel, Haesu drives efforts to support anticolonial liberation movements. The particularly strong sense of identity as Korean that Haesu assumes is in fact partly the product of the Japanese colonialism that would eradicate that identity altogether. Anticolonial nationalism provides Haesu with a sense of connection to Korea despite her physical removal from the peninsula, a continuity with the country to which she refers throughout as "home." In this way, the novel underscores the imagined nature of home, the irrelevance of physical location in defining home for the immigrant who is also in exile.¹⁴

At the same time, however, *Clay Walls* draws attention to the significance and consequentiality of location by its critique of America's treatment of its racialized inhabitants. The repeated rejections that Haesu faces from landlords who do not want "orientals" and from schools that refuse admittance to her children on the same grounds compound and contribute to Haesu's growing certainty of her Koreanness. And yet, even as Haesu grows increasingly sure that she is "one hundred percent Korean," readers come to question what that in fact means. That it does not signify residence, ownership, or citizenship is clear. In this novel, Koreanness is defined only through negation: whatever it is, it has no substance, no immanent presence. Nonetheless, for Haesu, it is an enormously compelling construct. This element of the complicated admixture of colonial history, anticolonial nationalism, and U.S. racism that Kim offers highlights the inadequacy and partiality of any single explanatory narrative of identity.

Traceable through this tangled web is a constant sense of gender as productive constraint. Sometimes commenting directly upon the visceral consequences of patriarchal power, Kim herself employs a dichotomous logic of gender difference as a primary metaphor for delineating the multiple grids of relations of power that intersect to determine the meaning of Koreanness. The Korean woman's body catachrestically stands for Korea itself, as directly averred upon Haesu's recollections of her childhood home, provoked by a visit to that home with her children.

> Stopping in front of a newly varnished gate, Mama announced, "We're here."
>
> Everything inside the gate was hidden from the street. Secluded, Haesu thought, close to everything but secluded. Korean seclusion was intended to keep precious possessions hidden. As a young girl, she had been hidden from view, required to cover her face whenever she went outside the walls. As her sexuality increased, the greater was her concealment. The higher the woman's rank, the more she was sequestered, and hers was of the upper class. Her country had fought for its own seclusion, struggling against the penetration of eastern invaders and western ideology. A futile struggle, she thought. Korean walls were made of clay, crumbling under repeated blows, leaving nothing as it was before. Chun had wanted a wall around their house in Los Angeles, she remembered, and she had ridiculed him. (CW 104–105)

Haesu's thoughts recall an early scene in the novel in which Chun, returning home late one night, rapes Haesu, a decisive event that marks a new chronology for their relationship: "Grievances from then on were dated after 'what he did to me'" (CW 30). Like Haesu, who "did not know the word for what he had done to her" (CW 30) and is left with an unsatisfying euphemism, Kim seems also to struggle for a way to articulate the experience of Japanese colonialism, using in the end gender relations as a framework for figuring the experience of Japanese occupation. In Haesu's thoughts, her gendered body becomes the figure of the national body, the implications of which I consider further below. For now, I want to note that along these lines, even as the novel figures in Haesu significant power, it also emphasizes the circumscription of her agency ("A futile struggle, she thought.").

So too does the house itself symbolize the embodied, materialized nation. Haesu's mother had renovated the house prior to their visit, replacing the clay walls that had long stood with a wooden fence. She explains to Haesu that the other renovations were a consequence of having "studied pictures of American houses," exemplifying the "penetration of western ideology" upon which Haesu comments. Haesu, "confused by the architectural mix," experiences the uncanny as she wanders through the familiar spaces that are nonetheless utterly different. But as the visit progresses, readers become aware that it is not only home that has changed, but also Haesu herself. Like the house, she is the same and not. Literalized in Chun's rape of Haesu, Haesu can be recognized as having her own boundaries penetrated by forces that "leav[e] nothing as it was before," by the forces, that is, of colonialism and patriarchal power. Part of Haesu's transformation registers in the fact that she and the children have become part of the forces of "western" penetration. The children teach their friends "American" games, and, in response to repeated inquiries about life in the United States, Haesu affirms the myth of America rather than narrating the less than glamorous details of her family's life: "She gave in to their persistent inquiries and told them about the running water and flush toilets, about department stores and their bountiful goods, about paved streets and automobiles, about the varieties of food and opportunities to make money. Whatever they asked, she answered. It sounded like paradise to them" (*CW* 108).

Despite Haesu's initial relief at being "home," the novel's introduction of these changes to her family home presage its more directed dramatization of the transformations effected by Japanese occupation. Interrogated by police officers about her conversations with one of the stewards on the ship that had brought them to Korea, a man suspected of anti-Japanese espionage, Haesu is compelled to deromanticize her notion of home. These officers remind her to speak in Japanese and that she is still "under Japanese jurisdiction" (*CW* 109), evoking the jeopardy she is in and thus undermining her capacity to maintain the nostalgic link to home that had sustained her while in the United States. The narrator explains, "[Haesu] was confused and no longer sure of anything. She struggled to think clearly but nothing fell into place" (CW 112). In a rather Foucauldian manner, *Clay Walls* illustrates the ways that meaning and truth are produced by and contingent upon relations of power. Having decided "to tell the truth," Haesu finds that, when enjoined to do so by forces that she deeply believes erroneously and unjustly to be in power, she both cannot and will not say anything at all.

The boundaries of the self, of self-identity, metaphorized as bodily and mental integrity, remark in *Clay Walls* on the multiple and dissimilar forces that erect and erode those boundaries. Like clay walls, they require constant reconstruction and serve a double-edged purpose: protection but also constraint. The clay walls serve, too, as apt metaphor to reflect upon the discursive boundaries that delineate the parameters of Asian American studies. As *Clay Walls* travels across spaces to witness the shared temporalities of the historical era it encompasses, the flows of imagination across and transected by multiple and dissimilar regimes of power unravel the ability of physical location to direct the selection of objects of investigation. It unravels, that is, the ability to assert with certainty a stable difference between "Asians in Asia" and "Asians in America." Moreover, *Clay Walls* makes clear in its final section, focused around Faye, that it is not literal movement of bodies from one physical location to another that argues for a transnational perspective in explaining the formation of "Asian American" identities. Rather, according to this novel, it is the presentness of the past that calls for thinking transnationally about "Asian America."

Faye's friendship with Jane Nagano, a Japanese American schoolmate, highlights the intersecting vectors of "Korea," "Japan," and "America" as distinguishable but interrelated narratives. Waiting with Jane to sign up for a school activity, Faye learns of her newfound friend's connection to Japan: "Jane gave the teacher her full name and my heart sank into my shoes. Her last name was Nagano, a Japanese name. Every March First and just about every day in between, Koreans reminded each other to hate the Japanese" (CW 208). March 1, a reference to a historic, violently quashed anti-Japanese uprising in Korea in 1919, is a signal date in anticolonial Korean nationalism and here functions to identify Faye with that history. The naming of Jane as Japan-identified abruptly transforms Jane from schoolmate into hated enemy, and at the same time causes Faye to question her own faithfulness to an identity built upon anti-Japanese sentiment. Faye thus worries about associating with Jane, and "trie[s] to forget that she [is] Japanese" (CW 212).

Significantly, the Nagano family is responsible for Faye's introduction to Walt Whitman's poetry, which is literally performed for Faye by Jane's sisters. Where Japanese colonialism had precipitated Faye's family's removal to the United States, Japanese Americans further Faye's integration into America. Kim not only draws a contiguous line across time and space with this parallel, she also critiques nativity as a technology of "natural" participation in the nation.[15] It is rather through National Literature—through Whitman but also through Willa Cather and Mark Twain—that Faye learns what Americanness means.

This final section of the novel explores the construction of Korean American woman as a category of social identity. Faye's negotiation of gender relations expressed through a heightened awareness of sexuality unfolds within a frame of a desire to understand her mother. An early sexual encounter, when Willie "ran his hands over my body" and "plunged his tongue into my mouth" (CW 252), echoes Chun's rape of Haesu, mirroring Haesu's embodied experience of gender. Earlier, Willie had been castigated by Haesu for defying curfew in a scene where Faye's pleas to be heard ("'Don't ask him. Ask me'" (CW 241)) are ignored and she is "left . . . standing in the dark as if I wasn't there at all. . . . Willie had helped himself to my body and Momma put my reputation in his hands" (CW 242). This scene articulates the production of identity around the negotiation of control over sexuality, modeling negotiations of boundaries between private and public realms, between the putative autonomy of the private body and public governance of that body.

Through both Haesu's inability to name rape and Faye's sense of invisibility, *Clay Walls* suggests that the very experience of the body is discursively mediated. Moreover, the novel installs the difference between Haesu as "Korean woman" and Faye as "Korean American woman" as itself a discursive matter. No knowledge inherent in or emanating from them/their bodies gives rise to these categories. Nor does nativity imply or guarantee an immediate sense of national identity. Rather, according to this novel, the variegated relations and regimes of power that materialize imagined boundaries among "Korea," "Japan," and "America" intersect to distinguish between "Korean" and "Korean American."

history, memory, home

Like *Clay Walls*, *A Gesture Life* thematizes Japanese colonialism, but does so from an entirely different perspective, one that might be seen as "postcolonial." Dramatized through three distinctive spatiotemporal frames that ultimately converge though they never resolve, Franklin Hata's story makes almost impossible the use of such terms as "Korean," "Japanese," and "American" as signifiers of identity, for in many ways, for him, they are but empty gestures. The first of these frames encompasses Hata's life from the early 1960s to the present day, the duration of his life in Bedley Run. The second, which chronologically precedes the first but which is introduced later in the novel, captures his life from roughly the 1930s to World War II. This is the period of his life as an "ethnic Korean" who is a subject of the Japanese empire. The third is a bit sketchier, but involves his daughter, Sunny, and her son, Thomas. This last, for reasons I explain below, might be understood as a "post-identity" frame. Lee sets up these distinguishable frameworks only to demonstrate how intimately interwoven their constitutive narratives are.

The novel's opening statement, "People know me here," indicates an understanding of the inseparable link between knowledge and identity. The declaration proves in the end to be a wishful sentiment rather than a demonstrable claim. With it, Lee sets up the novel's investigative concerns. Can knowledge about another be attributed with such definitude? What does it mean to know another, or to be known by another? Is knowledge of self dependent upon or available only through others? By using especially the tropes of the heteronormative romance and the parent–child relationship, two constructs that refer metaphorically to intimate knowledge of another, Lee explores such questions and suggests finally the futility of a search for certainty. Instead, he offers an acceptance of undecidability as the mechanism for claiming agency in directing and being accountable for one's life.

The novel opens in the present day, and readers meet the protagonist and narrator, known in this setting as "Doc Hata," when he is closer to the end

on space and subjectivity 101

rather than the beginning of his life. Immediately, Hata explains how invisibly familiar he has become in Bedley Run, where he has lived for "thirty-odd years."

> In the course of such time, without even realizing it, one takes on the characteristics of the locality, the color and stamp of the prevailing dress and gait and even speech—those gentle bells of the sidewalk passersby, their *How are yous* and *Good days* and *Hellos*. And in kind there is a gradual and accruing recognition of one's face, of being, as far as anyone can recall, from around here. There's no longer a lingering or vacant stare, and you can taste the small but unequaled pleasure that comes with being a familiar sight to the eyes. In my case, everyone here knows perfectly who I am. It's a simple determination. Whenever I step into a shop in the main part of the village, invariably someone will say, "Hey, it's good Doc Hata." (GL 1)

The description is too pastoral to be accepted without question. With it, Lee establishes part of the interpretive challenge of the novel as the need to resist seduction into uncritical belief by the self-proclaimed and narratively manifested "open and friendly" demeanor that Hata strikes. It is not that Hata deliberately misleads his audience, but rather, that Lee leaves readers unsure about Hata's powers of perception and invites us to question the motives that drive and shape Hata's representations of his life's formative events. For, at the same time that Hata offers such an impossibly simplistic description of the nature of one's social identity, he has the acumen to recognize that "It seems difficult enough to consider one's own triumphs and failures with perfect verity, for it's no secret that the past proves a most unstable mirror, typically too severe and flattering all at once, and never as truth-reflecting as people would like to believe" (GL 5). Lee delivers his readers into the hands of a narrator in whom we might like to but cannot quite believe. In this way, we are invited to assume a critical but generous stance, one that neither presumptively accepts nor rejects the truthfulness of received information. Lee thus places responsibility for knowledge on readers, emphasizing the importance of the interpretive act.

This opening passage, too, resonates against the explanations later provided that indicate that "Doc Hata" is a multiply fabricated identity. In bits and pieces scattered along the way, readers learn that he is "not a physician of any kind, and that [he] only ran a medical and surgical supply store in town" (GL 4). Hata later explains that "Hata" is in fact a shortened form of

"Kurohata," the name he assumed upon adoption by a "well-to-do childless couple" in colonial Korea, which removed him at age twelve from "the narrow existence of [his] family" (72). He explains, "Most of us were ethnic Koreans, though we spoke and lived as Japanese, if ones in twilight" (72). Hata marks his adoption "as the true beginning of 'my life.' This was when I first appreciated the comforts of real personhood, and its attendant secrets, among which is the harmonious relation between a self and his society" (72). This, indeed, marks the beginning of the story of his past, a history firmly embedded in Japanese colonialism and conditioning his life as Lieutenant Jiro Kurohata in the service of the Japanese imperial army during World War II. That philosophy circles back to the novel's introductory paragraph, retrospectively explaining his pleasure at having become a seamless part of the town while at the same time undermining the claim of simplicity in determining his identity.

And finally, the novel's opening gestures toward the novel's post-identity frame, as Hata's unquestioned familiarity and belonging in Bedley Run becomes meaningless as he sells his home and looks toward the possibility of installing his long estranged daughter, Sunny, and her son, Thomas, in the apartments above his store. Thomas, the multiracial child whose biological father remains unknown, with "high, narrowing eyes and [Sunny's] black hair, though it's tightly curled, near-Afro" (GL 208), figures the literalized, physicalized hybridity that results from the convergence of multiple systems of subjectification. With the figure of Thomas, whose existence catalyzes a renewal of connection between Hata and Sunny, and who inspires community building by requiring the concerted and collective attention of the people around him, Lee augurs the possibility of a condition in which identity is not contingent upon narrow concepts of heritage. This might be seen as a condition of post-identity insofar as it moves toward a displacement of the epistemology that offers identity as self-evidently issuing from a clearly and legibly marked body.

That Doc Hata meets Thomas when he is already several years old is symptomatic of the ways that *A Gesture Life* refuses to offer origins, genetic or geographic, as the grounds for conceptualizing identity. Hata dates his own life's beginnings to his adoption, as noted above, and provides no details of his immigration to the United States. All we are told is that in 1963, he was driving around the nation and happened upon Bedley Run. Hata adopted Sunny at age five from an orphanage in Korea, and information about her biological parents is not forthcoming. Adoption itself metaphorically subordinates the importance of origins to identity as well. And none of the other characters peopling this world have distinctly identifiable births, either literal or metaphoric. Indeed, the novel witnesses deaths through diseases and sees the terminations of pregnancies but consistently and insistently refuses to locate origins. This rejection of a teleological model of identity formation effectively argues against essentialism, placing both the production and investigation of identity firmly within the historico-discursive realm. Hata, Sunny, and Thomas, as well as the other characters in the novel, come into being only relationally, and only in relation to Hata's efforts to narrativize his life, a conceptualization of identity that rejects the notion of the natural autonomy or sovereignty of individuals. Lee's use of first-person narration thus does more than provide specific insight into this character's mind; it also emphasizes the contingency of identity upon narrative.

So too does the uneven, disruptive way in which the novel's three spatiotemporal frames collide. The plot line of each becomes deeply entangled in the others such that following one trajectory alone is impossible. Nor is information provided linearly or chronologically. The backstory that fleshes out, for example, the nature and course of Hata's affair with Mary Burns, to which readers are introduced in the early part of the novel, remains unelaborated until near the book's end. And yet, enough information is provided along the way to provide for narrative coherency. The narrative structure of this novel thus requires the ability and the willingness to remain open to the circumstantiality of knowledge. In this way, the novel refuses to be read within the single-minded, closure-driven paradigms of development and progress.

For Hata, the most compelling stimulus that shifts his thoughts from one narrative frame to another is Sunny, especially his perception of her sexuality. Those images and memories touch off the recollection of the women he knew in his years of service as a lieutenant and medic in the Japanese imperial army. In a relatively early scene, Hata recalls going in search of Sunny after she has left home at 18 because, Hata implies, she can no longer stand the increasingly strained nature of their relationship. As he is looking for her, he stumbles into a memory "of another time . . . when I began my first weeks of service in the great Pacific war," as he and his "mates" were "on [their] way to a welcoming club, a grand house . . . now used as a semi-official officers' club, with the usual entertainment" (GL 105). The memory culminates in the image of a dead woman's body: "The girl was naked, and the skin of her young body looked smooth and perfect, except that her head was crooked too far upward. It was obvious her neck was cleanly broken. She was quite dead" (GL 107). Whether she has killed herself to escape enforced servitude as a sexual "partner" for the officers or whether she died at their hands remain unclear. For Lieutenant Kurohata, this incident serves as introduction to rape as a tool of war.

"I was thinking of that girl as I walked around the side of the Gizzi house [where Sunny was reported to have been seen] and its waist-high weeds and saplings," Hata explains (GL 112). Still musing upon her, Hata locates Sunny, "standing in the middle of the squarish room, her figure in profile. She had on only a gray tank-top and her underwear. She was dancing, slowly, by herself. . . . She was running her hands over herself, pressing across the skimpy shirting and down her naked thighs and up again. . . . [The men watching] weren't forcing her, or even goading her, or doing anything to coerce. She was moving and dancing with every suggestion, and then finally she was touching herself in places no decent woman would wish men to think about, much less see" (GL 114). Unable to reveal his presence to her, Hata quietly departs, "[his] blood already trying to forget, growing cold" (GL 116). Note here that it is Sunny's willingness to perform that particularly troubles Hata. As becomes clear later in the book, Hata's discomfort in this scene may be explained by the fact that Sunny's actions undermine his conception of the victimage of Korean women derived during the war.

This early conjunction between Sunny and the women of the war serves as a precursor for the stronger links to follow. As Hata remembers more of his experiences in the war, it becomes clear that he has been unable to disarticulate his understanding of the bodies of the women forced into sexual slavery during the war from his conception of Sunny's body. It is ultimately that conflation, that presumption of the sameness of these bodies across space and time, that is offered as partial explanation for Hata's treatment of Sunny, as Mary Burns points out, "as if she's a woman to whom you're beholden, which I can't understand. I don't see the reason. You're the one who wanted her. You adopted her. But you act almost guilty, as if she's someone you hurt once, or betrayed, and now you're obliged to do whatever she wishes, which is never good for anyone, much less a child" (GL 60).

Literally in the middle of the novel, the "comfort woman" appears, the historical figure of the military sex slaves conscripted into service by the Japanese imperial government, whose stories have in recent years begun to emerge and circulate in U.S. public forums. In Lee's novel, this figure functions as representative of the radical power of systems of subjectification to produce embodied identities, to produce bodies themselves. Khutaeh, or "K," as Hata comes to call her, the particular "comfort woman" with whom Hata makes us familiar, might be read as, albeit distorted, a reflection of himself. She is quite literally the product of his imagination, as we only come to know her through his memory. But in that she stands as the logical conclusion of a colonial epistemology that produces the other as the less-than-self, the less-than-human, K also reflects though inexactly Hata's own position as the product of colonialism. To be "Korean" within this economy is to be the comfort woman; to be "Japanese" is to be the abuser. By rearing and habitus "Japanese" and yet coded by his ability to understand and speak in Korean as also "Korean," Hata uncomfortably resides at precisely the point at which these available subject positions collide. That in his memory Hata falls in love with K indicates his desire somehow to resolve these tensions. However, both through K's rejection of his emotional advances and by showing us her ultimate demise, Lee demonstrates the impossibility of fulfilling that desire. It is not until Hata gains this insight that he is able, with the reader, to recognize the fallacy of mapping onto Sunny the understanding of "woman" he derived from his experiences with K. Indeed, if the appearance of K provides a momentary sense of solid grounding in the still-murky motivations for Hata's self-reflective journey, that narrative does not come to explain the entirety of his life. In this way, Lee identifies Japanese colonialism as an immensely powerful but nonetheless not omnipotent force in the production and regulation of identity.

A Gesture Life does not resolve these different narratives by offering Hata, Sunny, and Thomas as a reunified family. Perhaps the signal characteristic of the novel's integrity is that to the last, it refuses to offer simplicity and closure. Instead, Hata's plans for the future are unsettled and firm only in his decision to leave Bedley Run and leave Sunny and Thomas behind. The novel closes, "Perhaps I'll travel to where Sunny wouldn't go, to the south and west and maybe farther still, across the oceans, to land on former shores. But I think it won't be any kind of pilgrimage. I won't be seeking out my destiny or fate. I won't attempt to find comfort in the visage of a creator or the forgiving dead. . . . I will circle round and arrive again. Come almost home" (GL 356). The subject, I, has disappeared altogether in this final sentence, leaving it to read ambiguously as imperative and declaration both. It is a conclusion that is not a closure, the infinity of the circle having replaced the definitude of linear narration.

Shadowing Lee's novel are historical narratives that are extensions and reconstitutions of those to which *Clay Walls* draws attention. Receding from prominence in *A Gesture Life* are signs of anticolonial nationalism. Concerned as this novel is with the historical period during occupation and following independence from Japan, in contrast to *Clay Walls*, Lee's work identifies a different set of imperatives underwriting and forestalling the emergence of Korean and Korean American identities. Here, the impulse is toward exploring coloniality and postcoloniality, the legacies of Japanese colonialism and their influences on materializing such identities. Doc Hata, as Jiro Kurohata, represents the colonial subject, the product of the disciplinary apparatuses installed by Japanese colonialism.

Japanese occupation meant among other things the dismantling of the educational systems that had been in place, the prohibition of the use of Korean language in public, and the conscription of young men for military service. Students in the newly established educational system under Japanese rule were taught to see themselves as "subjects of the Japanese Empire" (Kang 2000). The ideology underwriting Japanese colonization of Korea depended upon and offered understandings of the latter as a "backward" country in need of civilization, which was effected by the imposition of Japanese educational and political systems. Such an understanding of Korea, in combination with the demands for inexpensive labor that conditioned a pattern of exploitation of peoples on the peninsula for Japanese economic needs, precipitated the practice of the military sex slavery invoked in Lee's novel (Chung 1995). Through force and fraud, somewhere between 60,000 and 200,000 women were compelled into service as "comfort women," to sustain the morale of the Japanese army and to ensure against the spread of diseases that would ebb its strength.[16] *A Gesture*

Life clearly takes interest in these factors, deploying the figure of the "comfort woman" as a critique of Japanese colonialism.

In a way, this novel's interest in exploring the colonial rather than anticolonial or nationalist subject precipitates the indirect mediation—through the "comfort woman"—of its critique of Japanese colonialism. Otherwise, the colonial subject would merely invite a simplistic indictment that reiterates an "us"/"them" understanding of relations of power. Doc Hata, the representative colonial subject, is neither and both "us" and "them," a rendering that does not negate the wages of Japanese colonialism but allows for recognition of its ensuing and troubled hybridities. Lee's novel insists upon shifting toward a distinctly nonjudgmental, evaluative mode that is nonetheless capable of being critical of the abuses of power that the "comfort woman" signifies. As Doc Hata muses early on in the novel, "I think one person can hardly understand why another has conducted his life in such a way, how he came to commit certain actions and not others, whether he looks upon his past with mostly pleasure or equanimity or regret" (GL 5). In contrast to *Clay Walls*, whose preindependence chronological frame arguably compels the identification of anticolonial nationalism as a primary factor in the subjectification of Koreans and Korean Americans, *A Gesture Life*'s critical interests articulate the shifting historical conditions—from formal coloniality to postcoloniality—that its broader temporal frame encompasses.

What marks *A Gesture Life* as a specifically American novel is, I think, precisely that it conceptualizes Korea as postcolonial rather than neocolonial. Political independence from Japan inaugurated a new era of colonial relations for Korea, this time between the self-styled liberator, the United States, and the emancipated South Korea. Although popular narratives in both South Korea and the United States offer liberation as "a gift of the allied forces, especially the U.S.A." (Choi 1993, 80), increasing critical attention is being focused upon the ways that this " 'benefactor' . . . made South Korea into a neo-colony in order to create an anti-communist regime" (Kang 2000, 129).[17] The commonplace image of North Korea in the U.S. imagination as a country led by uncontrollable, putatively irrational figures clinging stubbornly and hopelessly to a world order no longer in existence supports the narrative of U.S.-as-liberator.[18] Contemporary interest in the U.S. mainstream media in the recent moves toward reunification of the peninsula seems driven to some extent by an understanding that reunification implies the capitulation of North Korea to a world order engineered in part by the United States following World War II (Cumings 1999a, c). It takes no special insight to recognize that this narrative masks U.S. responsibility for the division of the Korean peninsula in the first place. Alternatively, to see South Korea as neocolonial means recognizing the "colonization of consciousness," as Chungmoo Choi has put it, effected by the United States through a concerted effort at "Americanizing" South Korean politics and cultural practices.[19] Korean nationalism in this contemporary context emerges as heterogeneous and often conflicted as to objectives. And unlike the transnational solidarities to which *Clay Walls* points, Korean nationalism across borders faces difficulties in working collaboratively in part because of this neocolonial relation (see Jun 1997 and M. Kim 1997).

My point here is not that *A Gesture Life* should be responsible for or responsive to this way of conceiving postindependence Korea. Rather, it is to suggest that in its envisioning of postcolonial Korea, we can identify the Americanness of its perspective, the perpetuation of the invisibility of the United States' neocolonization. Americanness thus might be seen as an epistemological attitude, and I would suggest that it is because *A Gesture Life* works from such a critical perspective that the Korean and Korean American woman's body figures in it as a metaphor for nation. In Lee's novel, Doc Hata's ability finally to disarticulate his conception of Sunny from his memories of K is riven through Sunny's independence: her departure from home, her construction of a life deliberately separate from his. The manager of a clothing store in a shopping mall in the nearby working-class town of Ebbington, Sunny personifies the characteristics of consumerism and the bourgeois work ethic so closely affiliated with Americanness. The contrast between K and Sunny sediments an understanding of Korea as victim. Beaten and raped, driven to violence herself, K dies. "K" here easily refers both to this character and to Korea itself. "Khutaeh," meaning the end or the bottom piece, was the name given to her because she was the last of the children born to her family. It bears here even greater resonance as signifying the end of Korea. Sunny, on the other hand, liberated from Doc Hata, from a colonial past, promises and delivers—through Thomas—continuity into the future. Her name baldly gestures toward daybreak, a clearly forward-looking orientation.

In this way, the novel inclines toward reproducing knowledge of Korea as victim, as a story whose ability to self-generate has ended. Lee's representation of "comfort women" reinstalls neocolonial regimes of knowledge by privileging the distinction between the Korean and Korean American woman's body as a distinction of agency. Invited to condemn Japanese colonialism and experience pathos for K, *A Gesture Life* in this way works through the binary logic of narratives of victimization. As Leti Volpp has argued, such narratives can deflect attention from systemic conditions precipitating inequitable empowerment (1996).[20] "The condemnatory reaction," Volpp explains, "which distances the observer from the practice and defines the observer as the antithesis of that practice, relies upon and perpetuates a failure to see subordinating practices in our own culture" (2000b, 115). Especially around the issue of sexual violence, victimization as a technology of subjectification can proceed by installing and deploying "cultural difference" such that the culture of the "other" is seen as patriarchal and oppressive while the United States appears in contrast as liberating.[21] While *A Gesture Life* registers gendered sexual incursion by the United States through the implication that Sunny is the product of an "encounter between a GI and a local bar girl" (204), Hata's narrative nonetheless relies on distinguishing between K and Sunny as victim and agent, respectively.[22]

In both *Clay Walls* and *A Gesture Life*, that nationness is figured through the gendered body is suggestive about their respective understandings of the relationships between bodies and nation-states. They both imply in this manner that an isomorphic identification of body with nation would constitute the ability to be un-self-conscious, to be truly at home. As many critics have pointed out, this trope of woman-as-nation depends "on a particular image of woman as chaste, dutiful, daughterly or maternal" (Parker et al. 1992, 6).[23] The consequences of the mythification of both nation and woman consequent to this trope are obvious: erasure of complexity and contradiction, the ascription of a fictive unity/purity that cannot and does not exist, and, particularly with the category "woman," the effective undermining of an ability to have standing as a person. Even, or perhaps especially, when this trope appears as parts of narratives that ascribe complexity and agency to (some) women, as Kim's and Lee's novels arguably do, it requires particular identification and scrutiny for its mythifying tendencies to be forestalled.

heterotopic visions

I have offered the foregoing analyses to show that though engaging significantly different historical conditions, both *Clay Walls* and *A Gesture Life* imply the need for a transnational approach to conceiving the processes of "Asian American" subject formation. These novels make visible the "simultaneity of geographies," to borrow from Ketu Katrak (1996), the juxtapositionality of seemingly diachronically mappable historical frames. They thus register the inadequacy of U.S. nationalist accounts of immigration and settlement where arrival and achievement of identity with America stand as celebrated narrative closure. Neither common origin nor common destiny, the bookends that enclose such narratives of immigration and identity are to be found in these novels that leave us, finally, without resolution.

Moreover, that transnationalism not only describes cross-border flows but also much more radically, I think, prompts the deconstruction of common conceptions of space itself becomes evident through these novels. In other words, following through on these literary articulations of the convergence of seemingly spatially distinct historical fronts and narratives means disrupting the received conception of "Asia" as someplace and something that happens somewhere *over there*. If, as Alan Hyde has put it in the context of discussing treatments of "the body" in legal discourse, "seeing the world as socially constructed is a sort of academic fad" (1997, 6), it nonetheless takes a concerted effort to recognize the constructedness of what we may experience to be natural, real physical distances between places and peoples. Why do we experience physical location in terms of *distance*? And why and how does that experience of distance translate into *difference*?

As noted earlier, Asian American studies has employed such a spatial logic in its attempts to interrupt the racial essentialism of Asiatic racialization that homogenizes and offers "Asianness" as ahistorical and emanating from prediscursive bodies. In that way, the naturalized affiliation of territory with identity has been coopted and deployed to advance Asian Americanist efforts to contest anti-Asian racism in the U.S. frame. At the same time that Asian American studies continues its efforts to make visible the heterogeneity elided by Asiatic racialization, the insights of transnationalism and of postcolonial studies as articulated in the novels considered here compel a somewhat different response, one geared toward denaturalizing geography as the underwriting rationale for differences among "Asiannesses." I do not mean to suggest that there are not real and distinguishable territories in the world and that there are not real people who live in them. Nor am I arguing that those people in those places do not live lives particular to those locations. What I am getting at is that there is no reason that that place should be perceived necessarily as any more foreign by virtue of location than, say, California or Texas or Alaska. The territories designated by these names are effectively no more distant in my experience of them, sitting here at this moment in the place called Washington, D.C., than that place called Korea. All of which is to recall that the unity of the United States is a fictive unity, an imagined community, and one whose imagined boundaries have material consequences and are purposively constructed and deployed. The challenge before us is to identify what those consequences are and what and whose interests are served by maintaining a distance between "Asia" and "America."

To be clear, I am not arguing for the dissolution of Asian American studies. Rather, what I am suggesting is that critically acknowledging the material effectivity of multiply located histories and chronologies, which are themselves entangled as Kim's and Lee's works suggest, means recognizing the limitations of knowledge produced by distancing "America" from "Asia" as limitations that do ideological work. In that light, we might conceive "Asian America" as a heterotopic formation, one that enfigures the multiple and dissimilar spaces and places of discourse and history that collectively produce what seems at first glance, terminologically, to refer to a distinctly bounded site, "America." Foucault has theorized heterotopia as referencing both the real and unreal spaces that shape social relations (1994 [1967]). As in the reflection of a mirror, where knowledge of self derives from seeing that self where she is not, where understandings of real places are determined by seeing through unreal spaces, these novels may be seen to articulate the imagined spaces and material locations variously referenced by "home" and "nation," by "Korean" and "Korean American." Following their lead, we might understand that transnationalism in Asian American studies guides us to heterotopic visions of culture and politics.

4

(dis)owning America

I cannot go back—

I never left.

—Joseph P. Balaz, "Moeʻuhane" (1984)

In England and the United States, I may say perhaps without contradiction, the two freest and best governed countries on the face of the earth, the law is respected most, and the people bow to its supremacy, from the force of deep settled opinion, without the aid of cannon and bayonets to keep them in subjection. Their doctrine is, to obey the law while it is the law, so long as it accords with the constitution, and when wrong, to reform it through the legal channel of the Legislature.—William Little Lee, Chief Justice of the Supreme Court of Hawaiʻi (1852), quoted in Sally Engle Merry, *Colonizing Hawaiʻi: The Cultural Power of Law* (2000)

We need to know where we live in order to imagine living elsewhere. We need to imagine living elsewhere before we can live there.—Avery Gordon, *Ghostly Matters: Haunting and the Sociological Imagination* (1997)

(dis)owning America   113

Each of the preceding chapters has in its way pointed to the necessity of conceiving Asian American studies as a discourse that consistently mounts a twofold critique, of both U.S. nationalism and of Asian Americanist paradigms that replicate its apparatuses and objectives. We began, in chapters 1 and 2, by recognizing the impediments to acknowledging critically diversity and complexity imposed by uniform subjectivity as a cognate of U.S. nationalist and homologous Asian Americanist frames of knowledge. In chapter 1, we saw how "Filipino America" at once challenges dominant U.S. conceptualizations of racialized masculinities and contests the privileging of the trope of exclusion and the category of race as organizing concepts in Asian American studies. That consideration led to the exploration of the potential of the transnational as an analytic in Asian American studies that focused chapter 2. By recognizing how nikkei transnationality was constructed and made to operate in the historic instance of internment, we saw there the importance of persistently contesting racial essentialism, in part by embracing the undecidability and insubstantiality of "Asian American." In that light, rather than arguing for the (U.S.) nationality refused through Asiatic racialization, as exemplified in internment, that emphasizing the comparative dimensions of nation—of the transnational within the national—was a way of deploying the transnational as a critique of power became clear.

The arguments of these early chapters brought to surface the imperative to rethink the territorial imagination that has historically underwritten the coherency and distinctiveness of Asian American studies, the discussion that motivated chapter 3's analyses. There, we saw the ways that critical examination of "Korean America" pushes us toward adopting a heterotopic imagination that refutes the spatial logic of U.S. nationalism. Articulated through novelistic interrogations of the justifications for and effects of treating "Korean" and "Korean American" as naturally or appropriately distinct and separable constructs, chapter 3's argument pointed to how such a rationale sustains an arguably imperialist epistemology. Returned in this manner specifically to knowledge politics as a thematic focus of this book, in this final chapter, we return as well to the set of issues constellating around Lois Ann Yamanaka's novel *Blu's Hanging* (1997), invocation of which opened this study.

To examine those issues, I investigate with greater specificity the implications of the insights of postcolonial studies that have circulated throughout this book but as yet without particular remark. As a point of departure, I indicated that critical debates about the idea and form of the nation-state currently under way under the rubric of "postcolonial studies" problematize the grounds giving coherency to "Asian American." I explicate that claim in this chapter and, in so doing, explicitly think through what the "political" might mean for an Asian American studies conceived through a deconstructive account of "Asian American" and informed by postcolonial and transnationalist scholarship. The encounter of the "Asian American" with the "postcolonial" staged here, with Hawai'i as the locus of inquiry, radically destabilizes the kind of subjective, nation-oriented politics that have historically anchored Asian American studies. Doing so puts into question in other words a politics focused on working toward garnering the economic and social advantages that accrue to achieving the national subjectivity of Asian-raced peoples in the United States. In a particular way, as I explain below, the "postcolonial" limns the changing material bases for the emergence of Asian American identities under conditions of globalization. Those changes have been among the most compelling forces pressuring Asian Americanist critique to think outside the frame of nation. Literally/legally excluded from the U.S. nation and effectively externalized even within its spaces, Asian American studies has historically targeted national subjectivity as an objective in direct response to the juridically enforced impropriety of Asian-raced peoples in the United States. I argue here, as I have in this book as a whole, for an appropriation, for a deliberate cooptation of that impropriety as the critical edge necessary for Asian American studies to continue its work of challenging injustice in light of contemporary historical conditions. As the following discussions will show, the critical concerns that constitute postcolonial studies help Asian Americanist discourse hone that analytic edge in particular ways. The political emerges from this inquiry as a category refracted by complicated and often vexed questions of justice, of what justice means and of the instability of its meanings. The postcolonial in this sense functions as a device for illuminating that instability, recognition of which cautions against assuming a singular "correct" politics for Asian Americanist critique. This chapter advances this book's move toward identifying myriad and nonequivalent practices of liberation and freedom as the diversified political goals motivating Asian American studies.

I take this language from Michel Foucault's consideration of what liberation and freedom might mean in the context of understanding an individual's relation to "truth," given the fields of relations of power within which certain knowledges emerge to have the epistemic authority of "truth." Practices of freedom constitute an individual's ability to act upon the self, to exert control over one's relationship to others by means of having the freedom to behave in certain ways. "Freedom" here does not signify a position outside relations of power, conceived not only as political power but as the "whole range of power relations that may come into play among individuals, within families, in pedagogical relationships, political life, and so on" (Foucault 1994 [1984], 283). Rather, it names a condition within which an individual takes his or her self as object of epistemology, one inscribed by the uneven terrain constituted by the broad range of power relations. As both subject and object, this individual acts with deliberation as to how she presents her self to herself, in effect, to herself as other. This self-as-other thus translates into a model for behavior toward others. Such freedom of self-subjectification/-subjection is contingent upon some level of liberation from states of domination. Foucault explains that "When an individual or social group succeeds in blocking a field of power relations, immobilizing them and preventing any reversability of movement by economic, political, or military means, one is faced with what may be called a state of domination. In such a state, it is certain that practices of freedom do not exist or exist only unilaterally or are extremely constrained and limited" (Foucault 1994 [1984], 283). Liberation is a necessary condition, but practices of liberation are insufficient "to define the practices of freedom that will still be needed . . . to be able to define admissible and acceptable forms of existence or political society" (Foucault 1994 [1984], 282–283). Liberation in this context does not imply that once the power blockage constituting a state of domination has been dismantled, an essential, transcendent self/identity (re)emerges. Rather, it suggests that a given state of domination prohibits the effectivity of the range of relations of power. That is, such a state validates or recognizes only the subjectivity that issues from it, thus overshadowing or negating other forms resulting from the vast range of relations of power.

Conceiving of Asian American studies as advancing and engaging in practices of liberation and freedom facilitates critical acknowledgment of the vast diversity of the relations and blockages of power that underwrite the construction and legibility of political and social subjectivities, and that regulate social relations. Informing Asian American studies, in the face of that plurality, must be persistent remembrance that the freedom to self-subjectify is a beginning rather than an endpoint, a point of departure for formulating political, economic, and social structures that allow power to flow among individuals rather than unilaterally. This chapter suggests that this model addresses the multiple and variegated states of domination *and* liberation within and against which "Asian American" becomes intelligible as both coherent subjectivity and critical term of analysis.

As noted earlier, the radical diversity of Asian American identity formations registers in continuing debates about who and what "count" as "Asian American" in Asian American studies. Those debates have explicitly raised postcoloniality as an as yet underexamined topic important to Asian American studies. In this regard, this chapter contributes to efforts already under way to think through the postcolonial. These efforts have been largely focused around addressing the paradigmatic centrality of East Asian Americanness to Asian American studies. Such analyses have brought into the foreground postcoloniality as a historical and material base from which certain "Asian American" identity formations have emerged. As Lisa Lowe has argued,

> Post-1965 Asian immigrants are a contemporary group emerging out of colonialism in Asia as well as immigrant displacement to the United States, a group at once determined by the histories of Western expansionism in Asia and the racialization of working populations of color in the United States. Especially in light of post-1965 Asian immigrations to the United States, Asian American subjectivity is a complex site of different displacements, particularly the displacement from a decolonizing or neocolonized Asian society to a United States with whose sense of national identity the immigrants are often in contradiction. (1996, 103)

Postcoloniality in this context broadly refers to the histories and legacies of European and U.S. colonizations of especially South Asian and Southeast Asian countries, as well as the contemporary forms of uneven global relations of economic and political power.[1] The fringe status of studies of Filipino American formations in Asian American studies, for example, highlighted by the Yamanaka award controversy, points to the need for Asian Americanist paradigms to be informed by postcoloniality. Without such reshaping, the argument goes, analysis of Filipino Americanness *(dis)owning America* 117

can be mounted only at the expense of assimilating its unique historical groundings. In this regard, a call to consider postcoloniality translates into a call to take seriously historical differences.

But why postcoloniality as the rubric under which to highlight that necessity? What, in other words, is specifically useful about postcolonial and postcoloniality as critical terms of Asian Americanist analysis? These questions in part motivate the following discussion. This chapter confirms how the emphases of postcolonial studies on critiquing historic and current practices of economic and cultural globalization and attendant migratory patterns help provide insight into resulting subject formations and collectivities and into practices of U.S. imperialism.[2] Such insights bolster efforts by fields like Asian American studies to evaluate the material foundations of and justificatory ideologies underwriting racialization in the United States. Along these lines, postcolonial studies contributes to Asian Americanist discourse by highlighting the ways that national identities come into being through negotiations with global nexuses of relations of power.

Two additional concerns guide this discussion as well. First, the Yamanaka award controversy dramatically prompts focused critical attention on Hawai'i and Filipino Americanness and, by extension, on U.S. and Spanish colonialisms, thus initiating a dialogue between "Asian American" and postcolonial/postcoloniality as terms of critical practice. *Blu's Hanging*, the novel instigating debates about intra-field racisms, occasions an encounter between these terms and their epistemological limits. What they mean in a political and critical terrain characterized by Native Hawaiian sovereignty movements agitating for liberation from U.S. colonization and multiracial "local" identity formations that refuse "Asian American" identification is altogether unclear. For precisely that reason, undertaking to consider "Asian American" in relation to "postcolonial" in this context promises a radical exploration of the symbolic and political economies within which Asian American studies conducts its work. This book's first chapter looked specifically to Filipino Americanness. Here, I investigate how contestations over "Asian American," when the term is contextualized in Hawai'i, erode its descriptive aptitude. "Asian American" appears in this context as a term of domination and cooptation, recognition of which urges Asian American studies to find ways of ensuring that "Asian American" instead consistently refers to a commitment to contesting states of domination.

Second, the implications of postcolonialism for Asian American studies bear examination in a more institutional-level register. A principally 1980s and 1990s phenomenon driven largely by the migration to the "first world" and subsequent work of "third world" intellectuals, the establishment of postcolonialism in the U.S. academy has posed challenges for U.S. ethnic studies on that level. Since the publication of Edward Said's *Orientalism* in 1978, a wealth of critical literature has emerged that has come to be collected as postcolonial studies. Anchored by analysis of colonial epistemes and apparatuses of colonial domination, one of the signal characteristics of postcolonial theory has been sustained attention to the ways that academic disciplinary knowledge practices are implicated in the structures of colonialism. From critiques of the "postcolonial" itself as a term of criticism that intends to displace the center/periphery, self/other binaries of colonial thinking,[3] to questions about the possibilities of representing subalternity given the disciplinary and institutional demands of academic discourses,[4] postcolonial studies has been highly reflective about the politics of intellectual work. That discursive reflection has included analyzing how, in the U.S. context, postcolonialism's foundational interests in studying power dispersed differentially through the economic, cultural, and political machinery of colonialism may be depoliticized and turn into yet another discourse of otherness given the imperatives of U.S. multiculturalism (Sharpe 1995). This issue carries special significance given that postcolonialism's rapid institutional acceptance has been seen as suspect in some quarters—as symptomatic of deflection of attention to conditions of gendered racial inequality within the United States under the guise of attending to diversity, only located comfortably at a difference from "us"/the U.S.[5] To what extent and under what conditions are U.S. ethnic studies and postcolonial studies competitive discourses? What is at stake in maintaining distinctions between them, and how do their genealogical differences matter to understanding their positions in relation to each other?

The next section of this chapter engages such questions by offering an overview of the dominant critical interests of postcolonial studies. As with any effort to encapsulate a field, this overview is by no means exhaustive. Rather, it is geared toward identifying what I see to be central concerns of postcolonial discourses, especially as they articulate to Asian American studies. That discussion is followed by an examination of how Hawaiian history and context problematize both "postcolonial" and "Asian American." In that section, I am especially interested to recount how the United States continues to colonize Hawai'i, not only by means of refusing Hawaiian sovereignty, but also by deploying a "mainland"-derived binary paradigm of race relations through its state apparatus of the law. The Supreme Court decision in *Rice v. Cayetano* (2000), which anchors my discussion, illustrates the ways that a U.S. nationalist narrativization of history functions to sediment colonial relations between the United States and Hawai'i, thus arguing for counterhegemonic historiography in Asian Americanist practice. *Rice v. Cayetano* exemplifies the narrative naturalization of the (idea of) the U.S. nation by means of what Rob Wilson has described as "the conquest of space by time" (1996, 314), the production of ownership of territory (the nation), by control of history (nationalism). As the decision makes clear, contemporary hegemonic nationalist historiography reinstalls the material inequalities effected by the dual technologies of racism and colonialism. If, crudely put, Asian Americanists have been more immediately interested in the former and practitioners of postcolonial studies in the latter, then the fact of their interwoven texture as evidenced in this decision compels a collaborative effort. This chapter closes by returning attention to *Blu's Hanging* and to debates about the book's representational politics. I revisit what it may mean to identify the novel as "Asian American literature" in light of the complicated problematics laid out in the earlier parts of the chapter. I argue for interpreting the novel as "theoretical" in addition to "representational" and demonstrate how doing so enables Asian Americanist discourse to attend to the complexities of social subjectification.

"postcolonial" and Asian American studies

The following consideration of postcolonial and Asian American studies offers possibilities generated by tactical, "friendly" alliances between them.[6] I suggest here that the particular significance of the postcolonial and postcoloniality as terms of criticism for Asian American studies lies in their prompting of the deconstruction of the U.S. nation.

the United States isn't "postcolonial", but . . . In a 1995 essay, Jenny Sharpe posed the question, "Is the United States postcolonial?" The answer she offered was that it is not, or rather, that it is not postcolonial in an immediately critically meaningful way. Extending in some ways Ruth Frankenburg and Lata Mani's (1993) delineation of the differing meanings and periodizations accruing to "postcolonial," Sharpe rightly points out that applied to the United States, the term can lose its analytical edge and serve as yet another racialized identity in the catalogue of liberal multicultural enumerations of difference.[7] Descriptively, the "postcolonial" of "postcolonial studies" in the U.S. academy generally denotes the post–World War II proliferation of national independence (independence as nation-states) by the "Third World" through liberation movements and various projects of "decolonization." Rather than taking for granted a state of postcoloniality, however, postcolonial studies has put into question the aftermath of colonialism *and* liberation.[8] Postcolonial in this regard bears a silent but insistent question mark, serving as an inquiry rather than a description, an evaluative entry point rather than a conclusion. It recognizes the difficulties of decolonization given the impossibility of simply dissolving the effects of colonialism. Postcolonial studies confirms in this manner that colonized societies did not remain untransformed by colonialism to emerge after political liberation in some essential, "pure" form. Rather, the ways that the values and institutions accompanying colonial rule were grafted onto already dynamic and complex societies as part of the process of effectively instituting colonial domination condition the lack of "a clear focus and target of decolonization" (Pieterse and Parekh 1995). Under the rubric of postcolonial studies have accordingly emerged critiques of the various possibilities for and constraints on liberation and what follows thereafter, and the articulation and imagination of possibilities for forms of political and cultural life based on neither wholesale assimilation nor rejection of colonial life ways. This "postcolonial" invokes in the same breath colonization *and* decolonization. As Frankenburg and Mani have suggested, defining decolonization as referring to "a political, economic and discursive shift, one that is decisive without being definitive" positions the term as "enabl[ing] us to concede the shift effected by decolonization without claiming . . . a complete rupture in social, economic and political relations and forms of knowledge" (1993, 300).

At the same time, the frame of the postcolonial extends critical focus to imperial metropolitan spaces as well, to interrogate what cultural and political shifts the loss of empire might have set into motion in the "center" rather than "periphery." In this regard, the postcolonial as a term of criticism signals shifting locations, from nations-nee-colonies (from the Third World, from empire) to imperial metropoles-nee-nations (to the First World, to the heart of empire). These physical movements between "there" and "here" have found counterparts in theorizations of the mutual hybridization that also serve to blur distinctions between center and periphery. While such theories have importantly undermined essentialist notions of the purity of either metropolitan or colonial subjectivities, societies, and cultures, critical debates in postcolonial studies have made clear that the variegatedness of the historical foundations underwriting these "postcolonial" identities must be addressed.[9] "Postcolonial," even as it refers generally to Third World decolonization, cannot and does not have the same meaning across the differentiated histories that constitute India and Britain, for example (Frankenburg and Mani 1993; Sharpe 1995).

Already, the difficulties of applying this "postcolonial" meaningfully to the United States begin to become evident. For the histories of U.S. empire-building have unfolded in a manner and time scale different from those of its European analogs, resulting as a general rule not in the sovereignty of its colonies but in their absorption into the U.S. nation. Thus Hawai'i "became" the nation's fiftieth state, and Guam and Puerto Rico seemingly permanent protectorates, overseas extensions of the United States. Peoples indigenous to the continent continue to face the extinguishing of life ways in spite of having an official pseudo-sovereign status. The Philippines is a notable exception, though the continuing and insistent presence of U.S. military forces on the islands suggests that formal independence has not meant a total disconnection from U.S. power. I cite these examples to emphasize that U.S. colonialism and "postcoloniality" have been both *intra*territorial and extraterritorial, a condition that resists description by the Europe-based postcolonial. As Eva Cherniavsky has argued, "U.S. history is marked by a *convergence* of nationalism and colonialism, so that independence transfers power from imperialist interests abroad to imperialist interests on American soil—from white men to white men" (1996, 86; emphasis original). The celebrated liberation from England that genetically grounds U.S. national identity formation also marks the beginning of the story of colonization of the continent. But struggles for liberation in relation to the United States have largely been articulated as struggles for political and economic power by groups minoritized along racialized, gendered, and sexualized lines. While at times those struggles have been mounted in solidarity with and by using frameworks analogous to liberation movements in the Third World, they have been forwarded for the most part for the sake of gaining equality (civil rights) rather than sovereignty.[10]

To be sure, as noted above, Third World decolonization has had an impact on the United States as global migratory and economic patterns conditioned by colonialism and postcoloniality have resulted in changing gendered and sexualized race and class relations within the United States.[11] The United States may not be postcolonial in the ways that Britain or India may be, but it does nonetheless negotiate postcoloniality as a global condition. Along these lines, Sharpe has suggested with regard to the United States that "the 'postcolonial' be theorized as the point at which internal social relations intersect with global capitalism and the international division of labor" (1995, 184). She explains, "In other words, I want us to define the 'after' to colonialism as the neocolonial relations the United States entered into with decolonized nations" (1995, 184). This redefinition forms an axis of investigation for which the United States as a neocolonial power serves as target of inquiry. It emphasizes colonialism's imposition of capitalism on noncapitalist societies and underscores the United States' contemporary role in advancing and sustaining global capitalism.[12]

What does all of this mean for the various resistance discourses (antiracism, antisexism, antiheterosexism) in the United States? The danger here in emphasizing analysis of U.S. neocolonialism lies in its potential to hinder engagement with the particularities marking U.S. intraterritorial histories of racialized, patriarchal heteronormativity.[13] Vital to generative deployment of postcolonial critique in the U.S. frame is a reworking of the internal/external, center/periphery metaphor that organizes the "postcolonial" of postcolonial studies. That is, in the U.S. context, colonialism and decolonization cannot be understood primarily in terms of "here" and "there," metropole and distant colony. U.S. history is marked by an "internalization of 'extraterritorial' spaces and extroversion of colonized peoples" from the "space of an 'American' national politics and culture" (Cherniavsky 1996, 87). I am not arguing here for reintroduction of the model of "internal colonization" deployed in the 1960s and 1970s to "harness the language of decolonization" for politically strategic purposes (Sharpe 1995, 183).[14] Rather, I am emphasizing the need to pay equal attention to recognizing the United States as a historic as well as a "new" colonial power. In other words, for the postcolonial to be useful in articulation to the United States, it must contend with the nation's past in addition to present practices of empire. As Cherniavsky summarizes, "If postcolonial critical practice emerges in, and in response to, the failures of decolonization (to the impossibility of simply unraveling colonial power . . .), a postcolonial approach to U.S. history and culture would speak to the contradictions of a *naturalized/nationalized colonial domination*" (1996, 88; emphasis added). Accordingly, *denaturalization/denationalization* in this inseparably coupled form articulates the critical frame of empire in a way attentive to the specificities and generative for studies of U.S. culture and politics.

I would suggest that denaturalization/denationalization maps onto Asian American studies as a tactical orientation, one that urges Asian Americanist practice toward deconstruction. Postcolonial studies scholarship "about" postcoloniality helps Asian American studies understand the intranational social formations and relations consequent to the demographic impact of Third World decolonization and global capitalism. Decolonization initiated migratory patterns that include immigration from formerly colonized Asian countries, which in turn contributes to disassembling "Asian American" as a category of identity on the descriptive level alone. Moreover, postcolonial studies' demonstrations of the contingency of local socio-political/cultural identities on structures and relations of power both proximate and global underscore the constructedness of "Asian American" identities. "Indigenous" to "precolonial" to "colonial" to "national" to "immigrant" to "American" outlines the profound instability of and inscription by multiple kinds and registers of relations of power of such identities, narrativized through the developmental *telos* marking modernity. In this way, the limits of a politics of identity are firmly established. Postcolonial studies also, by marking the U.S. nation as simultaneously nation and empire, encourages the deconstruction of U.S. nation-ness itself, its seemingly inevitable status as nation, an insight crucial for Asian American studies, as I explain below.

"home"—place or desire? Despite the generations-long rootedness that characterizes significant portions of the populations of Asian-raced peoples in the United States, historically and currently, a sense of foreignness accompanies the racialization of certain individuals and groups as "Asian" or some specific iteration thereof.[15] Always there lingers the idea that those considered Asian can (or should, in some white supremacist renderings) go "home," which never refers in context to a location in the United States. As Lisa Lowe has so succinctly put it, "the American of Asian descent remains the symbolic 'alien,' the metonym for Asia who by definition cannot be imagined as sharing in America" (1996, 6). In a collapse of symbolic and political registers, the United States has codified this position by the numerous immigration exclusion laws enacted from the mid-nineteenth to the mid-twentieth centuries. These include the 1875 Page Law targeted at barring the immigration of prostitutes from China but effective in halting most entry by Chinese women; the prohibition of Chinese and Japanese laborers by, respectively, the 1882 Chinese Exclusion Act and the 1907–1908 "Gentleman's Agreement" between Japan and the United States; the creation of the Asiatic barred zone in 1917 that prohibited among others the entry of Indians; and the 1924 National Origins Quota Act, which limited the entry of "any alien ineligible to citizenship," a category that included those of Asian descent (see Hing 1993). The later twentieth century repeal of such laws, while allowing for increased numbers of migrants from Asia, have been marked as well by "more specifications and regulations for immigrants of Asian origins" (Lowe 1996, 9).[16] The internment of Japanese Americans during World War II also serves as an especially visible sign of the presumed foreignness of Asian-raced individuals living in the United States, as I discussed in chapter 2. For the activist-scholars of the 1960s and 1970s, this history, combined with the fact that most Asian-raced peoples in the United States at that time were native-born U.S. citizens, mobilized arguments that insisted upon belongingness.[17]

What, then, are the implications of highlighting the deconstruction of nation as the framing grounds for Asian American studies? They include, I believe, the imperative to disarticulate "nation" from "home." I want to suggest that Asian Americanists conceptually disown "America," the ideal, to further the work of creating home as a space relieved of states of domination. In other words, I am conceiving of home as that condition in which there is an equality of ability to participate in negotiating and constructing the ethos of the places in which we live. If there is something seemingly impossibly utopian about this sense of home, borrowing from Toni Morrison, I want to say that for those of us whose labor is a labor of language, it is vital to move "the job of unmattering race away from pathetic yearning and futile desire; away from an impossible future or an irretrievable and probably nonexistent Eden to a manageable, doable, modern human activity" (1997, 3–4). To "unmatter race" is a project of "depriving [race] of its lethal cling" (Morrison 1997, 5). To work at imagining this home in the present tense means concertedly dismantling those materially inscribed, epistemological constructs that make it seem inconceivable. This conception of home iterates, as Morrison explains, that "eliminating the potency of racist constructs in language is the work I can do. I can't wait for the ultimate liberation theory to imagine its practice and do its work" (1997, 4). If living in the U.S. nation means inhabiting "the house that race built,"[18] imagining an alternative to inaugurate its realization means distinguishing "nation" from "home."[19] As I have attempted to show throughout the preceding chapters, and as the following discussion explicitly argues, "nation," when it stands as a representative of the form of the modern nation-state, may be seen as a materially consequential epistemological construct that hinders imagining otherwise.

I argue for disowning America with the awareness that the freedom to disown, conceptually or otherwise, depends on to some extent already possessing the advantages that nation-as-home avails. I say this with the awareness that that necessary ownership has been afforded by the labors of those who have advanced and who continue to mount liberatory struggles that unblock socio-economic and juridical barriers to claiming America. That work remains invaluable in light of severe imbalances in access to America as home, exemplified by the contrast between the undocumented sweatshop worker and the "Asian Americans" currently serving as cabinet members in George W. Bush's administration. A determinate end, access to America, is not, however, the sought-after end. (That there are "Asian Americans" in the presidential cabinet is surely a sign of access, a certain recognition of belongingness, but equally surely, perhaps especially given this administration's conservative ideologies, it is not a condition of achieved justice.) National belongingness, in other words, does not solve injustice, and seeing America through the critical frame of empire makes that clear.

From a different but related point of entry, this move to disown America is driven by the need to challenge what Henry Schwarz has described as "the pervasive academic tradition of 'American exceptionalism' that has characterized much scholarly study in this country." That tradition gives rise to "the imaginary divide between postcolonial and other ethnic studies in the U.S." (Schwarz 2000, 9). American exceptionalism is the narrative that proclaims the distinctness of the United States in its break from the rigid hierarchies of Europe and especially England and forwards the foundational beliefs in justice and democracy as distinctly—*exceptionally*—American. Schwarz is persuasive in suggesting that the pervasiveness of this narrative has contributed to keeping postcolonial studies at arm's length from American studies, broadly construed. That separation enables the continued occlusion of the contradictions covered over by the narrative of American exceptionalism: "Both at home and abroad, America styled its image as the one place where diversity could exist. The irony of this image in light of its conquistadorial and slave-holding past required great ideological effort" (Schwarz 2000, 10). Investigating the United States along these lines has become a recognizable trend of contemporary American studies scholarship, and some of that work has significantly blurred distinctions between American studies and U.S. ethnic studies.[20] Such scholarship refuses the metaphorics of space, time, and subjectivity forwarded by what might be identified as the U.S. nationalist pedagogy through which American exceptionalism is promulgated. It offers instead an understanding of the United States as "the figure of an achieved colonial rule" (Cherniavsky 1996, 87). An American studies informed by the concerns of postcolonial critique betrays the ability of America to stand for and as its "noble achievements" of liberalism, democracy, and liberty by illuminating its "internalization of 'extraterritorial' spaces and extroversion [from American national politics and culture] of colonized peoples" (Cherniavsky 1996, 85–86).[21]

Certainly, Asian American studies, as well as other U.S. ethnic studies, has consistently argued the distance between America as the exceptional ideal and America as a lived form. Analyses of the myriad failures of America are commonplace and have advanced a kind of politics of recognition through which the presence and contributions of racialized groups to national life have been made visible.[22] In Asian American studies, for example, the absence of Chinese laborers in the "golden spike" photograph recording the completion of the transcontinental railroad has oft been cited in this regard. This kind of critique has been geared toward closing the gap between the ideal and reality of America and has contributed to effecting decisive (though again not definitive) shifts in U.S. culture and politics. The insights of postcolonial studies, however, suggest the need to interrogate the ideal itself.

In much postcolonial studies scholarship, the nation appears as a "form of struggle against imperialism" and "as a historically produced, unfinished, and contested terrain. The nation and the signs of its cultural life emerge as necessarily littered with unresolved contradictions and dilemmas" (Mufti and Shohat 1997, 3–4). Such an understanding transects ideas of nation as "imagined community" (Anderson 1991) and "invented tradition" (Hobsbawm 1983), deromanticizing them by force of historical, material specification.[23] Postcolonial studies has shown that while nationalism proved a powerful framework for mounting anticolonial struggles in the Third World to achieve formal political liberation, it has not delivered on its promised "mythos of hearth and home, [which] are now the property of national elites [who] have been increasingly revealed to be corrupt, capitulationist, undemocratic, patriarchal, and homophobic" (Mufti and Shohat 1997, 3). Nation, in this regard, emerges as a fiction around which practices of liberation organize under the name of nationalism. Specific to the particular collectivity denoted by nation in the modern era is its claim to a correlate political structure—the state—with an assumption of consensual membership in the polity. Nationalist projects do not inevitably result in or demand sovereignty as nation-states, but in modernity, the nation-state has been the dominant and dominating form of sociopolitical global ordering. Many liberation movements have had at least in part to adopt the economic and political and oftentimes educational infrastructures and epistemologies of the colonizer (the already "modern") to be recognized/recognizable as a legitimate authority. Nationalism in the context of decolonization is accordingly a problem, as Partha Chatterjee has put it, in that "Nationalism sets out to assert its freedom from European domination. But in the very conception of its project, it remains a prisoner of the prevalent European intellectual fashions" (1993b, 10). Chatterjee articulates the problem thus: "Why is it that non-European colonial countries have no historical alternative but to try to approximate the given attributes of modernity when that very process of approximation means their continued subjection under a world order which only sets their tasks for them and over which they have no control?" (1993b, 10). Accordingly, anticolonial nationalist thought may be seen to be not wholly an autonomous discourse, but rather, like the idea of nation-states itself, as conditioned by particular historical developments (see Anderson 1991).

Chatterjee argues that nationalism, to be a sustaining and sustainable framework, must inaugurate epistemologies and representational structures (both political and cultural) that are cognizant of the "problem of nationalist thought."

> The problem of nationalist thought becomes the particular manifestation of a much more general problem, namely, the problem of the bourgeois-rationalist conception of knowledge, established in the post-Enlightenment period of European intellectual history, as the moral and epistemic foundation for a supposedly universal framework of thought which perpetuates, in a real and not merely a metaphorical sense, colonial domination. It is a framework of knowledge which proclaims its own universality; its validity, it pronounces, is independent of cultures. Nationalist thought, in agreeing to become "modern," accepts the claim to universality of this "modern" framework of knowledge. Yet it also asserts the autonomous identity of a national culture. It thus simultaneously rejects and accepts the dominance, both epistemic and moral, of an alien culture. (Chatterjee 1993b, 11)

Effectively covering over its own historicity, Enlightenment epistemology delinks knowledge from cultural specificity. The modern nation-state as the avatar of those values is constitutively a contradictory form for the pursuit of freedom from colonial domination. As Chatterjee maps how the "post-Enlightenment telos begins to function as a freefloating signifier seeking universal confirmation" (Radhakrishnan 1992, 87), nationalism and nation appear as categories that are part of the hierarchization of culturally specific epistemologies that characterizes the logic of (post)colonial modernity.

Gayatri Spivak initiates a parallel if differently focused argument in asking "Can the Subaltern Speak?"; she demonstrates in the well-known essay by that name that what counts as knowledge in the "First World" academy is produced by epistemological categories foundationally incapable of representing (re-presenting) the "poor, black female" as exemplary subaltern. Collectively, these and other similarly oriented arguments[24] map onto Asian American studies in such a way as to insist that Asian Americanist discourse interrogate its epistemological assumptions. In other words, I am suggesting that the particular kinds of questions being raised in postcolonial studies about nation as an *epistemological* category provide a model through which Asian American studies might reflect upon its own work. Conceiving of nation in this manner means understanding the modern nation-state as inherently contradictory. The fundamental contradiction, in other words, is not between "America" the ideal and "America" the lived form, but rather is *internal* to the idea of the modern, sovereign, liberal nation-state itself. To summarize a bit schematically, liberalism provides for political sovereignty as the logical, natural extension of its ontological assumption of the autonomy of individuals. "Individual rights to property, speech, belief, association, and so on, as articulated by the Enlightenment thinkers . . . strongly implicated a private realm of autonomy and placed boundaries on intrusion into this private space by public authorities" (Aoki 1996, 1312). Homologously, this separation of public and private effected the consolidation of "political sovereignty along strict territorially justified lines" (Aoki 1996, 1312). Within this economy, "actors, whether individual contracting parties or nations, [are conceived] as abstract and formally equal" (Aoki 1998a, 13). In its abstractions and its claim to the universality of its ideas, liberalism creates its own contradiction. For, as Bhikhu Parekh has explained, "Liberals do believe in equal respect for all human beings, but they find it difficult to accord equal respect to those who do not value autonomy, individuality, self-determination, choice, secularism, ambition, competition and the pursuit of wealth" (1995, 37). In this regard, America as lived form, with all of its contradictions, *is* its ideal. It is already the exemplary manifestation of liberalism; it cannot be made any "better" by criticizing its contradictions alone.[25]

U.S. (neo)colonialism and Asian Americanist discourse

What I am suggesting is that taking seriously the insights of postcolonial studies results in an Asian Americanist discourse that employs empire not only as an analytic in studies of the United States, but also and equally importantly, in critical reflection of Asian American studies as well. Such moves illuminate the particularities of the history of U.S. imperialism (expansionism) and colonialism (occupation) and question a liberal politics that attempts to pursue justice without working toward a radical reformation of the structures that condition injustice.[26] I have suggested that embracing modernity's celebration of the nation-state is problematic for this reason and have emphasized the ways that understanding "nation" as an epistemological category of modernity, with its attendant universalist claims to truth, calls for interrogating the very ideals of "America."

In the remainder of this chapter, I particularize discussion of the United States as a colonial and neocolonial power by focusing inquiry on Hawai'i. I then show how Lois Ann Yamanaka's *Blu's Hanging* and the debates about it, contextualized by that foregoing discussion, help in the development of critical frameworks in difference from the imperatives of the liberal Enlightenment ideals embedded in the United States as exemplary modern nation-state.

history beyond control Native Hawaiian sovereignty movements continue to work toward both political and cultural liberation from U.S. colonialism. Hawaiian history—both its history of contact with exogamous powers and its endogamous history unrelated to such contact—has long precedence.[27] Modern Hawaiian history, which is to say, its history of compelled modernization, testifies to the familiar colonizing patterns of economic investments, bolstered by racialized and gendered ideological/religious justification and by military resources. Formally annexed in 1898, Hawai'i was but one of the overseas lands over which the United States took possession in that era. With the displacement of continental indigenous peoples as an available prototype, the United States was an experienced colonizing power by the end of the century. A snapshot portrait of the nation in 1890 offers insight into the forces motivating U.S. expansionism at the turn of the century: this movement saw a national economy over $65 billion, well above the national wealth of any single European nation; urbanization was proceeding apace, and electric and telephone technologies were changing social and business dynamics; industrialization, Wall Street economics, and monopoly capitalism created massive wealth for some and, in the South and Midwest agricultural arenas, poverty for others of the 75 million peopling the nation at that time.[28] That 75 million represents a population doubled in the span of a decade, largely as a result of immigration from eastern Europe as well as Japan. In short, by 1890, "the productive capacity of the nation had grown too large for the strictly continental market to absorb" (Musicant 1998, 9).

The United States became an increasingly assertive player in the global sphere during this era, leading for one to the Spanish-American War of 1898, which would result in the transfer of Guam, Puerto Rico, and the Philippines from Spanish to U.S. control—by peace treaty and payment of $20 million. Underwritten by racial and Christian-religious ideologies that infantilized Pacific Islander populations, the United States recognized both the strategic military position of Pacific locales and their potential as markets and as sources of raw materials for production. Claiming Hawai'i made sense in this logic of capital-driven expansionism that was also a logic of competition with European powers as well as Japan. Japan, undergoing its own modernization, had been building its own empire and was accordingly seen as a competitor. In 1897, as President McKinley renewed earlier failed efforts to annex Hawai'i, he wrote: "We cannot let these Islands go to Japan. . . . Japan has her eye on them. Her people are crowding in there. I am satisfied they do not go there voluntarily as ordinary immigrants, but that Japan is pressing them in there . . . to get possession before anybody can interfere" (quoted in Traxel 1998, 215).[29] This competition with Japan helped those in support of the idea of overseas expansion to overcome resistance to such a move, resistance that was variously grounded in anti-imperialism and in "Beliefs in the inferiority of barbarian societies and the alleged innate incapacity of nonwhite 'races' [which] rendered the incorporation of the islands deeply questionable" (Merry 2000, 21). In 1893, U.S. businessmen, primarily sugar planters, overthrew then reigning Queen Lili'uokalani with the support of U.S. military forces and established a provisional government in the islands. In June 1898, annexation to the United States was formalized by act of the U.S. Congress.

Formal territorialization by the United States followed a more than century-long negotiation with the forces of empire, and millennia-long independent existence characterized by dynamic negotiations of social and economic structures and practices of culture.[30] England's Captain James Cook first made landfall in the islands in 1778. His arrival heralded the development of an active sandalwood trade that resulted in extensive deforestation such that consequent environmental changes contributed significantly to the decimation of Hawaiian populations. It also augured the establishment of sugarcane plantations, which would ultimately lead to the importation of labor from Asian countries. Interactions with non-Hawaiians introduced diseases to which the native population had no immunity, a primary factor in the reduction of that population by 80 percent by the mid-nineteenth century. Throughout the 1800s, concurrent with the unification of the islands into one kingdom under King Kamehameha I (in 1810), Christian missionaries, primarily from the United States, arrived and imposed religious and cultural practices significantly different from those that had been in place in Hawai'i. "In Hawai'i, as in other societies penetrated by Western imperial power, the structural shift to capitalism involved major transformations in the ideological arenas of religion, language, and knowledge, and introduced new symbolic forms and practices of social representation" (Buck 1993, 60). The ideological systems of *mana*, a divinely provided life force, and *kapu*, the determination of sacred prohibitions, and cultural practices of *hula* among others, were forcibly rearticulated through the asymmetric relations of power between the material force underwriting missionary objectives and that of the increasingly literally diminished Hawaiian population. Pressure to allow land usage and ownership by non-Hawaiians steadily grew through this period, and the increasing commercialization of land culminated in the 1848 Great Mahele, or land redistribution: "land that hitherto had been communally held could thenceforth be sold" (Chan 1991, 26).

In 1993, in recognition of the fact that the annexation of Hawai'i took place without consent, the United States offered formal apology for this history.[31] What it did not do, however, was translate that recognition into Hawaiian sovereignty. Today, Hawaii's place in the frame of the U.S. imagination conceives it as "our own" paradise, one sufficiently different from "here" so as to be interesting, but not so different as to be threatening. Hula is commodified and sold with vacation packages that offer a "taste of Hawai'i," a construction that effaces ongoing struggles against material inequalities faced by native Hawaiian populations, to say nothing of the history of colonialism itself.[32] This is perhaps not surprising given that today's "mainland" envisionings of Hawai'i extend the "pastoralizing" of Hawai'i characterizing Western European and U.S. American narrativizations for centuries (Sumida 1991). From Melville to London to Michener to Elvis' *Blue Hawai'i*, these paradisical accounts of Hawai'i are familiar fare (Wilson 2000).

If culturally the United States continues to resist taking Hawai'i seriously as more than a source of tourist entertainment and dollars, politically it continues to recodify its position of dominance inaugurated in a specifically legal manner by William Little Lee's arrival in Hawai'i in 1846. As Sally Engle Merry (2000) recounts in her study of the cultural power of law in the colonization of Hawai'i, Lee, a lawyer trained at Harvard University, by 1847 had participated in drafting legislation to create a Superior Court of Law and Equity to which he was subsequently elected chief justice. By 1852, Lee was chief justice of the Supreme Court of Hawai'i and, in the speech that epigraphically introduces this chapter, celebrated the rule of law's newfound presence in Hawai'i. Merry explains that "Lee had arrived in Hawai'i at a critical time. Caught in the crosscurrents of global mercantile trade . . . the Kingdom of Hawai'i had become home to a large and fractious group of foreign merchants and sailors. As Britain, France, and the United States vied for power and influence in the Pacific, each sent warships to the islands demanding special treatment for its resident citizens and threatening to take over the kingdom" (2000, 4). Pressured by these conditions, King Kamehameha III "and the high-ranking chiefs were engaged in transforming the Hawaiian system of law and governance into an Anglo-American political system under the rule of law. Their strategy was to create a 'civilized' nation, in European terms, to induce those European and American powers whose recognition defined sovereign status to acknowledge the kingdom's independence" (Merry 2000, 4). For this reason, Lee's arrival appeared fortuitous.

This strange situation in which Hawaiian rulers were compelled to transform indigenous structures of governance to meet the demands of European and U.S. American modernity in order, paradoxically, to preserve independence resonates strikingly against the U.S. Supreme Court decision in Rice v. Cayetano (2000). The contradictoriness of reliance on the rule of law embedded in the nineteenth century Hawaiian rulers' welcome of Lee, manifests in this decision in the ways that the Ccurt recognizes only to moot the history of U.S. colonization of Hawai'i. This case bespeaks the United States's ability to withstand and absorb revelations of its contradictions, precisely by means of (in this instance) a discursively manifested power to define "history" as *nationalism*, as the narratives—and only those narratives—that consolidate the stability of the nation.

Rice v. Cayetano is a case that adjudicated the legality of Hawaii's voting limitations in elections for trustees to the Office of Hawaiian Affairs (OHA). The OHA had been established in 1978 through an amendment to the state constitution with the express mission of securing "The betterment of conditions of native Hawaiians . . . [and] Hawaiians" (508). In Rice, at issue was whether restrictions on the electorate voting for OHA trustees to "qualified voters who are Hawaiians, as provided by law" violated the U.S. Constitution's Fifteenth Amendment protection of the right to vote regardless of racial identity (509). Petitioner Harold Rice, whose familial roots in Hawai'i extended for generations but who did not meet the blood quantum designation required of qualified voters, sued Benjamin Cayetano in his capacity as governor of Hawai'i, upon denial of his application to vote in the trustee elections.³³ An attempt to preserve the cultural commonality associated with Hawaiian sovereignty pre-1778 (the date of Cook's arrival on the islands) motivated the establishment of the OHA and the gearing of the electoral franchise toward identifying those who would most directly benefit from its services.

Reversing the lower courts, the Supreme Court granted Harold Rice's petition to vote in the election by holding that these electoral restrictions did in fact violate his Fifteenth Amendment rights. The Court's decision in *Rice v. Cayetano* articulates—indeed codifies—the *national* historico-political framework within which *(post)colonial* conditions are adjudicated. The Court presents a history of the islands in some detail only to reinscribe colonial domination by mooting that history through its interpretation of "race," one derived from a specifically "mainland" history of race relations and one that discounts the material foundations of the emergence of racialized identities. In this way, the Court effectively masks even as it iterates the U.S. colonial past, by asserting the primacy of the present—of preserving the nation as it stands at present. Justice Kennedy, who authored the majority opinion, offered these concluding remarks:

> When the culture and way of life of a people are all but engulfed by a history beyond their control, their sense of loss may extend down through generations; and their dismay may be shared by many members of the larger community. As the State of Hawaii attempts to address these realities, it must, as always, seek the political consensus that begins with a sense of shared purpose. One of the necessary beginning points is this principle: The Constitution of the United States, too, has become the heritage of all the citizens of Hawaii. (524)

The passive construction of these comments, and indeed, of the decision overall, helps to efface U.S. accountability for precipitating the imposition of the Constitution on the islands' inhabitants. An assertion of "realities" displaces questions of power and agency in building a "political consensus" and replaces them with an appeal to common sense. As David Lionel Smith has explained, "Common sense is not critically self-conscious, and its function is to facilitate conformity and adaptation to familiar circumstances. It thrives on familiarity and fears change, and therefore common sense is profoundly conservative" (1997, 181).³⁴ The common sense invoked by the Court underwrites a historiography that deploys history to reinstall the primacy of the nation, once again placing history beyond control. It does so by means of facilitating a particular racialization, one that collapses distinctions between the ways in which racial categories became functional in the continental United States and how they came into being through the advent of colonialism in Hawai'i.

As Justice Stevens points out in his dissenting opinion, the Court can only arrive at its conclusion by "ignor[ing] the overwhelming differences between the Fifteenth Amendment case law on which it relies and the unique history of the State of Hawaii" (546). Criticizing the "wooden approach" adopted by Kennedy in the majority opinion, Stevens interprets these historical differences to argue for protection of self-determination. Stevens seeks judicial acknowledgment of what the majority refutes to be an analogous status between Native Hawaiians and continental indigenous peoples. As argued by respondent Hawai'i, the situation in this case approximates that of the relationship between the United States and continental indigenous populations as provided by Morton v. Mancari (1974). In Morton, Justice Blackmun explained that "As long as the special treatment [at issue] can be tied rationally to the fulfillment of Congress' unique obligation toward the Indians, such legislative judgments will not be disturbed. Here, where the preference is reasonable and rationally designed to further Indian self-government, we cannot say that Congress' classification violates" constitutionally protected rights (417 U.S. 484, 556). The Court in *Rice v. Cayetano* rejected the analogy, explaining that Native Hawaiians do not share the same "quasi-sovereign" status, evidenced in part by the fact that while the OHA has a "unique position under state law, it . . . remains an arm of the State" (521). This logic serves as a convenient rationale that enables the Court to avoid undertaking serious examination of the similarities between the histories of colonization marking the cultural and political statuses of Hawaiians and continental indigenous peoples.[35]

Rice works by making such distinctions and by simultaneously constructing Native Hawaiian identity by means of a continental racial discourse that erases colonialism. By validating Rice's invocation of Fifteenth Amendment rights, the Court effectively analogized his situation to that of Black Americans, flattening enormous and important differences along the way. This is not surprising, given that dehistoricization of race is an all too common contemporary phenomenon in legal discourse and elsewhere. The case is evidence of America's "retreat from race," in Dana Takagi's formulation (1992), the displacement (or "post"-ing) of civil rights rhetoric that plays out in part through the dehistoricization of racial categories. Rights rhetoric with respect to race, dislodged from historical specificity or sublated by nationalist historiography, reifies the notion central to the ideal of the nation that the accumulation of rights accruing to de jure citizenship means de facto equality. "Color-blindness" is offered as the remedy for racism, which in the Court's mind is defined by any racial classification.[36]

This dehistoricization of race enables the Court in *Rice* to invoke, perversely, *Hirabayashi v. United States* (1943), a case that codified the constitutionality of curfew laws applied to Japanese Americans during World War II, in its argument against racial classification in any form.[37] This flattening of racial categories finds precedence in *Adarand v. Pena*, a 1995 decision in which the Court similarly invoked a series of cases related to Japanese American internment as evidence of the ways that any recognition of racial difference is tantamount to racism.[38] Through such reasoning, the Court in *Adarand* advanced the defrayal of access to material resources through such strategies as affirmative action.[39] *Rice* and *Adarand* are in one sense simply contemporary manifestations of the ways that the judiciary has historically maintained the social and economic advantages of whiteness.[40] The challenge such iterations pose is twofold: first, they call for a methodology of comparative racialization that (re)historicizes race, and second, they insist upon recognition of the ways that the abstract, "universal" subject of the celebrated rule of law is effectively a white, male, property-owning heterosexual individual.[41]

In thinking through Hawai'i, what this means is recognizing the differential histories between the racialization of Native Hawaiians first through colonial discourse and then and currently through a continentally derived racial discourse. Part of this recognition entails acknowledging that in this locale, Americans of Asian descent are part of the presence and relations of power initiated by colonialism. As Haunani-Kay Trask explains, "Today, modern Hawai'i . . . is a settler society. Our Native people and territories have been overrun by non-Natives, including Asians. Calling themselves 'local,' the children of Asian settlers greatly outnumber us. They claim Hawai'i as their own, denying indigenous history, their long collaboration in our continued dispossession, and the benefits therefrom" (2000, 2).[42] Trask articulates deeply entrenched tensions between Native Hawaiian sovereignty movements and "local" cultural nationalisms that attempt to give voice to the distinctness of the identity formations emergent on Hawai'i.

> Part of this denial [of indigenous history and complicity in continued dispossession of Native Hawaiians] is the substitution of the term "local" for "immigrant," which is, itself, a particularly celebrated American gloss for "settler." As on the continent, so in our island home. Settlers and their children recast the American tale of nationhood: Hawai'i, like the continent, is naturalized as but another telling illustration of the uniqueness of America's "nation of immigrants." The ideology weaves a story of success: poor Japanese, Chinese, and Filipino settlers supplied the labor for wealthy, white sugar planters during the long period of the Territory (1900–1959). Exploitative plantation conditions thus underpin a master narrative of hard work and the endlessly celebrated triumph over anti-Asian racism. Settler children, ever industrious and deserving, obtain technical and liberal educations, thereby learning the political system through which they agitate for full voting rights as American citizens. Politically, the vehicle for Asian ascendancy is statehood. As a majority of voters at mid-century, the Japanese and other Asians moved into the middle class and eventually into seats of power in the legislature and the governor's house. (2000, 2)[43]

While Asian Americans, especially those of Japanese descent, "rise to dominance" on the islands, "Hawaiians remain a politically subordinated group suffering all the legacies of conquest: landlessness, disastrous health, diaspora, institutionalization in the military and prisons, poor educational attainment, and confinement to the service sector of employment" (Trask 2000, 3). From this perspective, the politics of anti-Asian racism are not only insufficient to contend with but in fact further consolidate the effects of colonialism on Hawai'i. Criticizing "local" identity movements, Trask asserts that "The [Native Hawaiian] struggle is not for a personal or group identity but for land, government, and international status as a recognized nation" (2000, 6).[44] Asian locals in this regard become analogous to "haoles," and those who would claim a progressive, liberatory politics must either "justify their continued benefit from Hawaiian subjugation, thus serving as support for that subjugation, or they must repudiate American hegemony and work with the Hawaiian nationalist movement. In plain

138   *imagine otherwise*

language, serious and thoughtful individuals, whether *haole* or Asian, must choose to support a form of Hawaiian self-determination created by Hawaiians" (2000, 20).⁴⁵

Even as "localism" is increasingly finding a material life in the form perhaps especially of literatures,⁴⁶ and even as Asian Americanists are increasingly "discovering" local literatures and investigating local histories and identity formations,⁴⁷ driven by such critical analyses as Trask's, Asian Americanist discourse—albeit unevenly—is taking up the gauntlet Trask throws down.⁴⁸ Is it possible to acknowledge and value a "local" identity as part of Asian Americanist discourse given the sharp criticisms offered by Trask? How can we account for/analyze/recognize the visions that emerge under the rubric of "local literature"? How can we account for/analyze/recognize the important differences between, for example, the political and economic power achieved by Americans of Filipino descent versus those of Japanese descent inhabiting the islands and the continent, while at the same time recognizing "Asian American"/"local" participation in "settler colonialism" both in Hawai'i and on the "mainland"? "Local identity," Candace Fujikane has explained, "is predicated precisely upon the fact that it is not a Native identity, and although Locals have a long history in the islands, their narratives are often marked by an uneasiness over the ways they claim an identity based on what is very specifically a Hawaiian homeland" (1994, 30).

"Home"—place or desire? Amid this tangled web of questions and problematics, one thing at least becomes clear: nationalism as a framework for Asian Americanist practice, or as a framework for driving local identity formations, appears rather awkward. For, as demanded by modernity, ownership of territory legitimates nations, and nationalisms, even if unintentionally (as in cultural nationalism), can lead to territorialization in ways that can resemble the practices of colonialism itself.⁴⁹ In Hawai'i, for example, some of the tensions between local Asians and Native Hawaiians result from the former's "champion[ing] of private property development . . . [an] idea[] once employed by the white oligarchy to dominate all aspects of the latters' lives" (E. Yamamoto 1999, 67). An Asian Americanist (as opposed to Native Hawaiianist) perspective informed by a postcolonial critique of colonialism in Hawai'i urges Asian American studies to broaden its objectives from combating anti-Asian racism to include challenging cooptation of its liberatory energies by the assimilative modes of nationalist

(dis)owning America 139

narration: by the bootstraps narrative celebrating individualism, the story of immigrant success defined as economic and political equality, and so on. In other words, the home Asian American studies pursues cannot be conceived as a desire for place.

These complexities get at the critical importance of what Lowe has described as "displacement, decolonization, and disidentification" as "crucial grounds for the emergence of Asian American critique" in the contemporary moment (1996, 104). In her study of Theresa Hak Kyung Cha's *Dictée* (1995 [1982]), Jessica Hagedorn's *Dogeaters* (1990), and Fae Myenne Ng's *Bone* (1993), Lowe demonstrates how "these Asian American works displace the representational regimes of the institutionalized novel and official historical narrative by writing out of the limits and breakdowns of those regimes. In their writing, these Asian immigrant and Asian American women explore other modes of retrieving and spatializing history. They offer other modes for imagining and narrating immigrant subjectivity and community . . . and refuse assimilation to the dominant narratives of integration, development, and identification" (1996, 101). These texts, according to Lowe, figure multiple and intersecting displacements by racialization and gendering, and by the decolonization of Asian countries and the rise of global capitalism. And, from those positions, they themselves mount "decolonizing projects" that displace colonial modes of knowledge and production. A postcolonial critique of U.S. colonialism challenges Asian American studies to conceive itself as a decolonizing project that, like the texts to which Lowe refers, works to displace and provide alternatives to dominant structures of knowledge.

This includes, in Lydia Liu's terms, the need "to question the legitimate politics of the state-representing-the-nation" (1994, 40). Liu argues that in such accounts as Chatterjee's discussed above, "the cultural domination of the West is homogenized and totalized to such a degree that alternative narratives within the nation-space [are] virtually written out as a theoretical possibility" (1994, 39). Postcolonial studies' identification and critique of modernity in this way can, ironically, result in positioning "the hegemonic discourse of the West . . . as an absolute power in constituting the native" (1994, 39). As Liu and others have demonstrated, such totalizing narratives reproduce the very epistemic conditions they intend to displace, erasing for one the ways that systems of gender and sexuality "specific to [their] own [respective] historical practices" have consequences in the formation of nations (Liu 1994, 39).[50] State power is vital to consider, but so, too, especially in generating alternative epistemological frames, are the other fields of power not directly named by nation and nationalism. In alliance with and extending the discussions initiated in earlier chapters, the following discussions show how *Blu's Hanging* may be read as making available such an alternative frame, one that is attentive simultaneously to the power of the nation-state and the lively practices ongoing in the nation-space.

hanging on—for justice, for all Here I revisit the debates about the awarding of the 1997 Best Fiction prize to Lois Ann Yamanaka's *Blu's Hanging* by the Association for Asian American Studies. The novel and these debates guide a theorization of a geographical sensibility that might potentially organize the spatial metaphorics of an Asian Americanist discourse informed by postcoloniality. Echoing the analyses offered in chapter 3, I suggest that this is a sensibility captured by the term "transnational," derived from analysis of the articulations of social relations mapped in Yamanaka's novel.

Set on the island of Molokaʻi, described by the narrator (Ivah) as "five years behind Hilo, and Hilo's five years behind Honolulu, and Honolulu's five years behind the mainland" (BH 136), *Blu's Hanging* unfolds in a literally and temporally peripheral location. The Ogata children, Ivah, Blu, and Maisie, who center the narrative, personify marginality: impoverished and socially outcast, mere survival in many ways defines their existence. Since their mother's death from an overuse of drugs she has relied on (unnecessarily, we learn) to stem recurrence of the leprosy that afflicted her and the children's father earlier in their lives, Maisie, the youngest, has been electively mute, and Blu, the middle child, attempts to satisfy an unnamed, devouring hunger by eating endlessly. Their mother's death marks a turning point for Ivah, a point after which she becomes, as eldest, responsible for her siblings and her father. Ivah at first reluctantly, then willingly, affirmatively, takes on the role of surrogate mother: the figurative rope that keeps the family together, "that Poppy tied to his body for his dream walk lies spiraled in a heap on the floor. I wrap it around my brother: keep him close to me always. I wrap it around Maisie: come home to us with words. I wrap it around Poppy: dream-walk, but come back to this kitchen. I wrap it around me. . . . Mama, let go of the rope" (BH 146).

(dis)owning America 141

Constrained choice, self-determination in the face of circumstances beyond individual control, characterize Ivah's development as character and narrator. At times seemingly unreliable and at others highly prescient, Ivah's narration emphasizes the difficulties of making legible knowledge of and produced in sharply disempowered, disenfranchised settings.

Criticisms of Blu's Hanging have focused around the figure of Uncle Paulo, the markedly rapacious local Filipino sexual predator who favors his nieces and Blu as victims of his inexplicable pathology. That Yamanaka's earlier work, Saturday Night at the Pahala Theatre, had been similarly critiqued for its putatively racist representations of local Filipinos, suggested that Uncle Paulo was not an exceptional but a characteristic rendering of local Filipinoness in this author's writings. In arguing for revoking the award, the local Filipino and Filipino American students, academic professionals, and community activists who led the movement reminded both the public at large and the Association members of the long history of specifically anti-Filipino racism that characterizes the formation of Filipino identities both in Hawai'i and on the continent. In that context, the Association's affirmation of the award committee's decision to name Blu's Hanging Best Fiction resonated sharply as yet another example of the effacement of anti-Filipino racism from the scene of Asian Americanist discourse.

As Fujikane has argued in her indictment of the novel and of those who deployed allegations of censorship to shut down its critics, Blu's Hanging's representation of Hawai'i itself is also open to critique. Fujikane explains that "The absence in Blu's Hanging of the predominantly Native Hawaiian population on the island of Moloka'i is ideological: the erasure of a Native Hawaiian presence in settler literature enacts a depopulation that renders Hawai'i an 'emptied' space open to settler claims of 'belonging' " (2000, 164). Indeed, the world of Blu's Hanging does not include Native Hawaiians. But in my reading, this effacement occurs not (only) by their literal absence but rather through a particular narrativization of history. Colonial history is obliquely invoked through the novel's criticism of the imposition of standard English and the transplanted "mainlander" teachers who stand as contemporary versions of the missionary invasion of Hawai'i that correlated with colonization. Both Miss Owens and Mrs. Nishimoto, "haole" teachers from Texas and Ohio, respectively, are wholly unsympathetic characters whose authority over the children is distinctly distasteful. Miss Owens on one occasion refers to the children as "Filthy-mouthed kids with limited vocabularies" (BH 46), and on several occasions Ivah shows us a direct connection among these teachers' stances on Hawaiian Pidgin English, their role as educators (state representatives), and the hypocrisy of a liberalism combined with a missionary zeal for salvation.[51] In Blu's Hanging, critique of colonialism focuses its effects on local Japanese as represented by the Ogata children, rather than on Native Hawaiians, arguably appropriating the history of U.S. colonialism for the purpose of reifying the claim to Hawaiʻi as home by local Asians. This is an appropriation that is perhaps especially striking given the political dominance of local Japanese in Hawaiʻi. "Local" here stands in direct competition with "Native Hawaiian."[52]

At the same time that Asian Americanist discourse carries on these kinds of representational critiques, I want to suggest that we must also be cognizant that prioritizing the politics of racial representation may occlude authorizing other, equally important interpretive registers. As I argued in this book's Introduction, the liberal multiculturalism that shapes the U.S. university effects the sedimentation of representations of racialized minorities as mimetic re-presentations, consolidating an essentialist understanding of racialized identities. In that context, given such effects, representational critiques must be complemented by analyses that foreground the *theoretical* work conducted in Asian American literatures. I want, in other words, to complicate the question raised by the award controversy—is *Blu's Hanging* racist or not?—by revising it to ask, what, in addition to race and racism, is this novel "about"? Or, perhaps more pointedly, what other work does it do? The passing of the resolution to rescind the award signals an affirmative desire to avoid even the possibility (given that many of those who voted for or against the resolution had not read the novel) of validating racist representations. Yet the articulation of that laudable desire in binary terms risks reducing an understanding of social subjectivities to race alone. As perhaps feminist scholarship in particular has made clear, such reductions can produce certain "truths" that mask other equally important matters, such as the situation and construction of "woman" as a social identity. Without detracting from the incisiveness of antiracist and anticolonial representational critiques, Asian American studies must be able also to function along a logic of *and*, as in, in this case, racism *and* what else?[53]

In my reading, *Blu's Hanging* theorizes an alternative epistemological space through its articulation of the failures of the heteronormative family as a construct that secures the promises of "home" as a space of fulfilled needs and safety. As Miss Ito, a local teacher sympathetic to and helpful in the Ogata children's lives, and Big Sis, their cousin, collect the children into a newly configured family at the novel's close, the possibility that a life alternative to that of struggle and impoverishment might be realized emerges. The novel guarantees nothing: Ivah's move to Mid-Pac, a college preparatory high school in Honolulu, may yet prove unsuccessful, and it remains unclear what that move will mean for Blu and Maisie. But just the possibility of a different life relieves the dense grief that comes with following these children's story to that point. Readers are invited to grieve not only with the children as they contend with life after their mother's death; we grieve also for the absence of innocence, of paradise, associated with childhood: "'Mama,' Blu yells into the night, 'Heaven ain't here'" (BH 260). The children's father has all but disappeared from their lives as Miss Ito and Big Sis increasingly perform parental roles in his stead. Though not explicitly erotic, Ivah's narration implies an eroticized pleasure between Big Sis and Miss Ito as shared intimate smiles and the familiarity of cohabitation (Big Sis moves in with Miss Ito upon moving to Moloka'i from another island to begin her work as a teacher) are recounted. For example, toward the end of the novel, Ivah recounts the following exchange between Big Sis and Miss Ito that takes place at the Ogata house. Significantly, this is the moment at which Big Sis and Miss Ito have brought Ivah the application to Mid-Pac and are encouraging her to take the step of applying, a clear moment of adopting a parenting function.

"What time Uncle coming home?" Big Sis asks, to change the subject.

"About nine," Blu tells her. "He cleaning at the Bank of Hawai'i tonight with Felix Furtado."

"Ooohh, thass the one checking you out, eh, Sandi?" Big Sis teases. The mood lightens up. That's how Big Sis is just like Mama. 'He get bubble eyes and bubble ass and he need one comb for Christmas."

"Faith Ann, you wait till we get home," Miss Ito says, and laughs as she shakes off the thought of ugly old Felix Furtado loving her.

"Sandi get the whole island, all the young guys checking her out still yet. But lucky thing she sharing cottage with me, so I run those horny buggas outta our yard, yeah, Sandi?"

"Faith Ann," she says, like she's pretending to run out of patience, "you're asking for a dirty lickens when we get home."

"Ooohh, I scared. I shakin'," says Big Sis, laughing. (BH 199)

What few moments of happiness there are in this novel surround and indeed are generated by the children's interaction with Big Sis and Miss Ito. Together, they are able to mitigate the harsh circumstances of the Ogata children's lives, something that neither the children's father nor the children themselves could do. By closing with a nonheteronormative family that functions as the mechanism for potential salvation, the novel interrogates the presumptive value of normatively wrought conceptions of family and home as the places and spaces of safety and innocence. Home and family, metaphors for national belongingness, are reconstituted in *Blu's Hanging* as processes that occur in negotiation with but in difference from heteronormativity. In other words, this newly formed family that augurs a hopeful future in *Blu's Hanging* is "queer" in the sense that David Eng (1997) has used the term to designate an alternative to the naturalized, heteronormative, masculinist social and political configurations installed by U.S. hegemonic nationalism.[54]

In this sense, I would argue that Yamanaka articulates what might be conceived as a transnational sensibility, one that recognizes and yet imagines beyond the material effectivity of the foundational epistemological structures (like heteronormativity) of the U.S. nation. Transnational here names a space that eludes conscription by the national imaginary, and one in which practices of subjectivity that cannot be represented within a national symbolic economy might find legibility. What strikes me as valuable about this particular iteration of this different epistemic terrain is that it identifies those subjectivities as complex and troubled, not as purely oppositional or liberating. That is, insofar as Miss Ito and Big Sis figure local Japanese-identified populations, their status as heroines in the novel bespeaks the novel's arguably problematic representational politics. Their privileged status manifests in other words the erasures of indigenous peoples and the effacement of anti-Filipino racism from the novel's scene of representation, as previously discussed. Nonheteronormativity neither trumps nor excuses these representational problematics. Accordingly, the transnational imaginary, that constructed frame of thought that designates the parameters of what can be conceived and what is rendered legible, emerges from *Blu's Hanging* as a space of complexity and contradiction. Recognition of this complexity argues for recoding "opposition" to reflect the multiple and heterogeneous forms of oppression and resistance, the multiple and dissimilar fields of power, involved in social subjectification.

The novel and debates about it, in combination with an Asian Americanist approach informed by postcolonial critique, illuminate the need for Asian American studies to revisit the implications of working with nation as its presumptive basis and parameters. I have attempted to show here the impossibility of understanding "Asian American" as an unproblematic designation, as a stable term of reference and politics that transcends context. And I have wanted to emphasize that given, as in the Hawaiian context, that Asian American studies stands as a discourse not of "minorities" but of the "emerging dominant," to borrow Gayatri Spivak's phrase (1997), Asian Americanist discourse must look to itself to ensure that the partial and variegated freedoms enjoyed by both Asian American studies and various Asian-raced peoples are not merely celebrated but are leading to an elsewhere.

conclusion:

when difference meets itself

In taking as my point of entry into this book's consideration of Asian American studies the tensions between "Filipino American" and "Asian American," I have tried to work with the ways that from that difference arises the imperative to rethink the political. Those kinds of antagonisms lead us to recognize anew the intractable diversities that "Asian American" attempts to render intelligible. From those differences, the necessity of reinventing our grounds for unification comes into sharp relief. As I have attempted to suggest through this book's arguments, the political may be seen to be animated by difference, not identity. Dissent, as difficult as it may be to confront, facilitates critical unification. Thinking in these terms allows us to take as motivating grounds for collaborative efforts to detoxify the relations of power that install difference as division, precisely our attempts to understand the investments and effects of differentiation. We can reinhabit and rearticulate difference not as the otherness constructed by certain practices of power, including certain paradigms of knowledge, but instead as the basis for unification. "Express solidarity, but as difference," Gayatri Spivak has enjoined (1996, 25); indeed, how we might go about doing so, and how the insights of literary texts and of poststructural theorizing might help us to do so, have served as driving forces for this book. Thinking deconstructively, we can understand that identity is contingent upon difference, that difference precedes and constitutes identity. By inverting the identity/difference hierarchy, we can, I think, conduct the destabilizing move of underscoring the fragile discursive stability of U.S. national identity and remain critically attentive to the difference that *is* "Asian American." To address, account for, and accommodate difference, we must remember that there is no common subject of Asian American studies; there are only infinite differences that we discursively cohere into epistemological objects.

In conceiving of multiple kinds of differences, we must of course recognize that they do not exist independently of each other. Rather, they converge and conflict and thus participate in shaping each other. And it is through those contacts, those meetings, that discursive and knowledge limitations can be recognized and interrogated. In the attempt to negotiate the confusion caused by the meeting of differently configured subjectivities and identity formations lies the catalyst for political mobilization. What is needed is not identity but a commitment to combating states of domination, to unifying for the sake not of the self but in the endless pursuit of justice. In its own way, each of this book's chapters has tried to make that point. And self-critique is surely a necessary part of examining how it is that we might produce knowledge about self and other, about other *as* self, that accords agency and power to the spaces of otherness. This is about trying to realize home as a place where complex personhood—selfhood and otherness, contradiction and commitment, community and difference—is always and immediately granted. As Avery Gordon has explained, "At the very least, complex personhood is about conferring the respect on others that comes from presuming that life and people's lives are simultaneously straightforward and full of enormously subtle meaning" (1997, 5).

On one level, the emergence of the discourses of transnationalism and postcolonial studies with which *Imagine Otherwise* has been engaged may be understood as efforts to make visible such complexities. Along these lines, we might recognize that the challenges such discourses pose for Asian American studies are not so new. Rather, they may be seen to make manifest in contemporary configurations various threads of ongoing critical debates in Asian American studies. It would in other words be a mistake to think that "Asian American" suddenly became unstable by force of globalization alone or that Asian American studies has been uninterested in global relations of power.[1] Asian Americanists have long been engaged in addressing the referential incapacity of "Asian American" as a term of identity, emphasizing its function as a political construct designed to challenge political and cultural anti-Asian racisms.[2] As a narrative of identity, "Asian American" has succeeded in mobilizing the field of Asian American studies by constructing and pointing to a common origin and gesturing toward a common destiny. Globalization and the establishment of transnationalism, in addition to poststructural and feminist insights into the problematics of totalizing narratives, however, have made it all the more difficult to unify around such a narrative. We find ourselves needing to rearticulate "Asian American" identity once again, to assess and address its utility under contemporary conditions.

In response, *Imagine Otherwise* has suggested embracing the a priori meaninglessness of "Asian American," the absence of an identity anterior to naming. "Interrogating identity-as-such," to reinvoke R. Radhakrishnan's earlier quoted articulation, may itself be conceived as that which serves as cohering grounds of Asian American studies. I have suggested that such a deconstructive approach to identity is particularly important to advance given the institutionalized setting of Asian American studies. The longer our collective history of establishment as an academic field, as with other disciplinary formations in the U.S. university, the more self-evident our object of knowledge, "Asian America," may seem to be. For it is the effect of disciplines, of departmental and other organizational divisions of the U.S. university, to naturalize and inhibit self-reflection—to naturalize, thus, the authority of various disciplinary formations to stand as sources of expert knowledge about an apparently discretely knowable prediscursive epistemological object (Weber 1987; Graff 1987). Because the legitimacy of Asian American studies has for so long been and continues yet to be challenged, the temptation exists to argue its merits by pointing to a common, understudied object, the "Asian American," whom we narrate into legibility through a narrative of identity. We willingly suspend differences to facilitate representational politics, and that strategy has been enormously important to catalyzing what changes Asian American studies has been able to effect in terms of curricular and pedagogical practices. But I am also increasingly convinced that one of the effects of such arguments may be to affirm the conception of "Asian America" as ahistorical, self-evident, and transparently knowable, thus effacing the dynamic complexity of Asian-raced peoples. In this light, I would like to suggest that persistently foregrounding the absence of "Asian America" and "Asian American identity" anterior to discourse through the practice of strategic anti-essentialism might be helpful in negotiating the effects and demands of our academic sites of practice.

If the academic setting of our knowledge practices would have us believe that our epistemological objects precede discourse, given the ways that institutionalization can rein in transformative energies, the challenge before us is endlessly to denaturalize the "Asian American" of Asian American studies. Insofar as literary texts are produced in spaces outside the U.S. university, they can help us identify the limitations of our academic disciplinary imperatives. The texts considered in this book take us outside the present; articulate a heterotopic, transnational imagination; and point to the macro- and microlevel registers within which the narrative dimensions of social subjectivities unfold. They speak of irremediable complexities and the impossibility of exhaustive narration, reminding us that knowledge is always only partial and situational, that it is constantly in need of revision and reinvention. Individually and collectively, these works argue for the development and practice of a politics of heterogeneity to address the infinite and arbitrary if materially circumscribed constructions of "Asian America." But as these texts also register, and as the legal articulations considered in this book make clear, because the politics of the U.S. nation-state is itself a politics of identity, of subjectivity understood in terms of identity, we cannot and should not altogether dismiss identity as a politicized construct to be negotiated.[3] To borrow again from Gayatri Spivak, identity is that which we cannot not want, given the centrality of subjectivity in modern political life and our locations within that political field. I have argued that for precisely this reason, assuming a deconstructive attitude is crucial. For within the logic of modern U.S. politics, as we have seen in the foregoing discussions, national identity/subjectivity is offered as a substitute for justice, and we must take care not to accept that logic as circumscribing our transformative politics.

When difference meets itself, to revisit Dana Takagi's elegant formulation (1996, 30), the necessary variability of justice comes to the fore, a vacillation that is necessarily present because of the acknowledged presence of diversity. Permanently fluctuating and irregular, justice cannot be conceived within a politics of heterogeneity as a fixed goal but emerges rather as an orientation, as a commitment to an indefatigable and illimitable interrogation of myriad relations of power and how they give, shape, and sometimes take life. When difference meets itself in the space of deconstructed identity, the complex personhood of every self and other rises to the surface. If "Asian American" could name such a space and Asian American studies could sustain it, we would make, I think, an important move toward imagining otherness otherwise, in ways that immediately accord agency, complexity, and contradiction.

In its material life, as Asian American studies so conceived might be the institutional and cognitive home for the pursuit of such work as studies in comparative racialization and intersectional projects that deliberately unravel seemingly stable distinctions among identificatory categories and disciplinary divisions. Even as our teaching and research continue to be informed by and anchored in the particularities marking Asiatic racialization, our efforts might in the embrace of the subjectlessness of discourse be organized, perhaps energized, by the limitless horizons of the possibilities of knowledge before us. What, finally, I think subjectlessness can help us to do is to articulate Asian American studies as an unbounded field, one that while in the structure of the academic institution is not structured by it.

A decade ago, Lisa Lowe suggested that "we can afford to rethink the notion of racialized ethnic identity in terms of differences of national origin, class, gender, and sexuality rather than presuming similarities and making the erasure of particularity the basis of unity" (1996, 83). The kinds of differences and dissent that have gained increasing visibility in the past decade as historical and discursive conditions have changed and continue to change suggest that in these opening years of the new century, we cannot afford not to. I have wanted to suggest, by way of this book, that conceptualizing Asian American studies as subjectless, as motivated by critique of subjectification rather than desire for subjectivity, may be one way to meet this challenge.

notes

introduction: on Asian Americanist critique

1. Protests over *Blu's Hanging*'s depiction of Filipino Americans culminated in the form of a resolution to rescind the award. Protestors, organized by the Filipino American Studies Caucus (FASC) of the Association and a group called the Anti-Racism Coalition (ARC), but numbering many others as well, argued that a book that figured Filipino Americans as animal torturers and child molesters, and that an author who had in other works offered arguably similarly problematic representations of Filipino Americans, should not be recognized as exemplary of the "best." Fifty-eight Filipino community organizations had expressed support for the FASC's and ARC's resolution to revoke the award. Despite these protests, AAAS's executive board affirmed the award committee's freedom to make its determination, and numerous efforts to find compromise positions failed. The resolution to revoke the award was introduced to the membership at the general business meeting held at the conference and passed by a vote of 90 or 91 (accounts differ) for to 55 against, with 19 abstentions. The vote was limited to those who were in attendance at the business meeting. The Association's executive board consequently resigned in the face of possible legal liability (for potential breach of contract, perhaps), and many members—both in support of the resolution and not—have declined continued participation in AAAS. I have drawn this summary from the chronology of events compiled principally by Daniel Kim for circulation among members of the East of California Caucus of the association. I am indebted to his hard work; errors in reporting are my own.

2. I am using "poststructuralism" and "postmodernism" rather loosely here. My interest is in pointing to these terms as identifying a particular discursive moment in which referentiality gives way to multiplicity. The terms are intimately related in that moment. Poststructuralism otherwise generally takes up language itself as its analytic focus, while postmodernism concerns itself more with representation—obviously, there are overlaps between these focuses. My immediate sources for poststructural theorizing are Judith Butler, Paul de Man, Jacques Derrida, Drucilla Cornell, Gilles Deleuze, and Diane Elam; and for postmodern theorizing my sources are David Harvey, Fredric Jameson, and Jean-Francois Lyotard.

notes to introduction

3   As R. Radhakrishnan has succinctly formulated, "The radical poststructuralist subject of epistemology, with its commitment to a nameless and open-ended process, finds itself at odds with the exigencies of political subjectivity, for the latter is not easily served by a deconstructive epistemology of perennial disaccomodation" (1996, 2).

4   See Derrida (1987) with respect to his theorization of subjectivity as a logocentric concept.

5   It is of course important to recognize that there are other kinds of multiculturalisms, "critical multiculturalisms," currently being theorized by such scholars as David Lloyd, Minoo Moallem, and Iain Boal, as well as under the auspices of such groups as the Chicago Cultural Studies Group. See Lloyd (1998), Moallem and Boal (1999), and Chicago Cultural Studies Group (1992).

6   This discussion draws on the vast and increasing body of scholarship on globalization. See, for example, Appadurai (1998), Cheng and Bonacich (1984), Dirlik (1996), Eisenstein (1998), Hall (1990), Harvey (1989), Lowe (1996, 2001), Lowe and Lloyd (1997), Miyoshi (1993), Ong (1999), Ong et al. (1994), Shohat (1998), Shohat and Stam (1994), and Tölöyan (1991). See also the review in chapter 2, note 1, of transnational studies scholarship.

7   Arjun Appadurai's concise synopsis of globalization is particularly helpful: "[Globalization] marks a set of transitions in the global political economy since the 1970s, in which multinational forms of capitalist organization began to be replaced by transnational, flexible, and irregular forms of organization, as labor, finance, technology, and technological capital began to be assembled in ways that treated national boundaries as mere constraints or fictions" (1998, 228; emphasis original). Appadurai cites Rouse (1995), Harvey (1989), and Lash and Urry (1987, 1994) in this summary. See also Coombe (1995), Dirlik (1993), Elkins (1995), Jameson (1994), Lim et al. (1999), Sassen (1996), Wallerstein (1990, 1991, 1995), and Wilson and Dissanayake (1996).

8   Zillah Eisenstein offers a stark summary of these conditions:

> Some 800 million people are starving across the globe. Women and girls represent approximately 60 percent of the billion or so people earning one dollar a day or less. However, in countries labeled democratic, a new kind of excessive wealth exists in which billionaires are allowed to amass as much as they can with few limits. . . . Meanwhile, corporations displace countries. Of the world's largest one hundred economies, fifty-one are corporations, not countries. The two hundred largest corporations hire less than three-fourths of one percent of the world's work force but account for 28 percent of the global market. The five hundred biggest corporations account for 70 percent of world trade. No surprise that Amnesty International now reports on corporations as well as nation-states. (1998, 1)

9 Lisa Lowe offers an especially eloquent understanding of the need for such a shift in relation specifically to Asian Americanist discourse: "In the face of the radical nonidentity of Asian racial formations globally, Asian American studies must develop . . . a shared language about exploitation within transnational capitalism, a language about economic and social justice rather than cultural or nationalist identity" (2001, 274).

10 As Diane Elam cogently explains, "No longer subject to a monarch, the modern citizen is now subject of a State. Yet this subjection is held to be freedom, since the State is nothing other than the collective will of its citizens" (1994, 70). See also Berlant (1991).

11 In this book, I follow Rey Chow's suggestion that "it is necessary to think primarily in terms of borders—of borders, that is, as *para-sites* that never take over a field in its entirety but erode it slowly and *tactically*" (2001, 201; emphases original). Chow, extending Michel de Certeau's work, explains that a "tactic" is "'calculated action determined by the absence of a proper locus'" (Chow 2001, 202; citing de Certeau 1984, 37). A tactical, parasitical approach does not seek a space of propriety; rather, tactical intervention intends to disrupt propriety itself, to avoid becoming itself a dominating discourse by disallowing its own borders to solidify. Here I employ this approach as part of this book's project of reflecting on Asian American studies and especially on its constitutive borders—the boundaries of inquiry considered "proper" to the field, and the spatial boundedness of its territorial imagination.

12 On law and literature generally, see Ferguson (1984), Gutierrez-Jones (1995), Leonard (1995), and Thomas (1987). On critical race theory, see Crenshaw et al. (1995), Chang (1993), and Johnson (1997). On feminist jurisprudence, see Cornell (1991, 1995), Crenshaw et al. (1995), Eisenstein (1988, 1994), Fineman and Thomadsen (1991), Frug (1992), Harris (1995), Matsuda (1995), Minow (1990), Schneider (1991), Volpp (1994, 1996, 2000b), West (1988), and Williams (1990). See also Tushnet (1984) and White (1988).

13 See Lauter (1991), Lloyd (1998), Lowe (1996), and Palumbo-Liu (1995a) on this issue.

14 David Palumbo-Liu offers an incisive discussion of the ways that this transparency is ascribed to U.S. ethnic literatures. See Palumbo-Liu (1995a).

15 Rey Chow points out that the idealization of otherness is related to a second kind of idealism—what she calls "mentalism, the tendency that treats the world as a result of ideas, which in turn are construed as the products of the human mind" (1998a, xx). She explains that "In the problematic of cultural otherness, the two senses of idealism come together: idealism in the sense of idealization, of valorization; but also in the sense of turning-into-an-idea" (1998a, xxi).

16 For further discussion of theory, authority, and power in relation to representing and researching raced, gendered, and classed identities, see Trinh (1989,

1991). Responses to earlier versions of this introduction prompt me to clarify that I do not believe or mean this ascription to Asian American literatures of this "theoretical" valence to detract from the complexities of other literatures, conventionally considered canonical or not. In particular, those texts that are considered canonical are read, I think, as the complex works that they may be. My point here is simply to try to underscore the importance of reading literatures collected under the rubric of "Asian American literature" with the same eye toward complexity to combat their conception as transparent.

17 This understanding of "culture" draws from and is aligned with that offered by Lowe (1996) and Omi and Winant (1994).

18 Sau-ling Wong attributes the phrase "claiming America" to Maxine Hong Kingston. Michael Omi and Howard Winant have shown that cultural nationalism may be "traced back at least to the Harlem Renaissance of the 1920s" (1994, 39). They explain that "Cultural nationalism found expression in every minority community. This was an explicit critique of the dominant Eurocentric (i.e., white) culture, understood to pervade both everyday life and 'high culture.' Cultural nationalists sought to redefine and recapture the specificity of their minority cultures, an objective which they identified as 'nationalist.' Painting, theater, dance, music, language, even cars and clothes, all became media through which a new style could be developed, and through which 'genuine' oppositional culture could be distinguished from assimilationist practices" (1994, 109).

19 On the masculinism of Asian American cultural nationalism, see Cheung (1990, 1993), E. Kim (1990), Lim (1993b), Lowe (1996), and Wong (1993). On its heteronormativity, see generally the essays collected in Eng and Hom (1998); see also Eng (1998), Leong (1996), and especially Takagi (1996).

20 For discussions of diversity among peoples of Asian descent in the United States, see Espiritu (1992, 1996a, b), Hing (1993), Palumbo-Liu (1999), Takagi (1992), and E. Yamamoto (1999). For discussions of a tacit East Asian American orientation in Asian American studies, see Campomanes (1992, 1995), Grewal (1994), Shankar and Srikanth (1998), and Visweswaran (1997). See also Davé et al. (2000), Katrak (1996), and Koshy (1996, 1998).

21 Susan Koshy is especially vigorous in her critique of "Asian American literature" along these lines. See Koshy (1996, 1998). See also Davé et al. (2000), Espiritu (1992, 1996a), Hirabayashi and Alquizola (1994), Hune (1995), Katrak (1996), Lim (1997), Osajima (1995), Palumbo-Liu (1999), Prashad (1998), and Wong (1995).

22 These terms closely approximate those in which Frank Chin articulates an influential definition of "Asian American." See Chin (1991).

23 As Rey Chow has put it, "For those groups on the side of non-white cultures—negotiating a point of entry into the multicultural scene means nothing less

notes to chapter one   157

than posing the question of rights—the right to representation and the right to culture. What this implies is much more than mere flight (by a particular non-white culture) for its 'freedom of speech,' because the very process of attaining 'speech' here is inextricably bound up with right, that is with the processes through which particular kinds of 'speeches' are legitimized in the first place" (1998a, 12). Chow summarizes: "To put it in very simple terms, a non-white culture, in order to 'be' or to 'speak,' must (1) seek legitimacy/recognition from white culture, which has denied the reality of the 'other' cultures all along; (2) use the language of white culture (since it is the dominant one) to produce itself (so that it could be recognized and thus legitimized); and yet (3) resist complete normativization by white culture" (1998a, 12). See also Bell (1995), Crenshaw (1995), Delgado (1995), Freeman (1995), Tushnet (1984), and especially Johnson (1997), Lloyd (1991), and Volpp (2000c).

24   The following chapters review this history more specifically.

25   Lowe provides a synopsis of the paradoxes inhering in the institutionalization of ethnic studies:

> Institutionalization provides a material base within the university for a transformative critique of traditional disciplines and their traditional separations; yet, on the other hand, the institutionalization of any field or curricula which establishes orthodox objects and methods submits in part to the demands of the university and its educative function of socializing subjects into the state. While institutionalizing interdisciplinarity study risks integrating it into a system which threatens to appropriate what is most critical and oppositional about that study, the logic through which the university incorporates areas of interdisciplinarity simultaneously provides for the possibility that these sites will remain oppositional forums, productively antagonistic to notions of autonomous culture and disciplinary regulation, and to the interpellation of students as univocal subjects. (1996, 41)

26   I am reminded of Lawson Inada's poem, "From Live Do," which articulates the impossibility of defining "Asian American poetry" and proffers instead an understanding based upon the ways in which such terms cannot be understood outside of the materialities of life as conditioned by history.

chapter 1. against uniform subjectivity: remembering "Filipino America"

1   See especially Campomanes (1995) for a compelling discussion of the ways that "Filipino America" requires Asian American studies to shift its historic frames and terms of analysis. Taking as a point of departure "our seeming 'inability' to congeal the Filipino case in categorical terms," Campomanes demonstrates how that "inability" is directly related to the absence of empire as a central analytic in Asian American and American studies.

2   Campomanes explains how such formulations as "forgotten insurrection," "forgotten Philippines," "Filipinos: Forgotten Asian Americans," and "Forgotten Filipinos," lifted from a series of academic texts, fix the Philippines and "Filipinos" firmly and seemingly inescapably in a space of negation. (The phrases are drawn respectively from Leon Wolff's *Little Brown Brother* [1960], Peter Stanley's 1972 essay titled "The Forgotten Philippines, 1790–1946," Fred Cordova's *Filipinos: Forgotten Asian Americans* [1983], and Ronald Takaki's *Strangers from a Different Shore* [1989]. See Works Cited for full citation information.)

> Each object—whether a turn-of-the-century war of U.S. conquest and Filipino resistance, a national field in area studies, or a congeries of peoples who are thus referenced—is deemed unrecognizeable and doomed to perpetual neglect. These accounts themselves . . . yield few clues to the relentlessly active effects of what is otherwise posited as a descriptive adjective ("forgotten") in a whole series of transitive trajectories by which the Philippines/Filipinos become "direct" and "indirect" objects of powerfully amnesiac acts. (1995)

3   See Okihiro (1994) and Wong (1999 [1996]).
4   See Berlant (1993) on amnesia and national identity formation. See also Anderson (1991, 1994).
5   See Lowe (1996) for an illuminating discussion of the ways the identity/difference dialectic has shaped Asian Americanist discourse.
6   See Lloyd (1991) for discussion of the ways that "radical politics [can] become all the more confined to the issue of civil rights, that is, to the extension of representation and the implicit affirmation of assimilation" (88).
7   On sexuality and Asian American studies, in addition to Takagi (1996), see Leong (1996), Eng and Hom (1998), and Ting (1995, 1998). Collectively, this body of work recognizes that Asian American studies has long been interested in questions of sexuality but has posed those questions in effectively heteronormative terms.
8   On the popular representational emasculation of "Asian American" men, see Hamamoto (1994), Hamamoto and Liu (2000), Lee (1999), Ling (1997), and Xing (1998). See also Chin (1991) for a provocative example of how belief in this sexualization of "Asian America" can shape Asian Americanist discourse.
9   As Jenny Sharpe has summarized, "Given its history of imported slave and contract labor, continental expansion, and overseas imperialism, an implication of American culture in the postcolonial study of empires is perhaps long overdue" (1995, 181).
10 While U.S ethnic studies has a long history of criticizing U.S. imperialism, as, for example, in the consolidation of activists of the 1960s under the rubric of the Third World Liberation Front, American studies genealogically traces to

different grounds, by some accounts to the effective support of that ideology (Kaplan 1993). The Third World Liberation Front identified the segregated spaces of racialized lives in the United States to be "internal colonies," which resulted in identifying nationalism as a correlate strategy for liberation. Black American, Latino and Latina, Native American, and Asian American students who agitated for the establishment of U.S. ethnic studies in U.S. universities in the 1960s coalesced as the Third World Liberation Front, explicitly purposeful in "fusing" with the "masses of Third World people" (Omatsu 1994, 25–26). As one statement of purpose offered by student activists explained:

> We seek . . . simply to function as human beings, to control our own lives. Initially, following the myth of the American Dream, we worked to attend predominantly white colleges, but we have learned through direct analysis that it is impossible for our people, so-called minorities, to function as human beings, in a racist society in which white always comes first. . . . So we have decided to fuse ourselves with the masses of Third World people, which [sic] are the majority of the world's peoples, to create, through struggle, a new humanity, a new humanism, a New World Consciousness, and within that context collectively control our own destinies. (quoted in Omatsu 1994, 25–26)

See also Wong (1995). For discussions of American studies and new directions in the field, see also Kaplan and Pease (1993), Kelley (2000), Maddox (1999), Pease (1994), Washington (1998), and Wiegman (1998).

11 See especially Campomanes (1997), Davé et al. (2000), and Grewal (1994).
12 See Shimakawa (2002) for a discussion of performance and performativity in relation to "Asian American" identities. See also Kondo (1997).
13 See Rafael (2000, chap. 2) for a discussion of the importance of "white" women in the "domestication" of the Philippines under U.S. colonial rule.
14 Lowe's reading of the driving force of the novel as emergent from precisely the contradictions inhering in the paradoxes between the mythic American ideal and the realities faced by "Filipinos" in the United States incisively establishes this point. See also Alquizola (1989, 1991), Mostern (1995), and San Juan (1991).
15 As E. Kim explains, "The white woman is a dream, an ideal. She symbolizes the contradiction between what is brutal in America and what is kind and beautiful" (1982, 52).
16 At one point, the novel explicitly points to the Roldan case discussed later in the chapter:

> Prior to the Roldan . . . case, Filipinos were considered Mongolians. Since there is a law which forbids the marriage between members of the Mongolian and Caucasian races, those who hated Filipinos wanted them to be included in

this discriminatory legislation. Anthropologists and other experts maintained that the Filipinos are not Mongolians, but members of the Malayan race. It was then a simple thing for the state legislature to pass a law forbidding marriage between members of the Malayan and Caucasian races. (*A* 143)

17 See Sedgwick (1985).
18 See Gonzales and Campomanes (1997); see also Roces (1994) and Santos (1976).
19 The phrase, "civilizing love and love of civilization," is Vicente Rafael's and is drawn from his analysis of the "white love" that characterized the United States' policy of "benevolent bondage" in occupying the Philippine islands (2000, 21).
20 See Schirmer (1972) and Tomkins (1970).
21 The geopolitical boundaries of what we now refer to as the Philippines shifted through the period of Spanish colonization. The Spanish colony existed in various permutations as *las islas Filipinas* until the late nineteenth century, when anticolonial nationalism against Spain and anti-imperial nationalism against the United States conditioned the sedimenting of boundaries. Indigenous islanders, Vicente Rafael explains, were "tendentiously misnamed [by Spaniards] . . . indios, placing them in the same racial pot as the inhabitants of the New World" (2000, 6). The term *Filipino* until near the end of the nineteenth century thus referred not to native populations but to the offspring of Spanish parents born in the colony (Rafael 2000, 6). Rafael explains that "Like the Americano, the Filipino was thought to be racially distinct and consequently inferior to the Spaniard who hailed from the peninsula regardless of his or her educational attainment or class background. At the same time, he or she enjoyed a more privileged social position in a plural society compared to the lowly indio, the untrusted but economically essential *Sangley*, or Chinese, and the equally educated and Hispanicized mestizos, both Spanish and Chinese" (2000, 6). This genealogy contributes to the terminological challenges of speaking of "Filipinos" and "Filipino Americans." Other terms used include Pilipino, U.S. Filipino, and Pilipino American. I have chosen to use Filipino and Filipino American here to refer to the peoples, histories, and cultures that are constructed as racialized natives of the Philippines from the U.S. perspective.
22 See Constantino (1975) and Delmendo (1998).
23 See Miller (1982). Indigenous peoples of the Philippines were couched as "savages" fairly regularly in U.S. popular discourse and were put on display as such in such events as the 1904 World Exposition.
24 See Rafael (2000, chap. 1) for an insightful discussion of the establishment of this paternalistic relationship.

25 Tracing the development of political and economic power in the islands through the territory's 300 years of Spanish colonization and beyond, Benedict Anderson explains that a visible and "self-conscious ruling class" among Filipinos did not emerge until U.S. occupation (1995, 11; emphasis original). What had until then been a social stratum primarily constituted by wealthy and educated *mestizos* who nonetheless lacked political power under Spanish rule, under U.S. control, gained access to the political machinery of the Philippines. A "national oligarchy" emerged that effectively ran the Philippines for the United States. As Anderson explains, "unlike all other modern colonial regimes in twentieth century Southeast Asia, which operated through huge, autocratic, white-run bureaucracies, the American authorities in Manila, once assured of the mestizos' self-interested loyalty to the motherland, . . . quickly turned over most of its component positions to the natives" (1995, 11–12). The United States, with its proven threat of military domination, needed only representative supervision of the quotidian operations of its colony. The new oligarchs quickly learned to use this governmental style to consolidate their own positions: "congressional control of the purse, and of senior judicial appointments, taught the oligarchy that the 'rule of law,' provided it made and managed this law, was the firmest *general* guarantee of its property and political hegemony" (Anderson 1995, 12; emphasis original). Established as they were, according to Anderson, it was "with real reluctance that in 1935 they accepted commonwealth status" (1995, 13). See also Karnow (1989) and Pomeroy (1992) on similar matters.

26 San Juan explains that "while the U.S. altered the economic-juridical mechanisms and adapted the feudal institutions [that had been in place during Spanish rule] to serve the paramount goal of capital/profit accumulation, the Philippines did not metamorphose into a full-fledged industrial state. . . . The circuit of commodity circulation needed the metropolis to complete it, and the surplus generated in the colony was not reinvested there to develop generalized commodity production and an independent, expanding internal market, but instead the surplus was transferred to the metropolis" (1992, 73).

27 See also Jeffords (1989). For discussions of gender and empire-building in other frames, see McClintock (1995) and Stoler (1991).

28 See Shah (2001) for a discussion of the threat of "contamination" with respect to Chinese immigrants.

29 The Act of July 1, 1902 provided for administration of the Philippines, stating in part:

> All inhabitants of the Philippine Islands continuing to reside therein, who were Spanish subjects on the 11th day of April, 1899, and then resided in said islands, and their children born subsequent thereto, shall be deemed and

held to be citizens of the Philippine Islands, and as such entitled to the protection of the United States, except such as shall have elected to preserve their allegiance to the crown of Spain in accordance with the provisions of the treaty of peace between the United States and Spain, signed at Paris December 10th, 1898. (32 Stat. section 1369)

30 See Lopez (1996).
31 For example, In re Ah Yup, 1 F. Cas. 223 (D. Cal. 1878) (Chinese are not white); In re Kanaka Nian, 21 Pac. 993 (1889) (Hawaiians are not white); In re Saito, 62 F. 126 (D. Mass. 1894) (Japanese are not white); United States v. Balsara, 180 F. 694 (2d Cir. 1910) (Asian Indians are white); United States v. Thind, 261 U.S. 204 (1923) (Asian Indians are not white). Ian Haney Lopez provides an extended table of racial prerequisite cases in Lopez (1996).
32 According to the Congressional Record, Senator Foraker, who introduced the language of Section 30, explained the provisions, which were initially drafted in relation to Puerto Rico:

> I do not know why it should not apply to a citizen of the Philippines living there, an inhabitant there, and owing allegiance to us, owing permanent allegiance to us as a people. That expression was furnished us by the State Department. This measure was referred to the State Department and very carefully considered there. If my memory does not serve me incorrectly, it originated with the State Department. They communicated to us in regard to it, saying that this trouble constantly arises. The citizens of Porto Rico and the citizens of the Philippines also, for I think it would have equal application to them, owe us permanent allegiance; and yet if they see fit to come here and reside in good faith and for all time they never can become naturalized. Their condition is worst [sic] than the condition of their fellow citizens who, under the terms of the treaty of peace, elected to retain their allegiance to Spain. (Vol. 38, Part 2, 58th Congress, 2d session, pp. 1254–1255)

33 On this point, the court had a significant train of precedent cases upon which to draw and from which it drew. In particular, it cited United States v. Balsara, 180 F. 694; In re Ah Yup, 1 F. Cas. 223 (D. Cal. 1878); In re Knight, 171 F. 299 (D.C. 1909); and In re Buntaro Kumagai, 163 F. 922 (D.C. 1908).
34 The Court in In re Rallos specifically follows In re Alverto.
35 The 1894 Act provides:

> Any alien of the age of twenty-one years and upwards who has enlisted or may enlist in the United States navy or marine corps, and has served or may hereafter serve five consecutive years in the United States navy or on enlistment in the United States marine corps, and has been or may hereafter be honorably discharged, shall be admitted to become a citizen of the United States upon his petition, without any previous declaration of his intention to

become such; and the court admitting such alien shall, in addition to proof of good moral character, be satisfied by competent proof of such person's service in and honorable discharge from the United States navy, or marine corps. (28 Stat. 124, section 165)

36 See Gonzalves (1995/1996) for contextualization of the issues of citizenship and race and military service evoked by these cases.
37 See Melendy (1977) and Parrenas (1998). As quoted by Volpp, the Resolution of the Northern Monterey Chamber of Commerce, which is summarized by Schirmer and Shalom (1987), identifies precisely these concerns:

> The charges made against the Filipinos in this Resolution were as follows: (1) Economic. They accept, it is alleged, lower wages than the American standards allow. The new immigrants coming in each month increase the labor supply and hold wages down. They live on fish and rice, and a dozen may occupy one or two rooms only. The cost of living is very low, hence, Americans cannot compete with them. (2) Health. Some Filipinos bring in meningitis, and other dangerous diseases. Some live unhealthily. Sometimes fifteen or more sleep in one or two rooms. (3) Intermarriage. A few have married white girls. Others will. "If the present state of affairs continues there will be 40,000 half-breed[s] in California before ten years have passed,"—is the dire prediction. (Volpp 2000a, 835, n.45)

> As Volpp explains, "The Resolution continued: 'We do not advocate violence but we do feel that the United States should give the Filipinos their liberty and send those unwelcome inhabitants from our shores that the white people have inherited this country for themselves and their offspring might live'" (Volpp 2000a, 835, n.45, quoting Schirmer and Shalom 1987, 59–60).

38 See Parrenas (1998) for discussion of "interracial and gender alliances between white working class women and Filipino immigrant men in the 1920s and 1930s" (115).
39 See also Melendy (1977, 55).
40 See Volpp (2000a, 801–802).
41 See Volpp (2000a, 817–822).
42 I thank Leti Volpp for her enormous help in recognizing this legislative history.
43 The Act states in part:

> On the 4th day of July immediately following the expiration of a period of ten years from the date of the inauguration of the new government under the constitution provided for in this Act the President of the United States shall by proclamation withdraw and surrender all right of possession, supervision, jurisdiction, control, or sovereignty then existing and exercised by the United States in and over the territory and people of the Philippine Islands. (quoted in Hing 1993, 214)

chapter 2. nikkei internment: determined identities/undecidable meanings

1 Transnationalism is an ungainly discourse, with so many and sometimes conflicting understandings of globalization that it resists succinct encapsulation. In a general sense, transnationalism might be understood as identifying and evaluating the possibilities of postnationality, of a particularized understanding of what postmodernity might mean, or, more specifically, of a condition in which nation-states have become vestigial traces of a past global ordering. (On connections among transnationalism and postmodernism, see Grewal and Kaplan [1994], Kaplan and Grewal [1999], Kaplan [1996], and hooks [1997]. See also Appiah [1997] on postcolonialism and postmodernism for further consideration of the varying functions of "post-.") Even on this point, though, there are vast differences in levels of optimism regarding such possibilities and in definitions of these terms. Perhaps, then, transnationalism might better be broadly conceived as an academic discourse that responds to and generates the sense that globalization refers to a distinct but not discontinuous shift in historical conditions and relations of power. Accordingly, transnationalism implies that our means to knowledge must likewise change to correlate with such transforming conditions. Globalization and its effects are perhaps the only commonalities among the wide array of methods and interests that could be classified under this rubric. Under this broad definition, transnationalism manifests variously, sometimes as critiques of transnational capitalism per se, sometimes as social scientific studies of migrations and diasporas initiated by globalization, and at others, with particular focus on the hybridization of cultures under globalization. (Dirlik's work may be seen as an example of transnationalism as critique of transnational capitalism (1992), while Cheng and Bonacich's study (1984) is an example of transnationalism as migration studies. On transnationalism as cultural studies, or studies of cultural hybridization, see Appadurai [1996], Featherstone [1990], Hall [1990, 1997], and Shohat and Stam [1994].) As the name itself implies, transnationalism terminologically and often substantively engages transformations to nation-states and their relationships with their inhabitants in part effected by transnational capitalism. Aihwa Ong's attentiveness to the prefix *trans* is helpful in understanding these emphases: "*Trans* denotes both moving through space and across lines, as well as changing the nature of something. Besides suggesting new relations between nation-states and capital, transnationality also alludes to the *trans*versal, the *trans*actional, the *trans*lational, and the *trans*gressive aspects of contemporary behavior and imagination that are incited, enabled, and regulated by the changing logics of states and capitalism" (1999, 4). Citizenship's significance as an identificatory category appears to be mutating as the forces compelling and

desires inciting contemporary migrations seem not so regularly to lead to settlement in and attachment to a given place, a given nation-state. The status and boundaries of nation-states themselves have been put into question by the growth of corporate economies and flows of capital and information across seemingly ineffectual national borders. As an academic discourse, transnationalism highlights and interrogates these phenomena.

Some practitioners of transnationalism deliberately rewrite the critical concerns of postcolonial studies in an attempt to displace (post)coloniality as the construct through which global relations of power are understood. Resisting the developmental telos connoted by a literal reading of "postcolonial," they promote transnationalism as part of a strategy designed to focus more directly on capitalism's structuring influences. Arjun Appadurai, for example, has argued the need for "widening . . . the sphere of the postcolony, to extend it beyond the geographical spaces of the ex-colonial world" to better account for globalized flows of economic, political, and cultural power (1993, 412). Arif Dirlik's criticism of postcolonialism likewise attempts such a shift: "the complicity of the postcolonial in hegemony lies in postcolonialism's diversion of attention from contemporary problems of social, political, and cultural domination, and its obfuscation of its own relationship to . . . a global capitalism . . . that serves as the structuring principle of global relations" (1992, 331).

In what are to my mind its most generative iterations, which are notably feminist in orientation, transnationalism utilizes multiple critical approaches in producing knowledge of what are recognized to be highly diversified and specifically located political, cultural, and social formations and practices. These versions are exemplified by Inderpal Grewal and Caren Kaplan's edited collection, *Scattered Hegemonies* (1994), *Between Woman and Nation*, edited by Caren Kaplan, Norma Alarcón, and Minoo Moallem (1999), and Lisa Lowe and David Lloyd's edited collection, *The Politics of Culture in the Shadow of Capital* (1997). They mine "the survival of alternatives in . . . locations worldwide" to identify "what arises historically, in contestation, and 'in difference' to capitalism" (Lowe and Lloyd 1997, 2). These practices of transnationalism seem generally to work with the understanding of the contemporary global terrain theorized by Grewal and Kaplan as constituted by " 'scattered hegemonies,' which are the effects of mobile capital as well as the multiple subjectivities that replace the European unitary subject" (1994, 7). In their study, Grewal and Kaplan are interested in deploying transnational feminism to respond to the effects of globalization as they articulate in dissimilar ways to the particular dynamics of the societies and cultures of myriad locations. The global terrain of "scattered hegemonies" accordingly requires that "feminist political practices . . . acknowledge transnational cultural flows . . . [in order to] understand the material conditions that structure women's lives in diverse locations. If feminist movements cannot understand the dynamics of these material conditions, they will be unable to construct an effective opposition to current economic and cultural hegemonies that are taking new global forms" (1994, 17).

Transnationalism thus may be seen to generate critical paradigms for investigating multifaceted, dissimilar, and specifically located alternative or resistant social practices that emerge simultaneously with globalization. As Lisa Lowe and David Lloyd have summarized, the "transnational" is one of several theoretical frameworks (including "international" and "global") "within which intersecting sets of social practices can be grasped. These practices include anticolonial and antiracist struggles, feminist struggles, labor organizing, cultural movements—all of which challenge contemporary neocolonial capitalism as a highly differentiated mode of production" (1997, 1). Or, in other words, derived in this vein, a transnational paradigm may be understood to advance comparative, dialogically oriented inquiry that recognizes the changing nature of the material and discursive significance of national borders. Perhaps for this reason, anthologies and academic journals constituted by multiply authored essays appear to be favored forms and forums for transnationalist discourse, which has a growing material life in such publications. I have already noted several of the recently emergent anthologies that engage and employ transnationalism. The journals *Public Culture, positions,* and *Diaspora* are notable for this as well as for their explicit and sustained interest in the critical concerns of the discourse. *Amerasia Journal* has recently published several issues focused around transnationalism, testifying to the growing interest in Asian American studies in the issues this discourse raises. Thus transnationalism does not imply that critical attentiveness to proximate conditions should be replaced by investigations of globalization per se. Rather, it advances efforts to work toward more particularized understandings of specific situations, which are then brought into conversation to provide a constellated picture of what globalization has—and has not—meant for various peoples and cultures around the world. M. Jacqui Alexander and Chandra Talpade Mohanty's introduction to their edited volume, *Feminist Genealogies, Colonial Legacies, Democratic Futures,* provides a thoughtful discussion of the ways that considering both the specific effects and immediate irrelevance of globalization is necessary for transformative critical and political practices (1997).

2 Gotanda explains that Asiatic racialization unfolds through a "group of related yet distinct ideas—Asiatic inassimilability, the conflation of Asian Americans with Asian citizens, and the perception of Asians as a threat to the American nation" (1999, 1). This process effects at various moments *citizenship nullification,* the prohibition of "the exercise of citizenship rights through the use of the implicit link between an Asiatic racial category and foreignness" (1999, 2). According to Gotanda, this "distinct mode of racialization of Americans of

Asian ancestry" developed "in the late nineteenth century during campaigns for Chinese exclusion. Asiatic racialization linked the idea of permanent foreignness—inassimilability to America—with national or ethnic categories such as Chinese, Japanese, or Korean. Asiatic racialization is thus characterized by a distinctive form of racial category linked to the idea that those so categorized are permanently foreign and inassimilable" (1999, 2). As referenced earlier, Lisa Lowe's work in *Immigrant Acts* (1996) persuasively establishes the ways that Asian-raced individuals have stood as metonyms for Asia. Gotanda's argument provides the particular vocabulary I will use, but the ideas I rely on are derived from the work of both of these critics.

3 To be clear, this is but one example of the broad-scale "crisis of identity" that, as Minoo Moallem summarizes, is conditioned by "the expansion of new forms of print and visual media, [together] with globalization, and with the erosion of the nation-state" characterizing the closing decades of the twentieth century (1999, 320). The distinctness and knowability of social and cultural identities for many have been called into question by these factors. As indicated in this book's introductory chapter, these shifts in part motivate this present project. The introduction by Elaine Kim and Lisa Lowe to a special issue of the journal *positions*, dedicated to "new formations" in Asian American studies, incisively explains the particular pressures on the reformulation of narratives of "Asian American" subject formations. See Kim and Lowe (1997).

4 With respect to "transnation" in particular, my definition draws from Arjun Appadurai's conceptualization. He explains, "For every nation-state that has exported significant numbers of its populations to the United States as refugees, tourists, or students, there is now a delocalized *transnation*, which retains a special ideological link to a putative place of origin but is otherwise a thoroughly diasporic collectivity" (1996, 172). According to Appadurai, diverse loyalties—familial and economic as well as patriotic—condition membership in these transnations. They are peopled by those "who love America but are not necessarily attached to the United States" (Appadurai 1996, 171). Where my definition departs from his is a shift in emphasis, from an understanding of transnations as formed by the migrants themselves, to one in which the coercive power of the nation-state compels membership in the transnation and prohibits formal attachment to the United States.

5 Numerous texts recount the villification of Asian-raced individuals. See, for example, Chan (1991), E. Kim (1982), Lee (1999), Hamamoto (1994), Hamamoto and Liu (2000), and Xing (1998).

6 Sucheng Chan reports that "A Gallup poll taken in 1942 showed that the images of Chinese and Japanese had bifurcated. Respondents characterized the Chinese as 'hardworking, honest, brave, religious, intelligent, and practical.' Japanese, on the other hand, were said to be 'treacherous, sly, cruel, and warlike'" (1991,

121). These images were given material life by the rescinding of the Chinese exclusion acts in 1943 and, on the other hand, by the internment of nikkei. This is not to suggest, however, that this shift in the perception of Chinese in America signaled the end of anti-Chinese discrimination. Rather, it indicates the flexibility of racism in identifying its targets, driven by its contemporaneous needs.

It should be noted that Asians of non-Japanese ancestry participated in the perpetuation of these fantasies. For example, "Fearful they would be targets of anti-Japanese hate and violence, many Chinese shopkeepers displayed signs announcing, 'This is a Chinese shop.' In the Chinese community, thousands of buttons were distributed: 'I am Chinese'" (Takaki 1989, 371).

7   Takaki reports that as early as 1936, Roosevelt had considered the possibility of nikkei internment: "One obvious thought occurs to me—that every Japanese citizen or non-citizen on the island of Oahu who meets . . . Japanese ships or has any connection with their officers or men should be secretly but definitely identified and his or her name placed on a special list of those who would be first to be placed in a concentration camp in the event of trouble" (1989, 390). Japan's modernization positioned that nation as a potential threat to the United States from the turn of the century forward. A history of national competitiveness between Japan and the United States undergirded Roosevelt's preparedness to move forward with internment.

8   In an illuminating argument, George Lipsitz explains how Japan's status enabled certain Black Americans to challenge white supremacy in the United States with the threat of transnational alliances between domestic antiracist struggles and Japanese efforts to contest the international power of the United States (1997).

9   Howard Zinn emphasizes the economic rather than humanitarian interests driving the United States' entry into the war:

> It was not Hitler's attacks on the Jews that brought the United States into World War II, any more than the enslavement of 4 million blacks brought Civil War in 1861. Italy's attack on Ethiopia, Hitler's invasion of Austria, his takeover of Czechoslovakia, his attack on Poland—none of those events caused the United States to enter the war, although Roosevelt did begin to give important aid to England. What brought the United States fully into the war was the Japanese attack on the American naval base at Pearl Harbor, Hawaii, on December 7, 1941. Surely it was not the humane concern for Japan's bombing of civilians that led to Roosevelt's outraged call for war—Japan's attack on China in 1937, her bombing of civilians at Nanking, had not provoked the United States to war. It was the Japanese attack on a link in the American Pacific Empire that did it. (1995, 401)

10   My discussion of the legal issues surrounding internment is informed by work by Peter Irons (1983), Neil Gotanda (1997), and Natsu Saito (1997).

notes to chapter two   169

11 This citation refers to Peter Irons's *Justice at War: The Story of the Japanese American Internment Cases*. All subsequent references to this text will be noted as *JAW*.
12 See *United States v. Hirabayashi*, 46 F. Supp. 657 (W.D. Wash. 1942), Brief in Support of Amended Demurrer to Indictment.
13 *United States v. Hirabayashi*, 46 F. Supp. 657. My citations to these cases are from Peter Irons' edited *Justice Denied*, which collects the texts of the decisions in various legal suits brought in relation to internment. All subsequent references to this text will be noted as *JD*.
14 *Hirabayashi v. United States*, 320 U.S. 81 (1943).
15 For example, *Korematsu v. United States*, 323 U.S. 214 (1944), and *Yasui v. United States*, 320 U.S. 115 (1943).
16 See Chang and Aoki (1998), Ancheta (1998), and Lopez (1996). Examples of such laws and cases include the Chinese Exclusion Act of 1882, *In re Ah Yup* (1878) (determining Chinese ineligibility for citizenship), *Takao Ozawa v. United States* (1922) (determining Japanese ineligibility for citizenship), and *United States v. Thind* (1923) (determining Asian Indians' ineligibility for citizenship in spite of their categorization as "caucasian").
17 Priscilla Wald's work historicizes this juridical dispossession in illuminating ways. She shows how the Supreme Court "attempt[ed] to legislate the disappearance of the 'Indians' [specifically, the Cherokee] and the 'descendants of Africans,' . . . by judging them neither citizens nor aliens and therefore not legally representable" (1993, 59). Referring specifically to *Cherokee Nation v. Georgia*, 30 U.S. 1 (1831) and *Scott v. Sanford*, 60 U.S. 691 (1857), Wald submits that the courts "turn[ed] the Cherokee and slaves into uncanny figures who mirror the legal contingency—and the potential fate—of all subjects in the Union, a fate made all the more plausible by the instability of the Union and the tenuousness of national identity" (1993, 59). These juridical machinations, she concludes, "profoundly troubled the concept of natural law—particularly the rights to own and inherit property, including property in the self. The dispossessed subjects embody—or disembody—an important representational threat: human beings to whom *natural* property rights do not extend" (1993, 61; emphasis original).
18 Naoki Sakai's (1997) theorization of the ways that the idea of a national literature relies upon an assumed comparative to other national literatures and thus may be understood as formally comparative informs my discussion on this point.
19 Robyn Wiegman's theorization of an "economy of visibility" through which physical markings are read as signs of ontological difference within U.S. discourses of race offers an illuminating explanation of how constructedness disappears under the pressure of various cultural forces. See Wiegman (1995).
20 According to Takaki, the questionnaire had a dual purpose: "(1) to enable

camp authorities to process individual internees for work furloughs as well as for resettlement outside of the restricted zones, and (2) to register Nisei for the draft" (1989, 397).

21. For issei, who were ineligible for U.S. citizenship and were "aliens" by legal definition, answering "yes" to question 28 would have meant choosing a condition of statelessness: they would literally have become citizens of nowhere. And in any case, as a matter of principle for many of the internees regardless of formal citizenship, because an affirmative answer suggested previous (and contemporaneous) disloyalty to the United States, they declined to respond (Takaki 1989). Moreover, as the issei were physically residents of the United States who were tied to it in material forms, the question posed significant practical problems for them.

22. About one-fifth of the men eligible to register for the draft declined to do so, responded with an explanation, or simply gave no response (Takaki 1989). In early 1944, the Selective Service began reclassifying the draft status of nisei men who has answered "yes" to both questions 27 and 28. Some of those who were drafted refused to be inducted, "protesting the violation of their Constitutional rights" (Takaki 1989, 398). Encouraged by the nisei-led Japanese American Citizens League, which, according to Chan, "wanted so badly to be accepted as Americans that they acted as the U.S. government's most ardent apologists" (1991, 129), some 30,000 nisei men ultimately served in the armed forces, as translators, decoders, and in combat in the 100th Battalion and 442d Regimental Combat Team, which became two of the most highly decorated units of the war (Chan 1991, 134–135).

23. See Probyn (1999) on ordinariness and the experience of nation.

24. See Anderson (1991) on the particular power of the imagined community of nation to effect a willingness to die.

25. See Jeffords (1997) on the ways that these transferrals of patriarchal power work.

26. The phrase is King-kok Cheung's, who in her study of Yamamoto's work describes the writer as one "who excels in coding through muted plots and innocent disguise" (1993, 28).

27. See also Luibheid (1997) for discussion of the ways that the 1965 Immigration and Nationality Act did not open borders quite as "freely" as generally conceived.

28. They draw on Chantal Mouffe's work in arguing this point. Writing about the European context, Mouffe observes:

> Now that the enemy [of the Cold War] has been defeated, the meaning of democracy itself has become blurred and needs to be redefined by the creation of a new frontier. This is much more difficult for the moderate right

and for the left than for the radical right. For the latter has already found its enemy. It is provided by the "enemy within," the immigrants, which are presented by the different movements of the extreme right as a threat to the cultural identity and national sovereignty of the "true" Europeans. (quoted in Chang and Aoki 1998, 321).

29 Chang and Aoki cite a 1996 *New York Times* poll indicating a widespread belief that "the 'invasion' or coming majority of color, has already eclipsed the numerical White majority" (1998, 321). Significant gaps between the perceived percentage of the U.S. population who are "Hispanic," "black," "Asian," and "white" and census figures of those populations, they suggest, imply that "many White Americans think that the 'conquest' is well under way" (1998, 322).

chapter 3. "one hundred percent Korean": on space and subjectivity

1 See Soja (1989) for further discussion of space as a social cognate.
2 One of the effects of reconceptualizing the spatial imagination of Asian American studies is the advancement of the realignment of Asian American studies with Asian studies, a field with which Asian American studies historically has had an uneasy relationship. The heightened visibility that post-1965 immigrants from Asia have given to the significance of pre-migration histories and cultural practices has elicited in Asian American studies a growing interest in revisiting relations between these historically distinguishable fields. As Elaine Kim and Lisa Lowe have summarized, "To account for the historical pasts and presents of these new immigrants, . . . there will need to be a variety of connections between Asian studies and Asian American studies" (1997, viii). The challenge before us is to make such connections while attending carefully to the differing genealogical groundings of these fields and while conscientiously remembering that there is no discursively transcendent "Asian" to serve as an immediately available common epistemological object. By thinking through the implications of a transnational territorial imagination for the relationship between Asian American studies and Asian studies as part of this chapter's work, I explore the disciplinary significance of following through on the insights offered by the novels considered here. Recognizing the homology between the spatial logic of U.S. nationalism and nation-based Asian Americanist paradigms, and using these literary texts to help us imagine otherwise, I suggest that deliberately bringing to surface the transnational imaginaries suppressed under such paradigms facilitates the establishment of grounds for cross-field linkages. Such links can thus translate into powerful collaborative critiques of both U.S. nationalism and imperialism. In part, I encourage Asian

American studies to pursue links with Asian studies to ensure, as R. Radhakrishnan has cautioned, against "a certain poststructuralist smugness about autocritiques and rigorous protocols of self-reflexivity." Such is an effect, he submits, that issues from a failure to follow through on self-critique with self-reinvention, which includes establishing a "different relationality" with other locations (1996, 170).

Along these lines, this chapter's discussions continue arguments that Karen Shimakawa and I have offered in our co-written introduction to *Orientations: Mapping Studies in the Asian Diaspora* (2001). I am grateful to her for allowing me to use our collaborative work freely here. My own contribution to that volume considered Ronyoung Kim's *Clay Walls* in conjunction with Theresa Hak Kyung Cha's *Dictée* in an essay geared toward considering the implications of thinking through Asian studies to the position of Asian American literatures in relation to American literary studies. My discussion of *Clay Walls* here draws from that essay but appears here in significantly revised form.

3   Unlike Asian American studies, the commonly accepted narrative of Asian studies locates its genesis in the establishment of area studies in U.S. universities in the context of the Cold War politics characterizing the aftermath of World War II. During the war, U.S. universities had been tasked with and found to be only moderately successful in providing the U.S. military with "knowledge of different areas and their peoples," knowledge valuable for the purposes of maintaining the security of the nation (Hall 1947, 22). Found "wanting in the accumulation of materials which would have made sound research or analysis possible," the Exploratory Committee on World Area Research formed immediately following the war advised the establishment of area studies to create "a vast body of knowledge about [other peoples]" in order to secure "national welfare in the postwar period" (Hall 1947, 22). As Vicente Rafael has summarized, "area studies [were to] develop a body of elite scholars capable of producing knowledge about other nations to the benefit of 'our' nation" (1994, 93). Asian studies as an academic field thus traces to this self/other way of envisioning the world deeply entrenched in U.S. Cold War politics, an epistemology that, thanks to Edward Said, is often shorthanded as "orientalism." See Chakrabarty (1998) for further discussion on these matters.

During the past few decades, in this post–Cold War era in which the historical mandate of area studies no longer has immediate currency, a vocal cohort of scholars working in Asian studies has emerged to challenge orientalism both as it structures Asian studies and as it circulates more broadly. They are reconfiguring the field such that the rather commonplace assumption of the orientalist tendencies in Asian studies that used to circulate without remark in Asian American studies appears markedly out of date. Moreover, these new directions in Asian studies coincide with Asian American studies' growing interests in internationalizing its scope of critical inquiry and its heightened self-reflectivity about its own assumptions and practices (see note 2, above). This is, in short, a moment at which both fields are currently undergoing fairly intensive and extensive reinvention. I mean here neither to compare nor to legislate relations between these fields. Instead, I take as a point of departure the ways that their coincidental self-critique enables us to conceive common grounds without relying on an essentialized understanding of "Asian-ness," and to think through what such linkages might mean for Asian Americanist critique.

4 These areas/the non-West follow no consistent pattern of delimitation. "Area" sometimes refers to nations, sometimes to a "world area" defined by one early practitioner as "an area of world importance (importance to the United States or its international relations)" (Steward 1950, in Cheah 2000, 40), and sometimes a "culture area," which appears to designate a perceived geographic region that has in common certain cultural practices or characteristics. Areas, in short, were conceived as "rough and ready delimitations serving chiefly the practical needs of military and political operations" (Singer 1964, in Cheah 2000, 40). Rapidly established by force of governmental/military support, area studies have in recent decades faced sharp critique for these connections between its intellectual objectives and governmental political interests (Cheah 2000; Rafael 1994; Said 1978).

5 For further discussion on this point, see Sakai (2000b), Hall (1996), Chow (1995).

6 Cheah further explains:

> Since these are, by definition, particular areas, they can only know themselves through area research as empirical data and as particular bounded objects. Put another way, the only knowledge they can have of themselves comes from apprehending themselves through the eyes of the West, which amounts to saying that they can never fully know themselves. Thus these areas must either give up the aim of self-knowledge, in which case they must remain mired in self-incurred tutelage because they have not achieved self-determination, or they can attain self-determination only by being enthralled or possessed by the specter of the West, since they can only know themselves as its other. (2000, 48)

And furthermore,

> Part of the dilemma is precisely that as U.S. area studies becomes disseminated throughout the globe, either through policy-making or through the training of indigenous area experts by the U.S. academic industry, the inhabitants of these places are constitutively made to cathect the space of the world area, the space of the particularistic object of factual information, and are

thus barred from genuine self-knowledge and self-determination. The problem is not necessarily solved by the fact that there are more and more Western-trained indigenous scholars based in their "home" areas and who write in the vernacular for local audiences. This in itself—physical or geographical location—is no guarantee that the conceptual matrix distinguishing areas from the universal knowing subject of the disciplines and subordinating them to it will be overturned. . . . One would need to ask: who is this "they" (indigenous scholars) who have become much better at studying "themselves"? How is this "they" formed by the "we" of area studies' institutional origin, and how is this "they" constitutively constrained by its conceptual matrix? (2000, 48)

See also Kang (2000) for a discussion of "neo-colonial intellectual," a consideration that explicitly undertakes to examine the "aporia of decolonization" in the South Korean context.

7   Problematic on its own terms, such support boomerangs in that the "ethnic" of ethnic studies shares much in common with the "area" of area studies. It is the particular to the universal in a way recognizably analogous to the "non-West" / "West" algorithm that has organized area studies. While the "ethnic" of ethnic studies has been formulated in response to the fact that the universal is not actually universal even within the confines of the "West," it translates through the logic of liberalism as that which *cannot* be universal.

8   Laura Hyun Yi Kang's work has helped me formulate this argument in this way. Kang "track[s] the peculiar yet resonant enfigurations of 'Asian/American women' in five select discursive terrains: literary, cinematic, historiographical, economic/ethnographic, and finally, a field delineated as 'self-representations.' This project investigates how 'Asian/American women' as both subject *and* problem of knowledge production can critically highlight the discursive limits of each terrain. The unbecoming slash of my naming," Kang explains, "marks the differential tensions as well as the shifting separations and crossings between the geopolitical locations of Asia and the United States and between the social and discursive categories of 'Asian women' and 'Asian American women'" (1997, 405). See Kang (1997, 2002).

9   See de Man (1996, 1983) for discussions of irony.

10 The phrase "shared temporality" is Marilyn Ivy's. She uses it as part of her argument about the "co-occurrence—the coevalness—of the problem of Japanese modernity with that of modernities elsewhere, and the shared temporality that implies" (1995, 5). Ivy clarifies "That coevalness does not imply the collapsing of differences within an undifferentiated global modernity, although I would argue that we ignore the homogenizing trajectories of advanced capitalism at our peril. Japan is not merely the same as other nation-states within this global order by virtue of its modernity, nor is it just a variation on the larger

modernization theme" (1995, 5–6). Naoki Sakai puts forward a similar argument: "I maintain that the coming of modernity can be attributed to no single cause, process, or territory. The time of modernity is never unitary; it is always in multiplicity. Modernity always appears in multiple histories" (2000a, viii).

11 Bill Ong Hing suggests that Commodore Matthew Perry's arrival, with four U.S. naval ships, in Tokyo Bay in 1854, "opened" Japan to the "West" and thus "helped bring about the Meiji Restoration" (1993, 26).

12 In this way, as Miriam Silverberg has argued, the incidence of Japanese modernity interrupts the conflation of "modern" with "Western." See Silverberg (1992, 1993).

13 See the discussion in chapter 2, note 1, regarding "transnational paradigm," especially with respect to Aihwa Ong's (1999) delineation.

14 In this sense, Kim's novel resonates against Anderson's work on exile and the ways that "home" comes into sharper focus from a position in exile. See Anderson (1994).

15 See Gotanda (1997) on nativity and citizenship.

16 The range in the numbers of "comfort women" is due to the unavailability of specific data and the reluctance of conscripted women who survived to come forward with their stories. Of the estimated numbers of "comfort women," Chin-sung Chung explains, some 80–90 percent are said to have been from Korea; women taken from other territories under Japanese control—Taiwan, China, the Philippines, and Indonesia—constituted the remaining population (1995). Ranging in age from 11 to 29, the average age of these women was 17. Chung explains that the recruitment of these women followed the pattern of "widespread recruitment of impoverished Korean women to work in Japanese factories during Japan's post–World War I industrial boom. From the beginning of colonization, Korean women were seen as inexpensive, easily controlled labor" (1995, 207). Dai-sil Kim-Gibson summarizes that "The most often cited reasons for establishing comfort houses in official reports of the Japanese government are: 1) to prevent soldiers from raping local women and incurring local opposition; 2) to protect them from venereal diseases and thereby avoiding the disablement of fighting men; and 3) to protect military secrets" (1999, 39). See also Chung (1995, 209–210) for elaboration on the rationale for the practice of military sex slavery.

17 See Cumings (1981).

18 See Lowe (1996) on U.S. imperialism's positioning of Korea as static victim.

19 See Choi (1993), Cumings (1981), and Kang (2000). "Soon," writes Choi, "American mass culture towered over Korea's desolate cultural landscape as South Korea became one of the most heavily armed fortresses of the vast American empire. To live in this state of internal displacement and external dependency is to live in a state of colonialism" (1993, 81).

176 notes to chapter four

20 Volpp, drawing on Mari Matsuda's work, addresses the ways that victimization rhetoric contributes to reinstalling racism and patriarchy endemic to the U.S. criminal justice system. See Volpp (1996, especially 1585–1588).

21 See also Volpp (1994) for further discussion of the ways that this rhetoric can perpetuate a colonial episteme of enhancing the self by denigrating the other. Volpp's work engages the ongoing critical conversations among feminist theorists likewise committed to the project of undermining systems that support imbalances of relations of power through various processes of engendering individuals. Much of this work has been targeted at critiquing the assumptions and implications of "white Western feminism." See, for example, Anzaldua (1987), hooks (1997), Mohanty (1991), Barlow (2000), Grewal and Kaplan (1994), Shohat (1998), Mufti and Shohat (1997).

22 This is not to deny the particular brutality of the practice of military sex slavery, but to recognize that that experience does not somehow negate the particular wages of U.S. racialized and heteronormative patriarchy. That the United States has not been the site of liberation for those engendered "women" and certainly for those "women" identified also as "Asian" is all too obvious; it is particularly evidenced in its legislative history. As noted in previous chapters, immigration regulation has included the 1875 Page Law, prohibiting "the importation into the United States of women for the purposes of prostitution," effectively defining women immigrants from China and Japan and those from any other "Oriental country" against whom the law was targeted as sex workers (Chan 1991, 105). The United States has also instituted laws that stripped citizenship from U.S. citizen women who married foreign-born men, subordinating by determining the identity of "woman" as legible only in relation to "man." The ongoing contestations over reproductive rights and legislation of heteronormativity sketch a terrain historically and currently not unhostile to "woman," one that argues against conceiving of the United States as the natural home of the liberated "woman." See Cornell (1991), Eisenstein (1988, 1994), Frug (1992), MacKinnon (1993), Schneider (1991), and West (1988).

23 See Ray (2000) and Kaplan et al. (1999) for discussions of the complicated connections between "woman" and "nation." See also Yuval-David (1997).

chapter 4. (dis)owning America

1 See Campomanes (1997), Davé et al. (2000), and Grewal (1994) for discussions of the transformative potential of the integration of postcolonial studies into the fabric of Asian Americanist discourse.

2 See Grewal (1994) for an illuminating argument regarding precisely this matter.

3   For example, see Appiah (1997), Dirlik (1992), Hall (1996), McClintock (1992), and Shohat (1992).
4   For example, see Chakrabarty (1997a, b), Chatterjee (1993a, b), Guha (1989), Prakash (1990, 1992), Rafael (1995), and Spivak (1988).
5   See Grewal (1994), Shohat (1992, 1998), and Mufti and Shohat (1997) for discussions of this tension.
6   I mean "friendship" as "a model for nonhierarchical, reciprocal relations that run counter to . . . hierarchical modes," as Irene Diamond and Lee Quinby have suggested (1988, ix). "Friendship's reciprocity takes the form of dialogue, what Foucault has called 'the work of reciprocal elucidation' in which 'the rights of each person are in some sense immanent in the discussion' " (Diamond and Quinby 1988, ix–x). Friendship is a model of nonassimilative and nondialectical relations. It does not seek synthesis or resolution of differences, but rather, produces knowledge in the spaces of those differences.
7   Sharpe explains that it has in some instances come merely to "designate the presence of racial minorities and Third World immigrants," flattening important distinctions between and among them (1995, 181).
8   Along these lines, Ella Shohat has suggested that "post-Third Worldism" serves as a more appropriate rubric, one that intends to get at the complex problematics of what follows after formal political independence. See Shohat and Stam (1994) and Mufti and Shohat (1997).
9   Homi Bhabha's (1994) and Trinh T. Minh-ha's (1989, 1991) respective works have been especially notable for their theorization of this kind of hybridity.
10 For this reason, Frankenburg and Mani (1993) suggest "post–civil rights" as an alternative term roughly analogous to "postcolonial."
11 Some of the most generative debates in postcolonial studies have been driven by feminist scholarship that thinks through the category "woman" as the locus of inquiry through which the complexities of colonization and decolonization must be understood. See, for example, essays in Alexander and Mohanty (1996), Grewal and Kaplan (1994), Kaplan et al. (1999), and Shohat (1998). See also Stoler (1991), Spivak (1989, 1992), and Ray (2000).
12 As is characteristic of much postcolonial studies scholarship, Sharpe's argument might be seen as "post-Marxist" insofar as it focuses on how capitalism as dominant global mode of production both conditions and negotiates locally specific cultural and political structures. This is not a version of "vulgar Marxism" that reduces the totality of life to economic explanation (economic determinism) or that offers history-as-class-struggle. Rather, postcolonial studies suggests that the imposition of structures of capitalism through colonialism marks a decisive though not definitive shift and that decolonization is especially complicated both to accomplish and to understand, given that capitalism is contemporarily an arguably global phenomenon.

178   notes to chapter four

13   To be clear, this axis of investigation does not preclude such an engagement. Rather, this is a matter of shifting emphasis in defining the locus of investigation.
14   Sharpe's summary of the weakness of the internal colonization model is incisive: "The weakness of the internal colonial model is that it draws too sharp a distinction between voluntary and involuntary movements of populations. In doing so, it equates immigration with assimilation and colonization with racism, thus neglecting racism in immigration. The limitations of this equation become evident in the historical example of Asians, for whom immigration was voluntary but who nonetheless experienced racism" (1995, 183). See also Omi and Winant (1994).
15   I take this subtitle from Aamir Mufti's and Ella Shohat's introduction to *Dangerous Liaisons: Gender, Nation, and Postcolonial Perspectives* (1997).
16   Lowe provides an incisive and detailed synopsis of these legislative acts in the first chapter of *Immigrant Acts* (1996). See especially notes 14–16, 27, and 33 to that chapter. Bill Ong Hing's *Making and Remaking Asian America through Immigration Policy, 1850–1990* (1993), offers an important review of such legislation. See also Ancheta (1998), Chang and Aoki (1998), Gotanda (1997, 1999), Johnson (1997), Lopez (1996).
17   To be clear, these were not assimilationist arguments but rather were geared toward claiming a literally/legally "rightful" place in America. By locating such claims to the United States as "home" in the 1960s and 1970s, I do not mean to imply that the kinds of challenges to the lives and livelihoods of Asian-raced individuals and communities are no longer relevant. Indeed, a contemporary resurgence of anti-Asian racism in the particularly publicized form of cloaking Chinese Americans in the mantle of traitorous spy suggests that belongingness remains a condition that cannot be taken for granted.
18   I take this phrase from the title of Wahneema Lubiano's (1997) edited collection.
19   See Morrison (1997). The Morrison essay with which I am working here is the opening piece to the Lubiano (1997) edited collection.
20   Examples include Kaplan (1993), Kaplan and Pease (1993), Lipsitz (1998), Lowe (1996, 1998a, b), Moon and Davidson (1995), Saldivar (1991, 1997), Spillers (1991), Wald (1993, 1995), and Wiegman (1995, 1998).
21   Taking as her point of departure Ranajit Guha's (1989) observation that none of the "noble achievements" of bourgeois culture "can survive the inexorable urge of capital to expand and reproduce itself by means of the politics of extraterritorial, colonial domination" (1996, 85–86), Cherniavsky explains: "In one sense, at least, in the case of the United States, capital appears effectively to exceed its own historical limit and assimilate the 'extraterritorial' to its logic. Significant classes of people whose land and/or labor is expropriated under this colonial rule, classes that comprise . . . the category of 'the people' as such, are, at various junctures of U.S. history, forcibly externalized with respect to

what is constituted as the space of an 'American' national politics and culture" (1996, 87). She further clarifies that "In Guha's use of the term, *the people* is synonymous with *the subaltern classes* and designates all those not included in the categories of (national, regional, or local) elite identity" (1996, 87; emphasis original).

22 This is what Oscar Campomanes has referred to as "contributionism" (1997).

23 To be clear, neither Anderson's nor Hobsbawm's studies are themselves especially romanticized understandings of "nation." Though in different ways, both historicize the emergence of the nation in ways that demonstrate its specific groundings in particular cultural values. Yet "imagined community" and "invented tradition" have found circulation free of these moorings such that they appear to have an idealized valence to them.

24 For example, Chakrabarty (1997a, b), Radkrishnan (1994), Yuval-Davis (1997), and Kaplan et al. (1999).

25 Accordingly, critiques of Asian American cultural nationalism might be extended beyond recognition of its representational failures—its heteronormative masculinism and homogenization of diversity—to interrogate its effective reliance on "nation" and "nationalism" as the objective and technological means for combating anti-Asian racism. See Sau-ling Wong's (1995) discussion; see also Cheung (1990), Eng (1997), E. Kim (1990), Lim (1993a, b), and Lowe (1996).

26 Here I follow Edward Said's distinction between imperialism and colonialism.

27 My focus here, which emphasizes post-contact and post-territorialized Hawai'i, in one sense problematically reiterates one of the conditions against which Native Hawaiian sovereignty movements are working. Elizabeth Buck offers an insightful consideration of this problematic in *Paradise Remade: The Politics of Culture and History in Hawai'i* (1993), one that informs my discussion here. Namely, in narrativizing Hawaiian history with this focus and in this manner, I am reproducing an arguably colonial episteme, one that validates knowledge produced only on its own terms. This is a version of the problem of thought that Chatterjee poses: a focus on post-contact history effectively centers "contact," effectively centers Western/colonial/Enlightenment epistemology, thereby effacing precisely the independent history that argues for Hawaiian sovereignty. Indeed, that such liberatory movements must make use of the language of sovereignty indicates the pervasiveness of this problem of thought. "History," to borrow from Dipesh Chakrabarty, "as a discourse produced at the institutional site of the university," is one that relies on understandings of subjectivities and social structures derived from and through "Europe," which are then made to stand for the universal (1997a, 263). Chakrabarty explains in his critique of "history as an academic discourse" that predominantly in that discourse, "Only 'Europe,' . . . is *theoretically* (i.e., at the level of the fundamental categories that

shape historical thinking) knowable; all other histories are matters of empirical research that fleshes out a theoretical skeleton that is substantially 'Europe'" (1997a, 263, 266). This is a problem of legibility, where even if documentable in accordance with the demands of this academic historiography (and that is a significant "even if" given oral cultures), history is narrativized in forms that foundationally cannot represent subjectivities and structures of life and culture alternative to those derived through "Europe." This kind of historiography that functionally supports and relies on colonial modes of knowledge has been critiqued by, in addition to Chakrabarty, Edward Said (1978, 1993), Gayatri Spivak (1988a), Chandra Mohanty (1991), Trinh Minh-Ha (1989), and Gyan Prakash (1990, 1992), among others. See Lowe (1996, 103–104) for a concise and thorough review of such work.

If my narrative of Hawaiian history is colonial in this regard, I think it is anticolonial (still within the framework of but in deliberate opposition to) in that by bringing into the foreground these problematics, I seek to undermine the idea that this (or any) historical narrative could stand as total knowledge of the past. As Greg Dening has noted, "The past is never contemporary, but history always is. History is always bound to the present in some way. History always represents the present in the ways that it re-presents the past" (1989, 134). In my discussion, the contemporary discursive conditions of postcolonial and Asian American studies and poststructural theorizing form the present context that articulates the past. Thus, and pursuing the tactic of denationalization/denaturalization argued above, this historicization of Hawai'i intends to facilitate the deconstruction of the naturalized history forwarded by the United States that continues to justify (from the U.S. perspective) colonization of Hawai'i.

28 See Musicant (1998) and Traxel (1998) for U.S. histories of this period.
29 The population of Japanese immigrants in Hawai'i numbered 25,000, roughly a quarter of the entire population and triple the population of whites (Musicant 1998, 105).
30 English language versions of Hawaiian history that do not center exogamous contact and discussions of Hawaiian culture may be found in Buck (1993), Kamahele (2000), Trask (1993), Stannard (1989), Charlot (1983), and Valeri (1985).
31 U.S. Public Law 103-150, 103d Congress, 1st Session, 107 Stat. 1510 (November 23, 1993).
32 Buck's work (1993) focuses in part on this history and this practice of commodification. See also Wilson (2000).
33 The suit was initially brought in 1997 in the District Court of Hawai'i. In that court's decision, the problematic of Rice's identity/ability to vote was explained thus: "Plaintiff [Rice] was born and currently lives in Hawaii as a citi-

zen, taxpayer and qualified elector of the United States, the State of Hawaii, and the County of Hawaii. He traces his ancestry to two members of the legislature of the Kingdom of Hawaii, prior to the Revolution of 1893 [when Queen Lili'uokalani was overthrown by the U.S. coup d'état]. Plaintiff, however, is Caucasian and is not within the definition of Hawaiian or Native Hawaiian" (963 F. Supp. 1547, 1548 (D. Hawai'i 1997)). "Hawaiian" and "Native Hawaiian" are defined statutorily:

> "Hawaiian" means any descendant of the aboriginal peoples inhabiting the Hawaiian Islands which exercised sovereignty and subsisted in the Hawaiian Islands in 1778, and which peoples thereafter have continued to reside in Hawaii (528 U.S. at 509),

and,

> "Native Hawaiian" means any descendant of not less than one-half part of the races inhabiting the Hawaiian Islands previous to 1778 . . . provided that the term identically refers to the descendants of such blood quantum of such aboriginal peoples which exercised sovereignty and subsisted in the Hawaiian Islands in 1778 and which peoples thereafter continued to reside in Hawaii (528 U.S. at 510).

34 Smith draws on Gramsci in his explanation of common sense, noting that Gramsci has defined common sense as

> the world conception absorbed uncritically by various social and cultural circles in which the moral individuality of the average man is developed. Common sense is not a single conception, identical in time and sense: it is the "folk-lore" of philosophy and like folk-lore it appears in innumerable forms: its fundamental and most characteristic trait is that of being (even in single brains) disintegrated, incoherent, inconsecutive, in keeping with the social and cultural position of the multitudes whose philosophy it is. (quoted in Smith 1997, 181)

Smith summarizes that because of the conservative effects of "common sense" logic, "paradoxically, those who wish to change the status quo must combat common sense and thereby risk acquiring the semblance of fools" (1997, 181).

35 I want to thank Leti Volpp for her valuable and timely insights into this case, which have helped to shape this analysis. See Volpp (2000c) for a discussion of this and related issues.

36 George Lipsitz has powerfully demonstrated precisely the ways that color-blindness is *not* the remedy to injustice in *The Possessive Investment in Whiteness* (1998). See Gotanda (1995) and Crenshaw (1995) for a critique of "color-blindness" in legal discourse.

notes to chapter four

37 The Court uses *Hirabayashi* in this manner:

> The ancestral inquiry mandated by the State is forbidden by the Fifteenth Amendment for the further reason that the use of racial classifications is corruptive of the whole legal order democratic elections seek to preserve. The law itself may not become the instrument for generating the prejudice and hostility all too often directed against persons whose particular ancestry is disclosed by their ethnic characteristics and cultural traditions. "Distinctions between citizens solely because of their ancestry are by their very nature odious to a free people whose institutions are founded upon the doctrine of equality." *Hirabayashi v. United States*, 320 U.S. 81, 100 (1943). Ancestral tracing of this sort achieves its purpose by creating a legal category which employs the same mechanisms, and causes the same injuries, as the laws or statutes that use race by name. (528 U.S. at 517)

38 *Adarand v. Pena*, 515 U.S. 200 (1995).
39 See Takagi (1992) for a discussion of the rollback of such strategies specifically in relation to education.
40 For this legal history, see Ancheta (1998), Freeman (1995), Gotanda (1997), Gutierrez-Jones (1995), Lopez (1996), Harris (1995), J. Lee (1995), Rosaldo (1997), and Saito (1997).
41 This kind of work is currently being undertaken in many different directions and discourses. For excellent examples, see Almaguer (1994), Chang and Aoki (1998), Espiritu (1992), Lopez (1996), Lipsitz (1998, 2001), and Parikh (1999). See also generally the essays collected in Gooding-Williams (1993).
42 To be clear, there are many different anticolonial movements in Hawai'i, and not all of them make a claim for political independence. Trask's work has been particularly visible in Asian Americanist discourse and has directly addressed the relationship of "local Asians" and "Asian Americans" to Native Hawaiian sovereignty efforts.
43 As Trask suggests, George Cooper and Gavan Daws offer a thorough analysis of Chinese and Japanese ascendancy to political power in Hawai'i in *Land and Power in Hawai'i* (1985).
44 Jonathan Okamura has historicized the emergence of "local" identities within the context of the capitalist practices structuring both the economic and social relations among the islands' inhabitants in the early twentieth century. "Viewed historically, the emergence of local culture and society represents an accommodation of ethnic groups to one another in the context of a social system primarily distinguished by the wide cleavage of the *Haole* planter and merchant oligarchy on the one hand, and the subordinate Hawaiian and immigrant plantation groups on the other" (1980, 122). "Local" identities have come to be viewed as alternatives to "Asian American," a designation seen as continent-

ally derived and one "that fails to recognize the anomalous status of Local Asians who are part of a non-Native Hawaiian, multiracial Local movement asserting its own cultural identity" (Fujikane 1994, 24). In this regard, "local" critiques "Asian American" for its effective inability to demonstrate diversity among the experiences and cultural practices of Asian-raced peoples in Hawai'i. In local literature, the common use of Hawaiian Pidgin English, a creole English that is the synthesis of the languages of the historic plantation groups (Portuguese, Japanese, Chinese, Filipino, Korean, and Native Hawaiian), signifies a difference from continental literatures written by immigrants from and descendants of Asian countries.

45 Such a challenge is being raised in other contexts and critiques as well. For example, Ruth Hsu asserts that "Asian Americans need to question not only what the American nation-state is doing, but also their own complicity in maintaining and furthering the West's colonialist policies" (1996, 46).

46 Rob Wilson points to Bamboo Ridge Press as a critical node of production and circulation of local literatures (2000).

47 Stephen Sumida's (1991, 1997) work stands as a hallmark in this regard. See also Fujikane (1994), Okamura (1980), E. Yamamoto (1999), and Wilson (2000).

48 *Amerasia Journal* has devoted an issue to these matters; see *Amerasia Journal* 26: 2(2000). See also Sumida (1997).

49 As Edward Said explains:

> Underlying social space are territories, lands, geographical domains, the actual geographical underpinnings of the imperial, and also the cultural contest. To think about distant places, to colonize them, to populate or depopulate them: all of this occurs on, about or because of land. The actual geographic possession of land is what empire in the final analysis is all about. . . . Imperialism and the culture associated with it affirm both the primacy of geography and an ideology about control of territory. The geographical sense makes projections—imaginative, cartographic, military, economic, historical, or in a general sense cultural. It also makes possible the construction of various kinds of knowledge, all of them in one way or another dependent upon the perceived character and destiny of a particular geography. (1993, 78)

Keith Aoki's (1996) work has led me to this particular quotation. He articulates the importance of territoriality in legal discourse of sovereignty and nation-states:

> In legal discourse, "the identification of the state with a territorially enclosed nation has infused jurisdictional rhetoric with metaphors of space, inclusion and exclusion. The state is thus depicted as a realm to which one belongs or

from which one is banned, whose interests one serves or one injures, and whose sovereignty should be respected but is persistently at risk. Territoriality, citizenship, and reasonableness categories all reiterate this dichotomy between what is and what is not in the nation-state's best interests." (Aoki 1996, 1303)

50 For further discussions on such matters, see the essays collected in Grewal and Kaplan (1994), Kaplan et al. (1999), and Lowe and Lloyd (1997).
51 See, for example, pp. 127–128 in Blu's Hanging, which offers a scene that is particularly notable for the explicitness of its politics.
52 This interpretation reminds us that, to borrow Sharpe's phrasing, the "intellectual antecedents" of postcolonial studies are the work that emerges from the specific sites of anticolonial struggle (1995, 187). In addition to Frantz Fanon, C. L. R. James, Aimé Césaire, Amilcar Cabral, Ngugi wa Thiongo, and Albert Memmi, whom Sharpe cites, we might include here, for example, Haunani-Kay Trask as an immediate intellectual antecedent of an Asian Americanist postcolonial critique. Interpreted through this postcolonial lens and contextualized by the history of anti-Filipino racism, the difficult representational effects of the novel surface sharply.
53 It is important to recognize that the forms of the award and the resolution to rescind the award to some extent made it impossible as a structural matter to attend to all of the complexities of the novel and the issues involved. Clearly, my own discussion is enabled by the luxury of a retrospective consideration.
54 See also Gopinath (1996) on the relationship among "queer," heteronormativity, and nation-building.

conclusion: when difference meets itself

1 As Sau-ling Wong among others has pointed out, it is inaccurate to suggest that Asian American studies has been disinterested or has in fact not been involved in investigating national-global relations and their implications for "Asian American" identity (1995). See also Leong (1996, 2001). Lisa Lowe's generative and oft-cited essay, "Heterogeneity, Hybridity, Multiplicity," first published in 1991 and forming a chapter in her 1996 book, stands as a particularly important hallmark in Asian Americanist theorizing on such critical interests. Likewise, Gary Okihiro's *Margins and Mainstreams: Asians in American History and Culture* (1994), "positing a global dimension to Asian American history from the Orientalism of the ancient Greeks to European imperialism and the world-system, from America to Asia, from the Pacific to the Indian and Atlantic oceans, from California to the Caribbean and American South" (xv), stands in this regard.

2 See Espiritu (1992, 1996b) and Lowe (1996). Karin Aguilar-San Juan offers an insightful discussion of identity in relation to authenticity and related problematics. See Aguilar-San Juan (1998).
3 As Diane Elam has noted, "the political subject is that which remains identical to itself," and, as well, to all other political subjects participating in or claiming a common political identity (1994, 71).

works cited

Adarand v. Pena, 515 U.S. 200 (1995).
Aguilar-San Juan, Karen, ed. 1994. *The State of Asian America: Activism and Resistance in the 1990s.* Boston: South End Press.
———. 1998. "Going Home: Enacting Justice in Queer Asian America." In *Q&A: Queer in Asian America*, ed. David Eng and Alice Hom. Philadelphia: Temple University Press.
Alexander, M. Jacqui, and Chandra Talpade Mohanty, eds. 1997. *Feminist Genealogies, Colonial Legacies, Democratic Futures.* New York: Routledge.
Almaguer, Tomas. 1994. *Racial Faultlines: The Historical Origins of White Supremacy in California.* Berkeley: University of California Press.
Alquizola, Marilyn. 1989. "The Fictive Narrator of *America Is in the Heart*." In *Frontiers of Asian American Studies: Writing, Research, and Commentary*, ed. Gail Nomura et al. Pullman, WA: Washington State University Press.
———. 1991. "Subversion of Affirmation: The Text and Subtext of *America Is in the Heart*." In *Asian Americans: Comparative and Global Perspectives*, ed. Shirley Hune, Stephen Fujita, and Amy Ling. Pullman, WA: Washington State University Press.
Althusser, Louis. 1971. "Ideology and Ideological State Apparatuses (Notes toward an Investigation)." In *Lenin and Philosophy and Other Essays*, trans. Ben Brewster. New York: Monthly Review Press.
Ancheta, Angelo N. 1998. *Race, Rights, and the Asian American Experience.* New Brunswick, NJ: Rutgers University Press.
Anderson, Benedict. 1991. *Imagined Communities: Reflections on the Origin and Spread of Nationalism.* Rev. ed. London: Verso.
———. 1994. "Exodus." *Critical Inquiry* 20: 314–327.
———. 1995. "Cacique Democracy in the Philippines: Origins and Dreams." In *Discrepant Histories: Translocal Essays on Filipino Cultures*, ed. Vicente Rafael. Philadelphia: Temple University Press.
Anzaldua, Gloria. 1987. *Borderlands/La Frontera: The New Mestiza.* San Francisco: Aunt Lute Book Co.
Aoki, Keith. 1996. "Intellectual Property and Sovereignty: Notes toward a Cultural Geography of Authorship." *Stanford Law Review* 48, no. 5: 1293–1355.
———. 1998a. "Considering Multiple and Overlapping Sovereignties: Liberalism, Libertarianism, National Sovereignty, 'Global' Intellectual Property, and the Internet." *Indiana Journal of Global Legal Studies* 5, no. 2: 443–473.

———. 1998b. "Neocolonialism, Anticommons Property, and Biopiracy in the (Not-So-Brave) New World Order of International Intellectual Property Protection." *Indiana Journal of Global Legal Studies* 6, no. 1: 11–58.

Appadurai, Arjun. 1993. "Patriotism and Its Futures." *Public Culture* 5, no. 3: 411–429.

———. 1996. *Modernity at Large: Cultural Dimensions of Globalization*. Minneapolis: University of Minnesota Press.

———. 1998. "Dead Certainty: Ethnic Violence in the Era of Globalization." *Public Culture* 10, no. 2: 225–247.

Appiah, Kwame Anthony. 1997. "Is the 'Post-' in 'Postcolonial' the 'Post-' in 'Postmodern'?" In *Dangerous Liaisons: Gender, Nation, and Postcolonial Perspectives*, ed. Anne McClintock, Aamir Mufti, and Ella Shohat. Minneapolis: University of Minnesota Press.

Balaz, Joseph P. 1984. "Moeʻuhane." In *Hoʻiʻhoʻihou: A Tribute to George Helm and Kimo Mitchell*, ed. Rodney Morales. Honolulu: Bamboo Ridge Press.

Balce-Cortes, Nerissa. 1995. "Imagining the Neocolony." *Critical Mass* 2, no. 2: 95–120.

Balibar, Etienne, and Immanuel Wallerstein. 1992. *Race, Nation, Class: Ambiguous Identities*. London: Verso.

Barlow, Tani. 2000. "Spheres of Debt and Feminist Ghosts in Area Studies of Women in China." *Traces: A Multilingual Journal of Translation and Theory* 1, 195–226.

Bederman, Gail. 1995. *Manliness and Civilization: A Cultural History of Gender and Race in the United States, 1880–1917*. Chicago: University of Chicago Press.

Bell, Derrick. 1995. "Brown v. Board of Education and the Interest Convergence Dilemma." In *Critical Race Theory: The Key Writings that Formed the Movement*, ed. Kimberle Crenshaw, Neil Gotanda, Gary Peller, and Kendall Thomas. New York: New Press.

Berlant, Lauren. 1991. *The Anatomy of National Fantasy: Hawthorne, Utopia, and Everyday Life*. Chicago: University of Chicago Press.

———. 1993. "The Theory of Infantile Citizenship." *Public Culture* 5, no. 3: 395–410.

Bhabha, Homi K., ed. 1990. *Nation and Narration*. London: Routledge.

———. 1994. *The Location of Culture*. New York: Routledge.

Brewer, Sarah E., David Kaib, and Karen O'Connor. 2000. "Sex and the Supreme Court: Gays, Lesbians, and Justice." In *The Politics of Gay Rights*, ed. Craig A. Rimmerman, Kenneth D. Wald, and Clyde Wilcox. Chicago: University of Chicago Press.

Buck, Elizabeth. 1993. *Paradise Remade: The Politics of Culture and History in Hawaiʻi*. Philadelphia: Temple University Press.

Bulosan, Carlos. 1988 [1943]. *America Is in the Heart*. Seattle: University of Washington Press.

Butler, Judith. 1990. *Gender Trouble: Feminism and the Subversion of Identity*. New York: Routledge.

———. 1993. *Bodies That Matter: On the Discursive Limits of "Sex."* New York: Routledge.

Campomanes, Oscar V. 1992. "Filipinos in the United States and Their Literature of Exile." In *Reading the Literatures of Asian America*, ed. Shirley Geok-lin Lim and Amy Ling. Philadelphia: Temple University Press.

———. 1995. "Afterword: The Empire's Forgetful and Forgotten Citizens: Unrepresentability and Unassimilability in Filipino-American Postcolonialities." *Critical Mass* 2, no. 2: 145–200.

———. 1997. "New Formations of Asian American Studies and the Question of U.S. Imperialism." *positions: east asia cultures critique* 5, no. 2: 523–550.

Cha, Theresa Hak Kyung. 1995 [1982]. *Dictée*. Berkeley: Third Woman Press.

Chakrabarty, Dipesh. 1997a. "Postcoloniality and the Artifice of History: Who Speaks for 'Indian' Pasts?" In *A Subaltern Studies Reader, 1986–1995*, ed. Ranajit Guha. Minneapolis: University of Minnesota Press.

———. 1997b. "The Time of History and the Times of Gods." In *The Politics of Culture in the Shadow of Late Capital*, ed. Lisa Lowe and David Lloyd. Durham, NC: Duke University Press.

———. 1998. "Reconstructing Liberalism? Notes toward a Conversation between Area Studies and Diasporic Studies." *Public Culture* 10, no. 3: 457–481.

Chan, Jeffrey Paul, Frank Chin, Lawson Inada, and Shawn Wong. 1991 [1974]. *Aiiieeeee! An Anthology of Asian American Writers*. New York: Penguin Books.

Chan, Sucheng. 1990. "Introduction." In *Quiet Odyssey: A Pioneer Korean Woman in America*, by Mary Paik Lee. Seattle: University of Washington Press.

———. 1991. *Asian Americans: An Interpretive History*. Boston: Twayne.

Chandra, Bipan. 1980. "Colonialism, Stages of Colonialism and the Colonial State." *Journal of Contemporary Asia* 10, no. 3: 272–285.

Chang, Jeff. 1996. "Local Knowledge(s): Notes on Race Relations, Panethnicity and History in Hawai'i." *Amerasia Journal* 22, no. 2: 1–29.

Chang, Robert S. 1993. "Toward an Asian American Legal Scholarship: Critical Race Theory, Post-Structuralism, and Narrative Space." *California Law Review* 81, 1241.

Chang, Robert S., and Keith Aoki. 1998. "Centering the Immigrant in the Inter/National Imagination." *La Raza Law Journal* 10, no. 1: 309–361.

Charlot, John. 1983. *Chanting the Universe: Hawaiian Religious Culture*. Hong Kong: Emphasis International.

Chatterjee, Partha. 1993a. *The Nation and Its Fragments: Colonial and Postcolonial Histories*. Princeton: Princeton University Press.

———. 1993b. *Nationalist Thought and the Colonial World: A Derivative Discourse?* Minneapolis: University of Minnesota Press.

Cheah, Pheng. 2000. "Universal Areas: Asian Studies in a World in Motion." *Traces: A Multilingual Journal of Theory and Translation* 1, 37–70.

Cheng, Lucie, and Edna Bonacich, eds. 1984. *Labor Immigration under Capitalism: Asian Workers in the United States before World War II.* Berkeley: University of California Press.

Cherniavsky, Eva. 1996. "Subaltern Studies in a U.S. Frame." *boundary 2* 2, no. 23: 85–110.

Cherokee Nation v. Georgia, 30 U.S. 1 (1831).

Cheung, King-kok. 1990. "The Woman Warrior versus the Chinaman Pacific: Must a Chinese American Critic Choose between Feminism and Heroism?" In *Conflicts in Feminism*, ed. Marianne Hirsch and Evelyn Fox Keller. New York: Routledge.

———. 1993. *Articulate Silences: Hisaye Yamamoto, Maxine Hong Kingston, Joy Kogawa.* Ithaca: Cornell University Press.

Chicago Cultural Studies Group. 1992. "Critical Multiculturalism." *Critical Inquiry* 18 (spring): 530–555.

Chin, Frank. 1991. "Come All Ye Asian American Writers of the Real and the Fake." In *The Big Aiiieeeee! An Anthology of Chinese American and Japanese American Literature*, ed. Jeffrey Paul Chan, Frank Chin, Lawson Fusao Inada, and Shawn Wong. New York: Meridian.

Choi, Chungmoo. 1993. "The Discourse of Decolonization and Popular Memory: South Korea." *positions: east asia cultures critique* 1, no. 1: 77–102.

Chow, Rey. 1993. *Writing Diaspora: Tactics of Intervention in Contemporary Cultural Studies.* Bloomington, IN: Indiana University Press.

———. 1995. *Primitive Passions: Visuality, Sexuality, Ethnography, and Contemporary Chinese Cinema.* New York: Columbia University Press.

———. 1998a. *Ethics After Idealism: Theory-Culture-Ethnicity-Reading.* Bloomington, IN: Indiana University Press.

———. 1998b. "Introduction: On Chineseness as a Theoretical Problem." *boundary 2* 25, no. 3: 1–24.

———. 2001. "Leading Questions." In *Orientations: Mapping Studies in the Asian Diaspora*, ed. Kandice Chuh and Karen Shimakawa. Durham, NC: Duke University Press.

Christian, Barbara. 1990. "The Race for Theory." In *The Nature and Context of Minority Discourse*, ed. Abdul R. JanMohamed and David Lloyd. London: Oxford University Press.

Chuh, Kandice and Karen Shimakawa, eds. 2001. *Orientations: Mapping Studies in the Asian Diaspora.* Durham, NC: Duke University Press.

Chung, Chin-sung. 1995. "An Overview of the Colonial and Socio-economic Background of Japanese Military Sex Slavery in Korea." *muae* 1: 204–215.

Clifford, James. 1992. "Traveling Cultures." In *Cultural Studies*, ed. Lawrence Grossberg, Cary Nelson, and Paula Treichler. New York: Routledge.

Connery, Christopher. 1995. "Pacific Rim Discourse: The U.S. Global Imaginary in the Late Cold War Years." In *Asia/Pacific as Space of Cultural Production*, ed. Rob Wilson and Arif Dirlik. Durham, NC: Duke University Press.

Constantino, Renato. 1975. *A History of the Philippines: From the Spanish Colonization to the Second World War*. New York: Monthly Review Press.

"Constructing the State Extraterritorially: Jurisdictional Discourse, the National Interest and the Transnational Norms." *Harvard Law Review* 103: 1273 (1990) [Note].

Coombe, Rosemary J. 1995. "The Cultural Life of Things: Anthropological Approaches to Law and Society in Conditions of Globalization." *American University Journal of International Law and Policy* 10, no. 2: 791–835.

Cooper, George and Gavan Daws. 1985. *Land and Power in Hawaii*. Honolulu: Benchmark Books.

Cordova, Fred. 1983. *Filipinos: Forgotten Asian Americans*. Seattle: Demonstration Project for Asian Americans.

Cornell, Drucilla. 1991. *Beyond Accommodation: Ethical Feminism, Deconstruction, and the Law*. New York: Routledge.

———. 1995. "What Is Ethical Feminism?" In *Feminist Contentions: A Philosophical Exchange*. New York: Routledge.

Crenshaw, Kimberle. 1995. "Mapping the Margins: Intersectionality, Identity Politics, and Violence Against Women of Color." In *Critical Race Theory: The Key Writings That Formed the Movement*, ed. Kimberle Crenshaw, Neil Gotanda, Gary Peller, and Kendall Thomas. New York: New Press.

Crenshaw, Kimberle, Neil Gotanda, Gary Peller, and Kendall Thomas, eds. 1995. *Critical Race Theory: The Key Writings That Formed the Movement*. New York: New Press.

Culler, Jonathan. 1982. *On Deconstruction: Theory and Criticism after Structuralism*. Ithaca: Cornell University Press.

———. 2000. "The Literary in Theory." In *What's Left of Theory? New Work on the Politics of Literary Theory*, ed. Judith Butler, John Guillory, and Kendall Thomas. New York: Routledge.

Cumings, Bruce. 1981. *The Origins of the Korean War: Liberation and the Emergence of Separate Regimes*. Princeton: Princeton University Press.

———. 1999a. "The End of History or the Return of Liberal Crisis?" *Current History* 98, no. 624: 9–16.

———. 1999b. *Parallax Visions: Making Sense of American-East Asian Relations at the End of the Century*. Durham, NC: Duke University Press.

———. 1999c. "Toward a Comprehensive Settlement of the Korea Problem." *Current History* 98, no. 632: 403.

Daniels, Roger. 1976. "American Historians and East Asian Immigrants." In *The Asian American*, ed. Norris Hundley, Jr. Santa Barbara, CA: CLIO Press.
Davé, Shilpa, Pawan Dhingra, et al. 2000. "De-Privileging Positions: Indian Americans, South Asian Americans, and the Politics of Asian American Studies." *Journal of Asian American Studies* 3, no. 1: 67–100.
de Certeau, Michel. 1984. *The Practice of Everyday Life*, trans. Steven Rendall. Berkeley: University of California Press.
Delgado, Richard. 1995. "The Imperial Scholar: Reflections on a Review of Civil Rights Literature." In *Critical Race Theory: The Key Writings That Formed the Movement*, ed. Kimberle Crenshaw, Neil Gotanda, Gary Peller, and Kendall Thomas. New York: New Press.
Delmendo, Sharon. 1998. "The American Factor in Jose Rizal's Nationalism." *Amerasia Journal* 24, no. 2: 35–63.
de Man, Paul. 1983. *Blindness and Insight: Essays in the Rhetoric of Contemporary Criticism*. Minneapolis: University of Minnesota Press.
———. 1996. *Aesthetic Ideology*. Minneapolis: University of Minnesota Press.
Dening, Greg. 1989. "History 'in' the Pacific." *Contemporary Pacific: A Journal of Island Affairs* 1, nos. 1–2: 134–140.
Derrida, 1987. "Deconstruction in America." An interview with James Creech, Peggy Kamuf, and Jane Todd. Trans. James Creech. *Critical Exchange* no. 17 (winter): 1–33.
———. 1988a. "Letter to a Japanese Friend," trans. Andrew Benjamin. In *Derrida and Différance*, ed. David Wood and Robert Bernasconi. Evanston, IL: Northwestern University Press.
———. 1988b. *Limited, Inc*. Evanston, IL: Northwestern University Press.
———. 1992. "Force of Law: The 'Mystical Foundation of Authority.'" In *Deconstruction and the Possibility of Justice*, ed. Drucilla Cornell, Michael Rosenfeld, and David Gray Carlson. New York: Routledge.
———. 1997 [1967]. ". . . That Dangerous Supplement . . ." In *Of Grammatology*, trans. Gayatri Chakravorty Spivak. Baltimore: Johns Hopkins University Press.
Diamond, Irene, and Lee Quinby, eds. 1988. *Feminism and Foucault: Reflections on Resistance*. Boston: Northeastern University Press.
Dirlik, Arif. 1992. "The Postcolonial Aura: Third World Criticism in the Age of Global Capitalism." *Critical Inquiry* 20, no. 2: 328–356.
———. 1993. "Asia-Pacific in Asian-American Perspective." In *What Is in a Rim? Critical Perspectives on the Pacific Region Idea*, ed. Arif Dirlik. Boulder, CO: Westview Press.
———. 1996. "Asians on the Rim: Transnational Capital and Local Community in the Making of Contemporary Asian America." *Amerasia Journal* 22, no. 3: 1–24.
Duus, Peter. 1995. *The Abacus and the Sword*. Berkeley: University of California Press.

Eisenstein, Zillah. 1988. *The Female Body and the Law*. Berkeley: University of California Press.
——. 1994. *The Color of Gender: Reimaging Democracy*. Berkeley: University of California Press.
——. 1998. *Global Obscenities: Patriarchy, Capitalism, and the Lure of Cyberfantasy*. New York: New York University Press.
Elam, Diane. 1994. *Feminism and Deconstruction: Ms. en abyme*. New York: Routledge.
Elkins, David J. 1995. *Beyond Sovereignty: Territory and Political Economy in the Twenty-First Century*. Toronto: University of Toronto Press.
Eng, David L. 1997. "Out Here and Over There: Queerness and Diaspora in Asian American Studies." *Social Text* 15, no. 3: 31–52.
——. 1998. "Heterosexuality in the Face of Whiteness: Divided Belief in M. Butterfly." In *Q&A: Queer in Asian America*, ed. David Eng and Alice Hom. Philadelphia: Temple University Press.
Eng, David L., and Alice Y. Hom, eds. 1998. *Q&A: Queer in Asian America*. Philadelphia: Temple University Press.
Espiritu, Yen Le. 1992. *Asian American Panethnicity: Bridging Institutions and Identities*. Philadelphia: Temple University Press.
——. 1996a. *Asian American Women and Men: Labor, Laws, and Love*. Thousand Oaks, CA: Sage Press.
——. 1996b. "Crossroads and Possibilities: Asian Americans on the Eve of the Twenty-First Century." *Amerasia Journal* 22, no. 2: vii–xii.
Evangelista, Susan. 1993. "Jessica Hagedorn and Manila Magic." *MELUS* 18, no. 4: 41–52.
Fanon, Frantz. 1968. *The Wretched of the Earth*. New York: Grove Press.
Featherstone, Mike, ed. 1990. *Global Culture: Nationalism, Globalization, and Modernity*. London: Sage.
Ferguson, Robert A. 1984. *Law and Letters in American Culture*. Cambridge, MA: Harvard University Press.
Fineman, Martha, and Nancy Thomadsen, eds. 1991. *At the Boundaries of Law: Feminism and Legal Theory*. New York: Routledge.
Foucault, Michel. 1990 [1978]. *The History of Sexuality*, Vol. 1. New York: Vintage Books.
——. 1994 [1967]. "Different Spaces." In *Aesthetics, Method, and Epistemology*, Vol. 2, ed. James D. Faubion, trans. Robert Hurley et al. New York: New Press.
——. 1994 [1984]. "The Ethics of the Concern of the Self as a Practice of Freedom." In *Michel Foucault: Ethics, Subjectivity and Truth*, ed. Paul Rabinow. New York: New Press.
Frankenburg, Ruth. 1993. *The Social Construction of Whiteness: White Women, Race Matters*. Minneapolis: University of Minnesota Press.

Frankenburg, Ruth, and Lata Mani. 1993. "Crosscurrents, Crosstalk: Race, 'Postcoloniality' and the Politics of Location." *Cultural Studies* 7, no. 2: 292–310.

Freeman, Alan David. 1995. "Legitimizing Racial Discrimination through Antidiscrimination Law: A Critical Review of Supreme Court Doctrine." In *Critical Race Theory: The Key Writings That Formed the Movement*, ed. Kimberle Crenshaw, Neil Gotanda, Gary Peller, and Kendall Thomas. New York: New Press.

Frug, Mary Joe. 1992. *Postmodern Legal Feminism*. New York: Routledge.

Fujikane, Candace. 1994. "Between Nationalisms: Hawai'i's Local Nation and Its Troubled Racial Paradise." *Critical Mass: A Journal of Asian American Cultural Criticism* 1, no. 2: 23–57.

———. 2000. "Sweeping Racism under the Rug of 'Censorship': The Controversy over Lois-Ann Yamanaka's Blu's Hanging." *Amerasia Journal* 26, no. 2: 158–194.

Goellnicht, Donald C. 1997. "Blurring Boundaries: Asian American Literature as Theory." In *An Interethnic Companion to Asian American Literature*, ed. King-Kok Cheung. Cambridge, UK: Cambridge University Press.

Gonzalez, N. V. M., and Oscar Campomanes. 1997. "Filipino American Literature." In *An Interethnic Companion to Asian American Literature*, ed. King-kok Cheung. Cambridge, UK: Cambridge University Press.

Gonzalves, Theo. 1995/1996. "'We hold a neatly folded hope': Filipino Veterans of World War II on Citizenship and Political Obligation." *Amerasia Journal* 21, no. 3: 155–174.

Gooding-Williams, Robert, ed. 1993. *Reading Rodney King/Reading Urban Uprising*. New York: Routledge.

Gopinath, Gayatri. 1996. "Funny Boys and Girls: Notes on a Queer South Asian Planet." In *Asian American Sexualities: Dimensions of the Gay and Lesbian Experience*, ed. Russell Leong. New York: Routledge.

Gordon, Avery. 1997. *Ghostly Matters: Haunting and the Sociological Imagination*. Minneapolis: University of Minnesota Press.

Gotanda, Neil. 1995. "A Critique of 'Our Constitution Is Color-Blind.'" In *Critical Race Theory: The Key Writings That Formed the Movement*, ed. Kimberle Crenshaw, Neil Gotanda, Gary Peller, and Kendall Thomas. New York: New Press.

———. 1997. "Race, Citizenship, and the Search for Political Community Among 'We the People.'" *Oregon Law Review* 76: 233.

———. 1999. "Citizenship Nullification: The Impossibility of Asian American Politics." Lecture delivered at the University of Maryland, College Park, 8 December.

Graff, Gerald. 1987. *Professing Literature*. Chicago: University of Chicago Press.

Grewal, Inderpal. 1994. "The 'Postcolonial,' Ethnic Studies, and the Diaspora: The Contexts of Ethnic Immigrant/Migrant Cultural Studies in the U.S." *Socialist Review* 24, no. 4: 45–74.

Grewal, Inderpal, and Caren Kaplan, eds. 1994. *Scattered Hegemonies: Postmodernity and Transnational Feminist Practices.* Minneapolis: University of Minnesota Press.

Guha, Ranajit. 1989. "Dominance without Hegemony and Its Historiography." In *Subaltern Studies 6,* ed. Ranajit Guha. Delhi: Oxford University Press.

Gutierrez-Jones, Carl. 1995. *Rethinking the Borderlands: Between Chicano Culture and Legal Discourse.* Berkeley: University of California Press.

Hagedorn, Jessica. 1990. *Dogeaters.* New York: Penguin Books.

Hall, Robert B. 1947. *Area Studies: With Special Reference to Their Implications for Research in the Social Sciences.* Social Sciences Research Council Pamphlet no. 3. New York: Social Sciences Research Council.

Hall, Stuart. 1990. "Cultural Identity and Diaspora." In *Identity: Community, Culture, Difference,* ed. Jonathan Rutherford. London: Lawrence and Wishart.

———. 1992. "Cultural Studies and Its Theoretical Legacies." In *Cultural Studies,* ed. Lawrence Grossberg, Cary Nelson, and Paula Treichler. New York: Routledge.

———. 1996. "When Was 'The Post-Colonial'? Thinking at the Limit." In *The Postcolonial Question: Common Skies, Divided Horizons,* ed. Iain Chambers and Lidia Curti. London: Routledge.

———. 1997. "Subjects in History: Making Diasporic Identities." In *The House That Race Built,* ed. Wahneema Lubiano. New York: Vintage Books.

Halperin, David. 1990. *One Hundred Years of Homosexuality.* New York: Routledge.

Hamamoto, Darrell Y. 1994. *Monitored Peril: Asian Americans and the Politics of TV Representation.* Minneapolis: University of Minnesota Press.

Hamamoto, Darrell Y., and Sandra Liu, eds. 2000. *Countervisions: Asian American Film Criticism.* Philadelphia: Temple University Press.

Harris, Cheryl. 1995. "Whiteness as Property." In *Critical Race Theory: The Key Writings That Formed the Movement,* ed. Kimberle Crenshaw, Neil Gotanda, Gary Peller, and Kendall Thomas. New York: New Press.

Hart, H. L. A. 1961. *The Concept of Law.* Oxford: Oxford University Press.

Harvey, David. 1989. *The Condition of Postmodernity: An Enquiry into the Origins of Cultural Change.* Cambridge, UK: Blackwell.

Hing, Bill Ong. 1993. *Making and Remaking Asian America Through Immigration Policy, 1850–1990.* Stanford: Stanford University Press.

Hirabayashi v. United States, 320 U.S. 81 (1943).

Hirabayashi, Lane Ryo, and Marilyn Alquizola. 1994. "Asian American Studies: Reevaluating for the 1990s." In *The State of Asian America: Activism and Resistance in the 1990s,* ed. Karin Aguilar-San Juan. Boston: South End Press.

Hobsbawm, Eric. 1990. *Nations and Nationalism Since 1780.* Cambridge, UK: Cambridge University Press.

Hobsbawm, Eric, and Terence Ranger, eds. 1983. *The Invention of Tradition.* Cambridge, UK: Cambridge University Press.

hooks, bell. 1997. "Sisterhood: Political Solidarity between Women." In *Dangerous Liaisons: Gender, Nation, and Postcolonial Perspectives*, ed. Anne McClintock, Aamir Mufti, and Ella Shohat. Minneapolis: University of Minnesota Press.

Hsu, Ruth. 1996. "Will the Model Minority Please Identify Itself? American Ethnic Identity and Its Discontents." *Diaspora: A Journal of Transnational Studies* 5, no. 1: 37–64.

Hune, Shirley. 1995. "Rethinking Race: Paradigms and Policy Formation." *Amerasia Journal* 21, nos. 1 and 2: 29–40.

Hyde, Alan. 1997. *Bodies of Law*. Princeton: Princeton University Press.

Igarashi, Yoshikuni. 1998. "The Bomb, Hirohito, and History: The Foundational Narrative of United States–Japan Postwar Relations." *positions: east asia cultures critique* 6, no. 2: 261–302.

Ileto, Reynaldo C. 1997. "Outlines of a Nonlinear Emplotment of Philippine History." In *The Politics of Culture in the Shadow of Late Capital*, ed. Lisa Lowe and David Lloyd. Durham, NC: Duke University Press.

Inada, Lawson Fusao. 1989. "From Live Do." In *Frontiers of Asian American Studies*, ed. Gail Nomura, Russell Endo, Stephen Sumida, and Russell Leong. Pullman, WA: Washington State University Press.

In re Ah Yup, 1 F. Cas. 223 (D. Cal. 1878).

In re Alverto, 198 Fed. 688 (E.D. Pa. 1912).

In re Bautista, 245 Fed. 765 (N.D. Cal. 1878).

In re Buntaro Kumagai, 163 F. 922 (D.C. 1908).

In re Kanaka Nian, 21 Pac. 993 (1889).

In re Knight, 171 F. 299 (D.C. 1909).

In re Rallos, 241 Fed. 686 (E.D. N.Y. 1917).

In re Saito, 62 F. 126 (D. Mass. 1894).

Irons, Peter. 1983. *Justice at War: The Story of the Japanese American Internment Cases*. New York: Oxford University Press.

———, ed. 1989. *Justice Delayed: The Record of the Japanese American Internment Cases*. New York: Oxford University Press.

Ivy, Marilyn. 1995. *Discourses of the Vanishing: Modernity, Phantasm, Japan*. Chicago: University of Chicago Press.

Jameson, Fredric. 1994. *Postmodernism, or the Cultural Logic of Late Capitalism*. Durham, NC: Duke University Press.

Jeffords, Susan. 1989. *The Remasculinization of America: Gender and the Vietnam War*. Bloomington, IN: Indiana University Press.

———. 1997. "Masculinity as Excess in Vietnam Films: The Father/Son Dynamic of American Culture." In *Feminisms: An Anthology of Literary Theory and Criticism*, ed. Robyn R. Warhol and Diane Price Herndl. New Brunswick, NJ: Rutgers University Press.

Johnson, Kevin R. 1997. "Racial Hierarchy, Asian Americans and Latinos as 'Foreigners,' and Social Change: Is Law the Way to Go?" *Oregon Law Review* 76: 347.

Jun, Helen Heran. 1997. "Contingent Nationalisms: Renegotiating Borders in Korean and Korean American Women's Oppositional Struggles." *positions: east asia cultures critique* 5, no. 2: 325–356.

Kamahele, Momiala. 2000. "'Īlio'ulaokalani: Defending Native Hawaiian Culture." *Amerasia Journal* 26, no. 2: 38–65.

Kang, Laura Hyun Yi. 1997. "Si(gh)ting Asian/American Women as Transnational Labor." *positions: east asia cultures critique* 5, no. 2: 403–438.

———. 2002. *Compositional Subjects: Enfiguring Asian/American Women*. Durham, NC: Duke University Press.

Kang, Nae-hui. 2000. "Mimicry and Difference: A Spectralogy for the Neocolonial Intellectual." *Traces: A Multilingual Journal of Theory and Translation* 1, 123–158.

Kaplan, Amy. 1990. "Romancing the Empire: The Embodiment of American Masculinity in the Popular Historical Novel of the 1850s." *American Literary History* 2, no. 4: 659–690.

———. 1993. "'Left Alone with America': The Absence of Empire in the Study of American Culture." In *The Cultures of United States Imperialism*, ed. Amy Kaplan and Donald Pease. Durham, NC: Duke University Press.

———. 1999. "The Birth of an Empire." *PMLA* 114, no. 5: 1068–1076.

Kaplan, Amy, and Donald Pease, eds. 1993. *The Cultures of United States Imperialism*. Durham, NC: Duke University Press.

Kaplan, Caren. 1996. *Questions of Travel: Postmodern Discourses of Displacement*. Durham, NC: Duke University Press.

Kaplan, Caren, Norma Alarcón, and Minoo Moallem, eds 1999. *Between Woman and Nation: Nationalisms, Transnational Feminisms, and the State*. Durham, NC: Duke University Press.

Kaplan, Caren, and Inderpal Grewal. 1999. "Transnational Feminist Cultural Studies: Beyond the Marxism/Poststructuralism/Feminism Divides." In *Between Woman and Nation: Nationalisms, Transnational Feminisms, and the State*, ed. Caren Kaplan, Norma Alarcón, and Minoo Moallem. Durham, NC: Duke University Press.

Karnow, Stanley. 1989. *In Our Image: America's Empire in the Philippines*. New York: Random Books.

Katrak, Ketu. 1996. "South Asian American Writers: Geography and Memory." *Amerasia Journal* 22, no. 3: 121–138.

Katsch, M. Ethan. 1995. *Law in a Digital World*. London: Oxford University Press.

Kelley, Mary. 2000. "Taking Stands: American Studies at Century's End/Presidential Address to the American Studies Association, October 29, 1999." *American Quarterly* 52, no. 1: 1–22.

Kim, Elaine H. 1982. *Asian American Literature: An Introduction to the Writings and Their Social Context*. Philadelphia: Temple University Press.

———. 1990. " 'Such Opposite Creatures': Men and Women in Asian American Literature." *Michigan Quarterly Review* 29: 68–93.

———. 1997. "Korean Americans in U.S. Race Relations: Some Considerations." *Amerasia Journal* 23, no. 2: 69–78.

Kim, Elaine H., and Lisa Lowe. 1997. "Guest Editors' Introduction." *positions: east asia cultures critique* 5, no. 2: v–xiv.

Kim, Min-Jung. 1997. "Moments of Danger in the (Dis)continuous Relation of Korean Nationalism and Korean American Nationalism." *positions: east asia cultures critique* 5, no. 2: 357–389.

Kim, Ronyoung. 1987. *Clay Walls*. Seattle: University of Washington Press.

Kim-Gibson, Dai Sil. 1999. *Silence Broken: Korean Comfort Women*. Parkersburg, IA: Mid-Prairie Books.

Kondo, Dorinne. 1997. *About Face: Performing Race in Fashion and Theatre*. New York: Routledge.

———. 2001. "(Un)Disciplined Subjects: (De)Colonizing the Academy?" In *Orientations: Mapping Studies in the Asian Diaspora*, ed. Kandice Chuh and Karen Shimakawa. Durham, NC: Duke University Press. 25–40.

Korematsu v. United States, 323 U.S. 214 (1944).

Koshy, Susan. 1996. "The Fiction of Asian American Literature." *Yale Journal of Criticism* 9, no. 2: 315–346.

———. 1998. "Category Crisis: South Asian Americans and Questions of Race and Ethnicity." *Diaspora* 7, no. 3: 285–320.

———. 1999. "From Cold War to Trade War: Neocolonialism and Human Rights." *Social Text* 17, no. 1: 1–32.

Laclau, Ernesto, and Chantal Mouffe. 1985. *Hegemony and Socialist Strategy: Towards a Radical Democracy*. London: Verso.

Lash, Scott, and John Urry. 1987. *The End of Organized Capitalism*. Madison, WI: University of Wisconsin Press.

———. 1994. *Economies of Signs and Space*. London: Sage.

Lauter, Paul. 1991. *Canons and Contexts*. New York: Oxford University Press.

Lavie, Smadar, and Ted Swedenburg, eds. 1996. *Displacement, Diaspora, and Geographies of Identity*. Durham, NC: Duke University Press.

Lee, Benjamin. 1998. "Peoples and Publics." *Public Culture* 10, no. 2: 371–394.

Lee, Chang-rae. 1999. *A Gesture Life*. New York: Riverhead Books.

Lee, Jayne Chong-Soon. 1995. "Navigating the Topology of Race." In *Critical Race Theory: The Key Writings That Formed the Movement*, ed. Kimberle Crenshaw, Neil Gotanda, Gary Peller, and Kendall Thomas. New York: New Press.

Lee, Robert G. 1999. *Orientals: Asian Americans in Popular Culture.* Philadelphia: Temple University Press.

Leon W., M. Consuelo. 1995. "Foundations of the American Image of the Pacific." In *Asia / Pacific as Space of Cultural Production,* ed. Rob Wilson and Arif Dirlik. Durham, NC: Duke University Press.

Leonard, Jerry D., ed. 1995. *Legal Studies as Cultural Studies: A Reader in (post)Modern Critical Theory.* Albany: State University of New York Press.

Leong, Russell. 1995. "Lived Theory (notes on the run)." *Amerasia Journal* 21, nos. 1 and 2: v–x.

———, ed. 1996. *Asian American Sexualities: Dimensions of the Gay and Lesbian Experience.* New York: Routledge.

———. 1998. "Beyond 'the lahar of colonizations': Filipino American Studies at UCLA." *Amerasia Journal* 24, no. 2: v–vii.

———. 2001. "Creating Performative Communities: Through Text, Time, and Space." In *Orientations: Mapping Studies in the Asian Diaspora,* ed. Kandice Chuh and Karen Shimakawa. Durham, NC: Duke University Press.

Lim, Shirley Geok-lin. 1992. "The Ambivalent American." In *Reading the Literatures of Asian America,* ed. Shirley Geok-lin Lim and Amy Ling. Philadelphia: Temple University Press.

———. 1993a. "Assaying the Gold: Or, Contesting the Ground of Asian American Literature." *New Literary History* 24: 147–169.

———. 1993b. "Feminist and Ethnic Literary Theories in Asian American Literature." *Feminist Studies* 19, no. 3: 571–595.

———. 1997. "Immigration and Diaspora." In *An Interethnic Companion to Asian American Literature,* ed. King-Kok Cheung. Cambridge, UK: Cambridge University Press.

Lim, Shirley Geok-lin, Larry E. Smith, and Wimal Dissanayake, eds. 1999. *Transnational Asia Pacific: Gender, Culture, and the Public Sphere.* Urbana, IL: University of Illinois Press.

Ling, Jinqui. 1997. "Identity Crisis and Gender Politics: Reappropriating Asian American Masculinity." In *An Interethnic Companion to Asian American Literature,* ed. King-Kok Cheung. Cambridge, UK: Cambridge University.

Lipsitz, George. 1997. "'Frantic to Join . . . the Japanese Army': The Asia Pacific War in the Lives of African American Soldiers and Civilians." In *The Politics of Culture in the Shadow of Late Capital,* ed. Lisa Lowe and David Lloyd. Durham, NC: Duke University Press.

———. 1998. *The Possessive Investment in Whiteness: How White People Profit from Identity Politics.* Philadelphia: Temple University Press.

———. 2001. "To Tell the Truth and Not Get Trapped: Why Inter-Ethnic Anti-Racism Matters Now." In *Orientations: Mapping Studies of the Asian Diaspora,* ed. Kandice Chuh and Karen Shimakawa. Durham, NC: Duke University Press.

Liu, Lydia. 1994. "The Female Body and Nationalist Discourse: *The Field of Life and Death* Revisited." In *Scattered Hegemonies: Postmodernity and Transnational Feminist Practices*, ed. Inderpal Grewal and Caren Kaplan. Minneapolis: University of Minnesota Press.

Lloyd, David. 1990. "Genet's Genealogy: European Minorities and the Ends of the Canon." In *The Nature and Context of Minority Discourse*, ed. Abdul R. JanMohamed and David Lloyd. London: Oxford University Press.

———. 1991. "Race Under Representation." *Oxford Literary Review* 13, nos. 1–2: 62–94.

———. 1997. "Nationalisms against the State." In *The Politics of Culture under the Shadow of Late Capital*, ed. Lisa Lowe and David Lloyd. Durham, NC: Duke University Press.

———. 1998. "Foundations of Diversity: Thinking the University in a Time of Multiculturalism." In *"Culture" and the Problem of the Disciplines*, ed. John Carlos Rowe. New York: Columbia University Press.

Lopez, Ian Haney. 1996. *White by Law: The Legal Construction of Race*. New York: New York University Press.

Lowe, Lisa. 1991. *Critical Terrains: French and British Orientalisms*. Ithaca: Cornell University Press.

———. 1996. *Immigrant Acts: On Asian American Cultural Politics*. Durham, NC: Duke University Press.

———. 1998a. "The International Within the National: American Studies and Asian American Critique." *Cultural Critique* 40: 29–47.

———. 1998b. "Memories of Colonial Modernity: *Dogeaters*." *Amerasia Journal* 24, no. 3: 161–164.

———. 2001. "Epistemological Shifts: National Ontology and the New Asian Immigrant." In *Orientations: Mapping Studies in the Asian Diaspora*, ed. Kandice Chuh and Karen Shimakawa. Durham, NC: Duke University Press.

Lowe, Lisa, and David Lloyd, eds. 1997. *The Politics of Culture in the Shadow of Capital*. Durham, NC: Duke University Press.

Luibheid, Eithne. 1997. "The 1965 Immigration and Nationality Act: An 'End' to Exclusion?" *positions: east asia cultures critique* 5, no. 2: 501–522.

Lubiano, Wahneema, ed. 1997. *The House That Race Built*. New York: Vintage Books.

MacKinnon, Catharine. 1993. *Only Words*. Cambridge, MA: Harvard University Press.

Maddox, Lucy, ed. 1999. *Locating American Studies: The Evolution of a Discipline*. Baltimore: Johns Hopkins University Press.

Matsuda, Mari. 1995. "Looking to the Bottom: Critical Legal Studies and Reparations." In *Critical Race Theory: The Key Writings That Formed the Movement*, ed. Kimberle Crenshaw, Neil Gotanda, Gary Peller, and Kendall Thomas. New York: New Press.

———. 1996. *Where Is Your Body? And Other Essays on Race, Gender, and the Law.* Boston: Beacon Press.

McClintock, Anne. 1992. "The Angel of Progress: Pitfalls of the Term 'Post-colonialism.'" *Social Text* 10, no. 2: 84–98.

———. 1995. *Imperial Leather: Race, Gender, and Sexuality in the Colonial Contest.* New York: Routledge.

McGregor, Davianna P. 1980. "Hawaiians: Organizing in the 1970s." *Amerasia Journal* 7, no. 2: 29–55.

Melendy, H. Brett. 1977. *Asians in America: Filipinos, Koreans, and East Indians.* Boston: Twayne.

Merry, Sally Engle. 2000. *Colonizing Hawai'i: The Cultural Power of Law.* Princeton: Princeton University Press.

Miller, Stuart Creighton. 1982. *"Benevolent Assimilation": The American Conquest of the Philippines, 1899–1903.* New Haven: Yale University Press.

Minoru Yasui v. United States, 320 U.S. 115 (1943).

Minow, Martha. 1990. *Making All the Difference: Inclusion, Exclusion, and American Law.* Ithaca: Cornell University Press.

Miyoshi, Masao. 1993. "A Borderless World? From Colonialism to Transnationalism and the Decline of the Nation-State." *Critical Inquiry* 19, no. 4: 726–751.

Moallem, Minoo. 1999. "Transnationalism, Feminism, and Fundamentalism." In *Between Woman and Nation: Nationalisms, Transnational Feminisms, and the State*, ed. Caren Kaplan, Norma Alarcón, and Minoo Moallem. Durham, NC: Duke University Press.

Moallem, Minoo, and Iain A. Boal. 1999. "Multicultural Nationalism and the Poetics of Inauguration." In *Between Woman and Nation: Nationalisms, Transnational Feminisms and the State*, ed. Caren Kaplan, Norma Alarcón, and Minoo Moallem. Durham, NC: Duke University Press.

Mohanty, Chandra Talpade. 1991. "Cartographies of Struggle: Third World Women and the Politics of Feminism." In *Third World Women and the Politics of Feminism*, ed. Chandra Talpade Mohanty, Anna Russo, and Lourdes Torres. Bloomington, IN: Indiana University Press.

Mohanty, Chandra Talpade, Ann Russo, and Lourdes Torres, eds. 1991. *Third World Women and the Politics of Feminism.* Bloomington, IN: Indiana University Press.

Moon, Michael, and Cathy Davidson, eds. 1995. *Subjects and Citizens: Nation, Race, and Gender from Oroonoko to Anita Hill.* Durham, NC: Duke University Press.

Morrison, Toni. 1997. "Home." In *The House That Race Built*, ed. Wahneema Lubiano. New York: Vintage Books.

Morton v. Mancari, 417 U.S. 484 (1974).

Mostern, Kenneth. 1995. "Why Is America in the Heart?" *Critical Mass* 2, no. 2: 35–66.

Mufti, Aamir, and Ella Shohat. 1997. "Introduction." In *Dangerous Liaisons: Gender, Nation, and Postcolonial Perspectives*, ed. Anne McClintock, Aamir Mufti, and Ella Shohat. Minneapolis: University of Minnesota Press.

Musicant, Ivan. 1998. *Empire by Default: The Spanish-American War and the Dawn of the American Century*. New York: Henry Holt.

Ng, Fae Myenne. 1993. *Bone*. New York: Hyperion.

Niranjana, Tejaswini. 1992. *Siting Translation: History, Post-structuralism, and the Colonial Context*. Berkeley: University of California Press.

Okada, John. 1992 [1957]. *No-No Boy*. Seattle: University of Washington Press.

Okamura, Jonathan. 1980. "Aloha Kanaka me ke Aloha 'Āina: Local Culture and Society in Hawai'i." *Amerasia* 7, no. 2: 119–137.

Okihiro, Gary. 1994. *Margins and Mainstreams: Asians in American History and Culture*. Seattle: University of Washington Press.

———. 1999. "Commentary." In *Locating American Studies: The Evolution of a Discipline*, ed. Lucy Maddox. Baltimore: Johns Hopkins University Press.

Okin, Susan Moller. 1999. *Is Multiculturalism Bad for Women?* Princeton: Princeton University Press.

Omatsu, Glenn. 1994. "The 'Four Prisons' and the Movements of Liberation: Asian American Activism from the 1960s to the 1990s." In *The State of Asian America: Activism and Resistance in the 1990s*, ed. Karen Aguilar-San Juan. Boston: South End Press.

Omi, Michael, and Dana Takagi. 1995. "Thinking Theory in Asian American Studies." *Amerasia Journal* 21, nos. 1 and 2: xi–xv.

Omi, Michael, and Howard Winant. 1994. *Racial Formation in the United States*, 2d ed. New York: Routledge.

Ong, Aihwa. 1999. *Flexible Citizenship: The Cultural Logic of Transnationality*. Durham, NC: Duke University Press.

Ong, Paul, Edna Bonacich, and Lucie Cheng, eds. 1994. *The New Asian Immigration in Los Angeles and Global Restructuring*. Philadelphia: Temple University Press.

Osajima, Keith. 1995. "Postmodern Possibilities: Theoretical and Political Directions for Asian American Studies." *Amerasia Journal* 21, nos. 1 and 2: 79–88.

Osumi, Megumi Dick. 1982. "California's Anti-Miscegenation Laws." In *Asian and Pacific American Experiences: Women's Perspectives*, ed. Nobuya Tsuchida. Minneapolis: Asian/Pacific American Learning Resource Center.

Palumbo-Liu, David, ed. 1995a. *The Ethnic Canon: Histories, Institutions, and Interventions*. Minneapolis: University of Minnesota Press.

———. 1995b. "Theory and the Subject of Asian American Studies." *Amerasia Journal* 21, nos. 1 and 2: 55–66.

———. 1999. *Asian/American: Historical Crossings of a Racial Frontier*. Stanford: Stanford University Press.

Parekh, Bhikhu. 1995. "Liberalism and Colonialism: A Critique of Locke and

Mill." In *The Decolonization of Imagination*, ed. Jan Nederveen Pieterse and Bhikhu Parekh. London: Zed Books.

Parikh, Crystal. 1999. "Betraying Identity: Emergent Articulations in U.S. Ethnic Literatures." Ph.D. Dissertation. University of Maryland, College Park, MD.

Parker, Andrew, Mary Russo, Doris Sommer, and Patricia Yaeger, eds. 1992. *Nationalisms and Sexualities*. New York: Routledge.

Parrenas, Rhacel Salazar. 1998. " 'White Trash' Meets the 'Little Brown Monkeys': The Taxi Dance Hall as a Site of Interracial and Gender Alliances between White Working Class Women and Filipino Immigrant Men in the 1920s and 1930s." *Amerasia Journal* 24, no. 2: 115–134.

Pease, Donald E., ed. 1994. *National Identities and Post-Americanist Narratives*. Durham, NC: Duke University Press.

Pieterse, Jan Nederveen, and Bhikhu Parekh. 1995. "Shifting Imaginaries: Decolonization, Internal Decolonization, Postcoloniality." In *The Decolonization of Imagination*, ed. Jan Nederveen Pieterse and Bhikhu Parekh. London: Zed Books.

Pomeroy, William J. 1992. *The Philippines: Colonialism, Collaboration, and Resistance*. New York: International Publishers.

Prakash, Gyan. 1990. "Writing Post-Orientalist Histories of the Third World: Perspectives from Indian Historiography." *Comparative Studies in Society and History* 32, no. 2: 383–408.

———. 1992. "Postcolonial Criticism and Indian Historiography." *Social Text* 10, no. 2: 8–19.

———. 1996. "Who's Afraid of Postcoloniality?" *Social Text* 14, no. 3: 187–203.

Prashad, Vijay. 1998. "Anti-D'Souza: The Ends of Racism and the Asian American." *Amerasia Journal* 24, no. 1: 23–40.

Probyn, Elspeth. 1999. "Bloody Metaphors and Other Allegories of the Ordinary." In *Between Woman and Nation: Nationalisms, Transnational Feminisms, and the State*, ed. Caren Kaplan, Norma Alarcón, and Minoo Moallem. Durham, NC: Duke University Press.

Radhakrishnan, R. 1992. "Nationalism, Gender, and the Narrative of Identity." In *Nationalisms and Sexualities*, ed. Andrew Parker, Mary Russo, Doris Sommer, and Patricia Yaeger. New York: Routledge.

———. 1994. "Postmodernism and the Rest of the World." *Organization* 1, no. 2: 305–340.

———. 1996. *Diasporic Mediations: Between Home and Location*. Minneapolis: University of Minnesota Press.

Rafael, Vicente. 1988. *Contracting Colonialism: Translation and Christian Conversion in Tagalog Society under Early Spanish Rule*. Ithaca: Cornell University Press.

———. 1994. "The Cultures of Area Studies in the United States." *Social Text* 12, no. 1: 91–111.

———, ed. 1995. *Discrepant Histories: Translocal Essays on Filipino Cultures.* Philadelphia: Temple University Press.

———. 2000. *White Love and Other Events in Filipino History.* Durham, NC: Duke University Press.

Ray, Sangeeta. 2000. *En-gendering India: Woman and Nation in Colonial and Postcolonial Narratives.* Durham, NC: Duke University Press.

Readings, Bill. 1996. *The University in Ruins.* Cambridge, MA: Harvard University Press.

Rice v. Cayetano, 528 U.S. 495 (2000).

Rich, Adrienne. 1993. "Compulsory Heterosexuality and Lesbian Existence." In *The Lesbian and Gay Studies Reader,* ed. Henry Abelove, Michele Aina Barale, and David Halperin. New York: Routledge.

Rimmerman, Craig A., Kenneth Wald, and Clyde Wilcox, eds. 2000. *The Politics of Gay Rights.* Chicago: University of Chicago Press.

Roces, Mina. 1994. "Filipino Identity in Fiction, 1945–1972." *Modern Asian Studies* 28, no. 2: 279–315.

Roldan v. Los Angeles County, 18 P.2d 706 (Cal. 1933).

Rosaldo, Renato. 1997. "Cultural Citizenship, Inequality, and Multiculturalism." In *Latino Cultural Citizenship: Claiming Identity, Space, and Rights,* ed. William V. Flores and Rina Benmayor. Boston: Beacon Press.

Rouse, Roger. 1995. "Thinking Through Transnationalism: Notes on the Cultural Politics of Class Relations in the Contemporary United States." *Public Culture* 7, no. 2: 353–402.

Rowe, John Carlos, ed. 1998. *"Culture" and the Problem of the Disciplines.* New York: Columbia University Press.

Said, Edward. 1978. *Orientalism.* New York: Pantheon Books.

———. 1993. *Culture and Imperialism.* New York: Alfred A. Knopf.

Saito, Natsu Taylor. 1997. "Alien and Non-Alien Alike: Citizenship, 'Foreignness,' and Racial Hierarchy in American Law." *Oregon Law Review* 76: 261.

Sakai, Naoki. 1991. *Voices of the Past: The Status of Language in Eighteenth-Century Japanese Discourse.* Ithaca: Cornell University Press.

———. 1997. *Translation and Subjectivity: On "Japan" and Cultural Nationalism.* Minneapolis: University of Minnesota Press.

———. 2000a. "Introduction." *Traces: A Multilingual Journal of Theory and Translation* 1: v–xiii.

———. 2000b. "The dislocation of the West." *Traces: A Multilingual Journal of Theory and Translation* 1: 71–94.

Saldivar, Jose David. 1991. *The Dialectics of Our America: Genealogy, Cultural Critique, and Literary History.* Durham, NC: Duke University Press.

———. 1997. *Border Matters: Remapping American Cultural Studies.* Berkeley: University of California Press.

San Buenaventura, Steffi. 1998. "The Colors of Manifest Destiny: Filipinos and the American Other(s)." *Amerasia Journal* 24, no. 3: 1–26.

San Juan, E., Jr. 1991. "Mapping the Boundaries: The Filipino Writer in the U.S.A." *Journal of Ethnic Studies* 19, no. 1: 117–131.

———. 1992. *Reading the West/Writing the East: Studies in Comparative Literature and Culture*. New York: Peter Lang.

Santos, Bienvenido. 1992 [1977]. "Immigration Blues." In *Scent of Apples: A Collection of Stories*. Seattle: University of Washington Press.

Santos, Tomas N. 1976. "The Filipino Writer in America—Old and New." *World Literature Written in English* 15: 406–414.

Sassen, Saskia. 1996. *Losing Control? Sovereignty in an Age of Globalization*. New York: Columbia University Press.

Schirmer, Daniel B. 1972. *Republic or Empire: American Resistance to the Philippine-American War*. Cambridge, MA: Schenkman Publishing.

Schirmer, Daniel B., and Stephen Rosskamm Shalom, eds. 1987. *The Philippines Reader: A History of Colonialism, Neocolonialism, Dictatorship, and Resistance*. Boston: South End Press.

Schneider, Elizabeth. 1991. "The Dialectics of Rights and Politics: Perspectives from the Women's Movement." In *At the Boundaries of Law*, ed. Martha Fineman and Nancy Thomadsen. New York: Routledge.

Schwarz, Henry. 2000. "Mission Impossible: Introducing Postcolonial Studies in the U.S. Academy." In *A Companion to Postcolonial Studies*, ed. Henry Schwarz and Sangeeta Ray. Oxford, UK: Blackwell Publishers.

Scott v. Sanford, 60 U.S. 691 (1857).

Sedgwick, Eve Kosofsky. 1985. *Between Men*. New York: Columbia University Press.

Shah, Nayan. 2001. *Contagious Divides: Epidemics and Race in San Francisco's Chinatown*. Berkeley: University of California Press.

Shankar, Lavina, and Rajini Srikanth, eds. 1998. *A Part, Yet Apart: South Asians in Asian America*. Philadelphia: Temple University Press.

Sharpe, Jenny. 1995. "Is the United States Postcolonial? Transnationalism, Immigration, and Race." *Diaspora* 4, no. 2: 181–199.

Shimakawa, Karen. 2002. *National Abjection: The Asian American Body On Stage*. Durham, NC: Duke University Press.

Shohat, Ella. 1992. "Notes on the 'Postcolonial.'" *Social Text* 10, no. 2: 99–113.

———, ed. 1998. *Talking Visions: Multicultural Feminism in a Transnational Age*. Cambridge, MA: The MIT Press.

Shohat, Ella, and Robert Stam. 1994. *Unthinking Eurocentrism: Multiculturalism and the Media*. New York: Routledge.

Silverberg, Miriam. 1992. "Constructing the Japanese Ethnography of Modernity." *Journal of Asian Studies* 51, no. 1: 30–54.

———. 1993. "Remembering Pearl Harbor, Forgetting Charlie Chaplin, and the Case of the Disappearing Western Woman: A Picture Story." *positions: east asia cultures critique* 1, no. 1: 24–76.

Singer, Milton. 1964. "The Social Sciences in Non-Western Studies." In *The Non-Western World in Higher Education: The Annals of the American Academy of Political and Social Science*, ed. Donald Bigelow and Lyman Legters. Philadelphia: American Academy of Political and Social Science.

Smith, David Lionel. 1997. "What Is Black Culture?" In *The House That Race Built*, ed. Wahneema Lubiano. New York: Vintage Books.

Soja, Edward. 1989. *Postmodern Geographies: The Reassertion of Space in Critical Social Theory*. London: Verso.

Spickard, Paul R. 2000. "What Must I Be? Asian Americans and the Question of Multiethnic Identity." In *Contemporary Asian America: A Multidisciplinary Reader*, ed. Min Zhou and James V. Gatewood. New York: New York University Press.

Spillers, Hortense, ed. 1991. *Comparative American Identities: Race, Sex, and Nationality in the Modern Text*. New York: Routledge.

Spivak, Gayatri. 1988a. "Subaltern Studies: Deconstructing Historiography." In *In Other Worlds*. New York: Routledge.

———. 1988b. "Can the Subaltern Speak?" In *Marxism and the Interpretation of Culture*, ed. Cary Nelson and Lawrence Grossberg. Chicago: University of Chicago Press.

———. 1989. "Feminism and Deconstruction, Again: Negotiating with Unacknowledged Masculinism." In *Between Feminism and Psychoanalysis*, ed. Teresa Brennan. New York: Routledge.

———. 1992. "Woman in Difference: Mahasweta Devi's 'Douloti the Beautiful.'" In *Nationalisms and Sexualities*, ed. Andrew Parker, Mary Russo, Doris Sommer, and Patricia Yaeger. New York: Routledge.

———. 1996. "Bonding in Difference: Interview with Alfred Arteaga." In *The Spivak Reader: Selected Works of Gayatri Chakravorty Spivak*, ed. Donna Landry and Gerald MacLean. New York: Routledge.

———. 1997. "Teaching for the Times." In *Dangerous Liaisons: Gender, Nation, and Postcolonial Perspectives*, ed. Anne McClintock, Aamir Mufti, and Ella Shohat. Minneapolis: University of Minnesota Press.

Stanley, Peter. 1972. "The Forgotten Philippines, 1790–1946." In *American-East Asian Relations: A Survey*, ed. Ernest May and James Thomson. Cambridge, MA: Harvard University Press.

Stannard, David. 1989. *Before the Horror: The Population of Hawai'i on the Eve of Western Contact*. Honolulu: Social Sciences Research Institute and University of Hawai'i Press.

Steward, Julian. 1950. *Area Research: Theory and Practice*. Social Science Research Council, Bulletin 63.

Stoler, Ann. 1991. "Carnal Knowledge and Imperial Power: Gender, Race, and Morality in Colonial Asia." In *Gender at the Crossroads of Knowledge: Feminist Anthropology in the Postmodern Era*, ed. Micaela Di Leonardo. Berkeley: University of California Press.

Sumida, Stephen. 1991. *And the View from the Shore*. Seattle: University of Washington Press.

———. 1997. "Postcolonialism, Nationalism, and the Emergence of Asian / Pacific American Literatures." In *An Interethnic Companion to Asian American Literature*, ed. King-Kok Cheung. Cambridge, UK: Cambridge University Press.

Takagi, Dana. 1992. *The Retreat from Race: Asian American Admissions and Racial Politics*. New Brunswick, NJ: Rutgers University Press.

———. 1996. "Maiden Voyage: Excursion into Sexuality and Identity Politics in Asian America." In *Asian American Sexualities: Dimensions of the Gay and Lesbian Experience*, ed. Russell Leong. New York: Routledge.

Takaki, Ronald. 1989. *Strangers from a Different Shore*. Boston: Little, Brown.

Takao Ozawa v. United States, 260 U.S. 178 (1922).

Thomas, Brook. 1987. *Cross-examinations of Law and Literature*. Cambridge, UK: Cambridge University Press.

Ting, Jennifer. 1995. "Bachelor Society: Deviant Heterosexuality and Asian American Historiography." In *Privileging Positions: The Sites of Asian American Studies*. Pullman, WA: Washington State University Press. 271–280.

———. 1998. "The Power of Sexuality." *Journal of Asian American Studies* 1, no. 1: 65–82.

Tölölyan, Khachig. 1991. "The Nation-State and Its Others: In Lieu of a Preface." *Diaspora* 1, no. 1: 3–7.

Tomkins, E. Berkeley. 1970. *Anti-Imperialism in the United States, 1890–1920*. Philadelphia: University of Pennsylvania Press.

Trask, Haunani-Kay. 1993. *From a Native Daughter: Colonialism and Sovereignty in the Pacific*. Monroe, ME: Common Cause Press.

———. 2000. "Settlers of Color and 'Immigrant' Hegemony: 'Locals' in Hawai'i." *Amerasia Journal* 26, no. 2: 1–26.

Traxel, David. 1998. *1898*. New York: Alfred A. Knopf.

Trinh, T. Minh-ha. 1989. *Woman, Native, Other*. Bloomington, IN: Indiana University Press.

———. 1991. *When the Moon Waxes Red: Representation, Gender, and Cultural Politics*. New York: Routledge.

Trucios-Haynes, Enid. 1997. "The Legacy of Racially Restrictive Immigration Laws and Policies on the Construction of an American National Identity." *Oregon Law Review* 76: 369.

Tushnet, Mark. 1984. "An Essay on Rights." *Texas Law Review* 62: 1363–1403.

United States v. Balsara, 180 F. 694 (2d Cir. 1910).

United States v. Hirabayashi, 46 F. Supp. 657 (W.D. Wash. 1942).
United States v. Thind, 261 U.S. 204 (1923).
Valeri, Valerio. 1985. Kingship and Sacrifice. Chicago: University of Chicago Press.
Visweswaran, Kamala. 1996. "Betrayal: An Analysis in Three Acts." In Scattered Hegemonies, ed. Inderpal Grewal and Caren Kaplan. Minneapolis: University of Minnesota Press.
———. 1997. "Diaspora by Design: Flexible Citizenship and South Asians in U.S. Racial Formations." Diaspora 6: 5–29.
Volpp, Leti. 1994. "(Mis)Identifying Culture: Asian Women and the 'Cultural' Defense." Harvard Women's Law Journal 17: 57.
———. 1996. "Talking 'Culture': Gender, Race, Nation, and the Politics of Multiculturalism." Columbia Law Review 96: 1573.
———. 2000a. "American Mestizo: Filipinos and Antimiscegenation Laws in California." U.C. Davis Law Review 33: 795.
———. 2000b. "Blaming Culture for Bad Behavior." Yale Journal of Law and the Humanities 12, no. 89: 89–116.
———. 2000c. "Righting Wrongs." UCLA Law Review 47: 1815.
Wagley, Charles. 1948. Area Research and Training: A Conference Report on the Study of World Areas. Social Science Research Council, Pamphlet 6.
Wald, Priscilla. 1993. "Terms of Assimilation: Legislating Subjectivity in the Emerging Nation." In The Cultures of United States Imperialism, ed. Amy Kaplan and Donald Pease. Durham, NC: Duke University Press.
———. 1995. Constituting Americans: Cultural Anxiety and Narrative Form. Durham, NC: Duke University Press.
Wallerstein, Immanuel. 1990. "Culture as the Ideological Battleground of the Modern World System." Theory, Culture and Society 7, nos. 2–3: 31–57.
———. 1991. Geopolitics and Geoculture: Essays on the Changing World-System. Cambridge, UK: Cambridge University Press.
———. 1995. After Liberalism. New York: The New Press.
Washington, Mary Helen. 1998. "Disturbing the Peace: What Happens to American Studies If You Put African American Studies at the Center?" American Quarterly 50: 1–23.
Weber, Samuel. 1987. Institution and Interpretation. Minneapolis: University of Minnesota Press.
West, Robin. 1988. "Jurisprudence and Gender." University of Chicago Law Review 55, no. 1: 1–72.
White, G. Edward. 1988. The Marshall Court and Cultural Change, 1815–35: The History of the Supreme Court of the United States, Vols. 3–4. New York: Macmillan.
Wiegman, Robyn. 1995. American Anatomies: Theorizing Race and Gender. Durham, NC: Duke University Press.

———. 1998. "Introduction: The Futures of American Studies." *Cultural Critique* 40: 5–10.
Williams, Patricia. 1990. *The Alchemy of Race and Rights*. Cambridge, MA: Harvard University Press.
Wilson, Rob. 1996. "*Goodbye Paradise*: Global/Localism in the American Pacific." In *Global/Local: Cultural Production and the Transnational Imaginary*, ed. Rob Wilson and Wimal Dissanayake. Durham, NC: Duke University Press.
———. 2000. *Reimagining the American Pacific*. Durham, NC: Duke University Press.
Wilson, Rob, and Wimal Dissanayake, eds. 1996. *Global/Local: Cultural Production and the Transnational Imaginary*. Durham, NC: Duke University Press.
Wolff, Leon. 1960. *Little Brown Brother*. New York: Doubleday.
Wong, K. Scott. 1999 [1996]. "The Transformation of Culture: Three Chinese Views of America." In *Locating American Studies: The Evolution of a Discipline*, ed. Lucy Maddox. Baltimore: Johns Hopkins University Press.
Wong, Sau-ling C. 1993. *Reading Asian American Literature: From Necessity to Extravagance*. Princeton: Princeton University Press.
———. 1995. "Denationalization Reconsidered: Asian American Cultural Criticism at a Theoretical Crossroads." *Amerasia Journal* 21, nos. 1 and 2: 1–27.
———. 2001. "The Stakes of Textual Border-Crossing: Hualing Nieh's *Mulberry and Peach* in Sinocentric, Asian American, and Feminist Critical Practices." In *Orientations: Mapping Studies in the Asian Diaspora*, ed. Kandice Chuh and Karen Shimakawa. Durham, NC: Duke University Press.
Worsley, Peter. 1984. *The Three Worlds*. Chicago: University of Chicago Press.
Xing, Jun. 1998. *Asian America Through the Lens: History, Representation, and Identities*. Walnut Creek, CA: AltaMira Press.
Yamamoto, Eric K. 1999. *Interracial Justice: Conflict and Reconciliation in Post-Civil Rights America*. New York: New York University Press.
Yamamoto, Hisaye. 1998 [1948]. "The High-Heeled Shoes: A Memoir." In *Seventeen Syllables and Other Stories*. New York: Routledge.
Yamamoto, Traise. 1999. *Masking Selves, Making Subjects: Japanese American Women, Identity, and the Body*. Berkeley: University of California Press.
Yamanaka, Lois Ann. 1997. *Blu's Hanging*. New York: Avon Books.
Yun, Chung-Hei. 1992. "Beyond 'Clay Walls': Korean American Literature." In *Reading the Literatures of Asian America*, ed. Shirley Geok-lin Lim and Amy Ling. Philadelphia: Temple University Press.
Yuval-David, Nira. 1997. *Gender and Nation*. London: Sage Publications.
Zinn, Howard. 1995. *A People's History of the United States: 1492–Present*. Rev. ed. New York: HarperCollins.

index

America Is in the Heart (Bulosan), 13, 35–44

Anti-racism: Asian American studies and, 3; "unmattering race" and, 124–25

"Asian American": as analytic category, 84; literariness of, 27; as object of knowledge, 2, 20–21, 116–17, 149–50

Asian American identity, 9–12, 148–59; decolonization and, 116; literariness of, 27; orientalism and, 20–21, 59–60. See also Identity; Race; Subjectivity

Asian Americanist discourse: cultural nationalism and, 20–21, 31, 156 n.18; East Asian orientation of, 2; globalization and, 6–7, 59–60 (see also Postcolonialism; Transnationalism); heteronormativity of, 2, 21, 34, 43 (see also Sexuality); masculinism of, 2, 21 (see also Gender); spatial imagination of, 87–91, 98 (see also Space). See also Knowledge, politics of

Asian American literature: American literature and, 4; politics of knowledge and, x, 4, 16–20; as theory, x, 15–20, 142, 155 n.16

Asian American studies, 150–51: Asian studies and, 88–91, 171 n.2, 171 n.3; as field of collaborative antagonisms, 28–29; gender and, 35–44; globalization and, 7, 59–60 (see also Postcolonialism; Transnationalism); history of, 5, 20–21, 23–24; institutional sites of, 3–6, 9–11, 13, 16–20, 24–27, 149, 157 n.25 (see also U.S. university); "marginalization" and, 2, 7, 21, 56–57 (see also Knowledge: politics of); multiculturalism and, 5, 16–20 (see also Multiculturalism); politics of, 2–4, 114–16 (see also Justice); sexuality and, 13, 34–44; spatial metaphorics of, 87–91 (see also Space); subjectlessness and, 9–14, 34, 82–83

Asiatic racialization. *See* Race

Association for Asian American Studies, 2, 3

Blu's Hanging (Yamanaka), 2, 113, 140–45; controversy around, 2, 12–14, 116, 141, 153 n.1. See also Hawai'i

Bulosan, Carlos, 13, 35–44

Campomanes, Oscar: on "Filipino America," 32; on Filipino/a American literatures, 26, 43; on U.S. imperialism, 43–49

Chow, Rey: on intellectual work, 1, 16, 18; on "otherness," 155 n.15, 156 n.23

Citizenship, U.S.: gender and, 109; modernity and, 10; race and, 49–50, 63–70, 94; rights and, 33–34, 63–70, 72–73; viscerality of, 74–75. See also U.S. nation(alism)

Clay Walls (Kim), 15, 87, 90–100. See also Korean America(ns)

Colonialism: epistemologies of, 88–91, 119–29, 139–40; problems of decolonization and, 120–29, 139–40; race and sexuality and, 44–48, 121–22, 129–45; U.S. neocolonialism as, 108, 122, 129–40; U.S. occupation of Hawaiʻi, 121; U.S. occupation of Philippines, 31–57 passim. See also Hawaiʻi; Philippines; U.S. nation(alism)

"Comfort Women," 105–9. See also Gesture Life, A; Korean America(ns): Japanese imperialism and

Deconstruction, 8–9, 58, 69, 82; "deconstructive attitude," 8–9, 26–27, 150; of U.S. nation-ness, 123–24. See also Derrida, Jacques; Spivak, Gayatri Chakravorty

Derrida, Jacques: on deconstruction, 8, 58 (see also Deconstruction); on justice, 1, 8; on undecidability, 70. See also Poststructural(ism)

Filipino/a America(ns), 13, 31–57 passim, 58–59, 86, 113; "American national" and, 48–51; anti-Filipino/a racism and, 12, 32–34, 39, 53–55, 153 n.1; as object of knowledge, 2, 116–17; U.S. citizenship and, 49–56. See also Blu's Hanging; Colonialism: U.S. occupation of Philippines; Philippines

Foucault, Michel: on practices of liberation and freedom, 114–15; on space, 85, 110–111

Gender. See Asian Americanist discourse; Asian American studies; Sexuality

Gesture Life, A (Lee), 15, 87, 90, 100–109. See also Korean America(ns)

Globalization, 6–7, 154 n.7, 154 n.8; Asian American studies and, 7.

See also Postcolonialism; Transnationalism

Gordon, Avery: on "complex personhood," 29, 148; on imagining otherwise, ix–x, 112

Hawaiʻi, 2, 14, 121: modern history of, 130–32, 179 n.27; Native Hawaiian sovereignty movements and, 117, 136–40, 180 n.33. See also Blu's Hanging; Colonialism: U.S. occupation of Hawaiʻi

Heterogeneity, politics of, 86, 150

"High-Heeled Shoes, The" (Yamamoto), 14–15, 62–63, 70. See also Japanese America(ns): internment of

Hirabayashi, Gordon, 66

Hirabayashi v. United States, 66–67, 136. See also Japanese America(ns): internment of

Identity: difference and, x, 4, 21, 86, 147; as narrative, 33–34, 103 (see also Citizenship, U.S.); "otherness" and, 9, 15, 18; politics of, 16–21, 150 (see also Subject(ivity)); racial essentialism and, 60, 81–83; undecidability and, 14, 61–63, 70, 71, 83. See also Asian American identity

"Immigration Blues" (Santos), 13, 35–44. See also Filipino/a America(ns)

Imperialism. See Colonialism

In re Alverto, 50–51. See also Filipino/a America(ns)

In re Bautista, 50–52. See also Filipino/a America(ns)

In re Rallos, 50–51. See also Filipino/a America(ns)

Interdisciplinarity, 9, 26–29

Japanese America(ns), 113; internment of, 14–15, 58–82 passim, 86,

124; Japanese modernity and, 65; transnationalization and, 63–70. *See also* Citizenship, U.S.: race and

Justice, 1; Asian American studies and, 4, 11; capitalism and, 25–26; colonial epistemology and, 15; deconstruction and, 8; globalization and, 8; postcolonial studies and, 114; subjectivity and, 22; variability of, 150

Kim, Ronyoung, 15, 87, 90–100. *See also* Korean America(ns)

Knowledge, politics of, x, 2, 21, 113; area studies and, 86–91; poststructuralism and, 4–6, 16–20; subjectivity and, 5, 21–29

Korean America(ns), 85–111 *passim*, 113; Japanese imperialism and, 15, 90–93, 95–97, 100, 105–9; Korean modernity and, 93; space and, 15; transnationalism and, 15. *See also Clay Walls; Gesture Life, A;* Military sex slavery

Law(s): antimiscegenation, 40–41, 53–55; Cable Act (1922), 55; Chinese Exclusion Act (1882), 94, 124; Executive Order 9066, 65; "Gentleman's Agreement" (1907–8), 52, 94, 124; Immigration and Nationality Act (1952), 49; Immigration and Nationality Act (1965), 7; Insular Cases, 48–49; Japanese American internment, 64–70; Naturalization Act (1790), 68; National Origins Quota Act (1924), 94, 124; Naturalization Act (1906), 49; Page Law (1875), 124; as state apparatus, 10; subjectivity and, 15–16, 21–23; Tydings-McDuffie Act (1934), 56. *See also* Justice

Lee, Chang-rae, 15, 87, 90, 100–109. *See also* Korean America(ns)

Liberalism, 29, 129. *See also* Colonialism

Lloyd, David: on identity, 33; on U.S. university, 13, 17–18

"Localism," 17, 138, 142, 182 n.44. *See also* Hawai'i

Lowe, Lisa: on Asian American culture, 1; on Asian American racialization, 22–23, 124; on decolonization, 139; on difference, 151; on "new immigrants," 116

Military sex slavery, 105–9. *See also Gesture Life, A;* Korean America(ns): Japanese imperialism and

Multiculturalism: Asian American studies and, 5–6; postmodernism and, 5, 16–20; race and, 5–20; U.S. academy influenced by, 5–6, 16–20, 118; varieties of, 154 n.5. *See also* Liberalism

Nation: Asian Americanist discourse and, 3, 124–25; as epistemological category, 11, 33–36, 48, 56–57, 58, 126–29; modernity and, 3, 127; as nation-state, 3, 127; transnation and, 69–70. *See also* Colonialism; Space; Transnationalism; U.S. nation(alism)

No-No Boy (Okada), 14–15, 62–63, 70–76. *See also* Japanese America(ns): internment of

Okada, John, 14–15, 62–63, 70–76. *See also* Japanese America(ns): internment of

Orientalism. *See* Colonialism: epistemologies of; Race

Palumbo-Liu, David, 11–12
Philippines, 121, 160 n.21. *See also*

Philippines (cont.)
  Colonialism: U.S. occupation of Philippines; Filipino/a America(ns)
Postcolonialism, 3; Asian American studies and, 112–45 passim; Hawai'i and, 14; postcoloniality and, 116–17; U.S. academy and, 36, 114, 125–26. See also Colonialism: epistemologies of; Globalization
Poststructural(ism), x; postmodernism and, 4–5, 153 n.2; U.S. academy influenced by, 4–6. See also Deconstruction; Derrida, Jacques; Foucault, Michel; Spivak, Gayatri Chakravorty

Race: as analytic category, 34; color-blindness and, 135–36; multiculturalism and, 6–21; orientalism and, 20–21; racial essentialism and, 14, 60, 81–82; racial formation and, 19; racialization and, 3, 11, 59–62; racism and, 14; sexuality and, 31, 34; whiteness and, 34, 38–40. See also Colonialism: epistemologies of
Rice v. Cayetano, 119, 133–36
Roldan v. Los Angeles County, 54–55. See also Filipino/a America(ns); Law(s): antimiscegenation

Santos, Bienvenidos. See "Immigration Blues"
Sexuality, 31, 34; heteronormativity and, 2, 21, 31–57 passim. See also Asian Americanist discourse; Asian American studies: sexuality and
Space: heterotopic, 110–11; territoriality and, 86–87; transnationalism and, 15, 85–111 passim; U.S. nation(alism) and, 1, 86–87, 138–39. See also Korean America(ns)

Spivak, Gayatri Chakravorty: on capitalism, 25–26, 28–29; on deconstruction, 58, 82; on difference, 147; on identity, 75, 82; on "otherness," 9, 145
Strategic anti-essentialism, 10, 149
Subject(ivity): citizenship and, 10; gender and, 73–81, 96–100; globalization and, 7; justice and, 5; knowledge and, 5; subjectlessness and, 9–14, 82–83; uniformity of, 21–23, 31–36, 58; U.S. nation(alism) and, 1, 15–16, 22–23. See also Identity; Law(s)

Takagi, Dana: on "Asian American," 31; on Asian American studies, 26; on difference, 150; on race, 136; sexuality and, 35
Transnationalism, 3, 6–7, 59–63, 164 n.1: Asiatic racialization and, 59–62; Filipino/a Americans and, 59; Japanese American internment and, 14; transnational feminism and, 7; transnational imaginary and, 76, 94–95, 110–11, 142–45. See also Korean America(ns); Nation

U.S. nation(alism), x, 1; "America(ns)" and, x, 36 (see also Citizenship; Identity; Subjectivity); Asian American studies and, 3–4, 13, 31–57 passim (see also Asian American identity); discourse of exceptionalism and, 32, 36, 43–44, 56–57, 125–26; gender and, 51–52, 109; heteronormativity and, 44–48; modernity and, 3, 6, 65; patriotism and, 3, 52, 61, 64–68, 70–76; the "postcolonial" and, 119–23 (see also Colonialism); racism and, 68–69; territoriality and, 86–87, 138–39. See also Race; Space

U.S. university, 4–6, 10, 13, 24–29, 149; liberalism and, 16–20; postcolonialism in, 118. *See also* Asian American studies: institutional sites of; Colonialism: epistemologies of; Multiculturalism

Victim(ization), 1, 109

Volpp, Leti: on Filipino/a Americans and antimiscegenation laws, 53–55; on narratives of victimization, 109

Wong, Sau-ling C., 22, 87

Yamamoto, Hisaye, 14–15, 62–63, 70. *See also* Japanese America(ns): internment of

Yamanaka, Lois Ann, 2, 12–14, 113, 116, 140–45

Kandice Chuh is Associate Professor of English at the University of Maryland, where she is also affiliated with the Asian American Studies Program and the American Studies Department. She is the coeditor (with Karen Shimakawa) of *Orientations: Mapping Studies in the Asian Diaspora* (Duke University Press, 2001).

Library of Congress Cataloging-in-Publication Data

Chuh, Kandice, 1968–
Imagine otherwise : on Asian Americanist critique / Kandice Chuh.
p. cm.
Includes bibliographical references (p.) and index.
ISBN 0-8223-3104-7 (cloth) —
ISBN 0-8223-3140-3 (pbk.)
1. Asian Americans—Study and teaching. 2. Asian Americans—Ethnic identity. 3. American literature—Asian American authors—History and criticism. I. Title.
E184.06 C497 2003
305.895'073—dc21   2002151598

www.ingramcontent.com/pod-product-compliance
Lightning Source LLC
Chambersburg PA
CBHW071818230426
43670CB00013B/2492